DATE DUE

APR 0 3 2001			
MAR 1 3 2002			
MAY 2 0 2002			
JUN 1 0 2003			
JUN 2 2 2005			
MAY 1 1 2007			
NOV 2 0 2009			
GAYLORD			PRINTED IN U.S.A.

Frederick Douglass

Engraving of Frederick Douglass from *Autographs for Freedom*, edited by Julia Griffiths, 1854.

FREDERICK DOUGLASS
Oratory from Slavery

David B. Chesebrough

Great American Orators, Number 26
Bernard K. Duffy and Halford R. Ryan, Series Advisers

GREENWOOD PRESS
Westport, Connecticut • London

Library of Congress Cataloging-in-Publication Data

Chesebrough, David B., 1932–
    Frederick Douglass : oratory from slavery / David B. Chesebrough.
        p. cm.—(Great American orators, ISSN 0898-8277 ; no. 26)
    Includes bibliographical references (p.   ) and index.
    ISBN 0–313–30287–1 (alk. paper)
    1. Douglass, Frederick, 1817?–1895—Oratory. I. Title.
    II. Series.
    E449.D75C47   1998
    973.8′092—dc21
    [B]   97–33138

British Library Cataloguing in Publication Data is available.

Library of Congress Catalog Card Number: 97–33138
ISBN: 0–313–30287–1
ISSN: 0898–8277

First published in 1998

Greenwood Press, 88 Post Road West, Westport, CT 06881
An imprint of Greenwood Publishing Group, Inc.

Printed in the United States of America

∞™

The paper used in this book complies with the
Permanent Paper Standard issued by the National
Information Standards Organization (Z39.48–1984).

10 9 8 7 6 5 4 3 2

Copyright Acknowledgment

The author and publisher gratefully acknowledge permission for use of the following material:

Excerpts from "Frederick Douglass and the Anti-Slavery Crusade: His Career and Speeches,"
by R. Gerald Fulkerson, Ph.D. dissertation, University of Illinois, 1971.

Excerpts from "A Rhetorical Analysis of the Speeches of Frederick Douglass during and after the
Civil War," by George A. Hinshaw, Ph.D. dissertation, University of Nebraska, 1972.

Dedicated to the memory of

Florence J. Chesebrough

Humanitarian,

pioneer in the care of mentally handicapped children,

my mother

CONTENTS

Contents

SERIES FOREWORD

The idea for a series of books on great American orators grew out of the recognition that there is a paucity of book-length studies on individual orators and their speeches. Apart from a few notable exceptions, the study of American public address has been pursued in scores of articles published in professional journals. As helpful as these studies have been, none has or can provide a complete analysis of a speaker's rhetoric. Book-length studies, such as those in this series, will help fill the void that has existed in the study of American public address and its related disciplines of politics and history, theology and sociology, communication and law. In a book, the critic can explicate a broader range of a speaker's persuasive discourse than reasonably could be treated in an article. The comprehensive research and sustained reflection that books require will undoubtedly yield many original and enduring insights concerning the nation's most important voices.

Public address has been a fertile ground for scholarly investigation. No matter how insightful their intellectual forebears, each generation of scholars must reexamine its universe of discourse, while expanding the compass of its researches and redefining its purpose and methods. To avoid intellectual torpor new scholars cannot be content simply to see through the eyes of those who have come before them. We hope that this series of books will stimulate important new understandings of the nature of persuasive discourse and provide opportunities for scholarship in the history and criticism of American public address.

This series examines the role of rhetoric in the United States. American speakers shaped the destiny of the colonies, the young republic, and the mature nation. During each stage of intellectual, political, and religious development of the United States, great orators, standing at the rostrum, on the stump, and in the pulpit, used words and gestures to influence their audiences. Usually striving for the noble, sometimes achieving the base, they urged their fellow citizens toward a more perfect Union. The books in this series chronicle and explain the accomplishments of representative American leaders as orators.

A series of book-length studies on American persuaders honors the role men and women have played in U.S. history. Previously, if one desired to assess the impact of a speaker or a speech upon history, the path was, at best, not well marked and, at worst, littered with obstacles. To be sure, one might turn to biographies and general histories to learn about an orator, but for the public address scholar these sources often prove unhelpful. Rhetorical topics, such as speech invention, style, delivery, organizational strategies, and persuasive effect, are often treated in passing, if mentioned at all. Authoritative speech texts are often difficult to locate, and the problem of textual accuracy is frequently encountered. This is especially true for those figures who spoke one or two hundred years ago or for those whose persuasive role, though significant was secondary to other leading lights of the age.

Each book in this series is organized to meet the needs of scholars and students of the history and criticism of public address. Part I is a critical analysis of the orator and his or her speeches. Within the format of a case study, one may expect considerable latitude. For instance, in a given chapter an author might explicate a single speech or a group of related speeches, or examine orations that comprise a genre of rhetoric such as forensic speaking. But the critic's focus remains on the rhetorical considerations of speaker, speech, occasion, and effect. Part II contains the texts of important addresses that are discussed in the critical analysis that precedes it. To the extent possible, each author has endeavored to collect authoritative speech texts, which have often been found through original research in collections of primary source material. In a few instances, because of the extreme length of a speech, texts have been edited, but the authors have been careful to delete material that is least important to the speech, and these deletions have been held to a minimum.

In each book thee is a chronology of major speeches that serves more purposes than may be apparent at first. Pragmatically, it typically lists all of the orator's known speeches and addresses. Places and dates of the speeches are also listed, although this is information that is sometimes difficult to determine precisely. But in a wider sense, the chronology attests to the scope of rhetoric in the United States. Certainly in quantity if not always in quality, Americans are historically talkers and listeners.

Because of the disparate nature of the speakers examined in this series, there is some latitude in the nature of the bibliographical materials that have been included in each book. But in every instance, authors have carefully described original historical materials and collections and gathered critical studies, biographies and autobiographies, and a variety of secondary sources that bear on the speaker and the oratory. By combining in each book bibliographical materials, speech texts, and critical chapters, this series notes that text and research sources are interwoven in the act of rhetorical criticism.

May the books in this series serve to memorialize the nation's greatest orators.

Bernard K. Duffy
Halford R. Ryan

ACKNOWLEDGMENTS

Though the research and writing of a book appears on the surface to be such a solitary effort, in reality, it has always been for me—and for most other writers, I suspect—a collaborative effort. It is, therefore, imperative that these others who have been a part of *Frederick Douglass: Oratory from Slavery* be acknowledged and thanked.

I begin with those at Greenwood Press who asked me to prepare a manuscript on Frederick Douglass. Though Douglass has long held a place of high esteem in my thoughts, it had never occurred to me to author anything on this great and noble nineteenth-century reformer. Greenwood's request was a challenge, and my life has been enriched in researching the life and words—both spoken and written—of Douglass.

The people associated with Greenwood have been helpful at every step during the process, beginning with Nita H. Romer, acquisitions editor in the social and political sciences. Dr. Bernard Duffy, an adviser of Greenwood's *Great American Orator Series,* was most helpful in suggesting various sources to be consulted.

I very much appreciate the efforts of Dr. Richard W. Leeman who read an early draft of this work and made some helpful suggestions, especially in terms of conceptualizing and organizing the material.

The staff of the Rush Rhees Library at the University of Rochester were most helpful when I went there to research their Douglass materials. My special thanks to Karl Kabelac, the manuscript librarian, who, in my estimation, went out of his way to help locate the information for which I was looking.

Deborah Burroughs, my colleague and friend at Illinois State University, appraised the manuscript at various stages and made several helpful suggestions.

Finally, Sharon Hagan Foiles, who has played such an important role in all my writings, continued to do so with this one. Sharon is the person who formats my material into a presentable manuscript. Her computer skills help to compensate for my technological deficiencies. I would think that my continuing requests of her time and talents would annoy her, but if so, Sharon has never let me know it. As always, I am greatly indebted to her.

All of these people share in whatever merits this book may have, and my cup of gratitude to them overflows.

INTRODUCTION

> Those who profess freedom and yet deprecate agitation are men who want crops without plowing up the ground, they want rain without thunder and lightning. They want the ocean without the awful roar of its many waters.
>
> Frederick Douglass, 1857 speech

Nineteenth-century America pulsated with great oratory. The American pulpit, as a whole, was never better than those years when preachers of the stature of Henry Ward Beecher, Phillips Brooks, William Ellery Channing, and Theodore Parker dominated the ecclesiastical scene. It was a time when national politics thundered with the voices of those who had mastered rhetorical eloquence—Daniel Webster, Stephen Douglas, and Abraham Lincoln, to name only a few. The antislavery movement brought to the forefront its own specialized orators, with Wendell Phillips as one of the best among several very talented public speakers who denounced slavery in fierce and uncompromising language. The women's movement provided a platform for the rhetorical skills of Elizabeth Cady Stanton and Susan B. Anthony. The names of Ralph Waldo Emerson and Edward Everett must of course be added to this pantheon of nineteenth-century rhetoricians. There were so many, many others in that era who had something to say and said it extremely well.

Standing at least the equal to any nineteenth-century orator was one who at first glance seemed most unlikely—Frederick Douglass. Douglass was unlikely, first of all, because he was a black man. In the mid-nineteenth century, even the most benevolent whites, such as Abraham Lincoln, considered blacks, at best, to be culturally inferior. Writing of that era, Robert T. Oliver has noted:

A Negro orator was as much an anomaly as a high school student urging his opinions about current issues to a general community audience. The adults might (and often do) admire the youngster's skill and praise his accomplishments, but this is far from taking seriously the advice he has to offer. What is being judged is a performance rather than an assertion of leadership. Negroes (and, parenthetically women) who sought to influence public opinion and policies in that time, through the influence of public speaking, were oddities to be observed and in some fashion perhaps even to be admired—but certainly not leaders to be followed. The wonder is not that there were few Negro orators but that there were any who attained to genuine distinction under such circumstances.[1]

Nevertheless, in spite of such discriminatory opinions, there were a few black orators who were eminently successful. These few were powerful, polished, and influential. They spoke with eloquent indignation against the institution of slavery. Their ranks included Charles Lennox Remond, Henry Highland Garnet, Samuel Ringgold Ward, John Mercer Langsdon, Nathaniel Paul, Alexander Crummell, James W.C. Pennington, and the greatest of them all, Frederick Douglass.

Race, however, was not the only factor that made Douglass an unlikely orator. There was background. For the first twenty-one years of his life, Douglass was a slave. He had no formal schooling in the art of rhetoric, or anything else for that matter. In contrast there was Remond, another superbly gifted black orator. Remond was born and raised in Massachusetts. At an early age he was recognized as possessing a gift of eloquent speech. In his formal education and other experiences he was encouraged and tutored in the development of this gift. For several years he was the most prominent and gifted black orator for the abolitionist cause. By the early 1840s, however, Remond became aware that he was taking a subordinate role to a newcomer who had escaped from slavery in 1838.

Douglass's oratorical skills were instrumental in breaking down many of the stereotypes and prejudices people held about blacks in the nineteenth century. A correspondent from the Nantucket *Islander* wrote of hearing Douglass in 1842. The reporter confessed that he went to hear the speech with "a bundle of prejudices," believing that blacks were mentally inferior, and expecting little from the Douglass speech. He attended, however, "for amusement and for recreation." What he heard that day was a "mental repast. Food for thought was showered . . . like manna from heaven." The reporter left the meeting hall "with a mountain load of prejudice" tumbling from his back. "Douglass," he wrote, "was chaste in language, brilliant in thought, and truly eloquent in delivery." In 1851 the Toronto *North American* declared that Douglass was "evidence in his own person of the falsity of the notion that the coloured race are incapable of high mental culture." Two years later, the *Journal*, of Freeport, Illinois, observed that Douglass "affords incontestable evidence of the capabilities of the African for intellectual culture."[2]

Soon after Douglass's death, the *Brooklyn Times* eulogized: "The superlative service which Frederick Douglass rendered to his mother's race was to dispel forever the fiction of the inferiority of the African race." At the same time, the *Indianapolis Times* similarly observed: "Frederick Douglass was the man who compelled a reluctant people to admit that a man of African blood could be an intellectual force."[3]

Douglass's oratory was the foundation for everything else he accomplished.

Waldo E. Martin Jr. has noted that "a significant measure of his [Douglass's] prestige and influence derived from the extraordinary power and range of his oratory. Indeed, his superb oratorical abilities and career dovetailed and enhanced his roles as race leader, abolitionist, social reformer, journalist, Republican, and government official."[4]

There are many excellent sources, both primary and secondary, for the researcher who wishes to learn about Frederick Douglass and his oratory. Some that this researcher found especially helpful are as follows. This best single source would be the five-volume work, *The Frederick Douglass Papers*, edited by John W. Blassingame, published in the years 1979 to 1992. Before Blassingame, Philip S. Foner had edited five volumes, *The Life and Writings of Frederick Douglass* (1950). This is still a very good and reliable collection of Douglass's writings and words, but it has been surpassed by Blassingame's efforts.

The three autobiographies of Douglass are indispensable for those who want to understand this black orator: *Narrative of the Life of Frederick Douglass: An American Slave* (1845); *My Bondage and My Freedom* (1855); and *The Life and Times of Frederick Douglass* (1881, 1892).

There are several good biographies of Frederick Douglass. Four that this writer found especially enlightening were *Frederick Douglass: The Colored Orator* (1891) by Frederick May Holland; *Frederick Douglass* (1948) by Benjamin Quarles; *Frederick Douglass: A Biography* (1964) by Philip S. Foner; and *Frederick Douglass* (1991) by William S. McFeely.

Two unpublished dissertations that lend special insight into the oratorical abilities and techniques of Douglass are "Frederick Douglass and the Anti-Slavery Crusade: His Career and Speeches" (1971) by R. Gerald Fulkerson; and "A Rhetorical Analysis of the Speeches of Frederick Douglass during and after the Civil War" (1972) by George A. Hinshaw.

Part I of this book sketches the important events of Douglass's life, with special focus on those various influences and circumstances, even in his days under slavery, that contributed to his reputation as one of the nineteenth century's greatest public speakers. Close examination will be made of his various oratorical experiences: the places he spoke, the audiences he addressed, the subjects about which he talked, and the mixed responses of his listeners to what he had to say.

Part II first of all, examines the many rhetorical techniques employed by Douglass, techniques that are organized under the general headings of ethos, pathos, and parallelism. This part concludes with three of Douglass's speeches, one each from three important epochs in his life: the prewar years, the war years, and the postwar years. Each speech, an important and noted address, will be recorded in its entirety, or nearly so. The mere reading of these speeches will enable the reader to understand how majestically Douglass used language to capture the attention of those who heard him. We must, of course, rely on the descriptions of others as to the experience of actually hearing Douglass deliver these orations, but the recorded words, in and of themselves, stand as a mighty testimony to the dynamic skills of this great man.

I

THE DEVELOPMENT
OF AN ORATOR

1

THE YEARS OF SLAVERY
(1818-1837)

It was 1818 when a slave woman, Harriet Bailey, gave birth to her fourth child, a boy, whom she named Frederick Augustus Washington Bailey. The place of birth was in Talbot County, on the eastern shore of Maryland. The father of the infant was an unknown white man. The whispered rumors, Frederick wrote in his first autobiography, "that my master was my father, may or may not be true . . . is of but little consequence. . . . The slaveholder, in cases not a few, sustains to his slaves the double relation of master and father."[1] Another uncertainty surrounding that birth was when it happened. Slave owners, as one more means of separating their slaves from their roots, kept their chattels in as much ignorance as possible concerning their roots. Douglass—the surname Frederick would later adopt—wrote:

By far the larger part of the slaves know as little of their ages as horses know of theirs, and it is the wish of most masters within my knowledge to keep their slaves thus ignorant. I do not remember to have ever met a slave who could tell of his birthday. . . . A want of information concerning my own was a source of unhappiness to me even during childhood. The white children could tell their ages. I could not tell why I ought to be deprived of the same privilege.[2]

When only a few months old, Frederick was separated from his mother to be raised by his elderly grandparents, Isaac and Betsey Bailey. This was a course of action often followed by slave owners. It served the dual purpose of loosening family ties among the slaves, and allowed for greater work from younger parents who would not be distracted with caring for their children. He recalled seeing his mother only four or five times in his life. She lived on a plantation twelve miles away, and on those few occasions she would walk the miles after work at night to be with her son, remain for a few hours, and then walk back, making sure that she arrived on time for work the following morning. Douglass wrote, "I do not recollect of ever seeing my mother by the light of day." In that first autobiography, Douglass pondered the purpose of separating a mother from her child. "For what this separation is done, I do not know," he mused, "unless it be to hinder the development of the child's affection toward its mother, and to blunt and destroy the natural affection of the mother for the child. This is the inevitable result."[3] Harriet Bailey died when her son was seven. If slave owners desired to break the natural bonds of affection between a mother and child by early separating them, they were, in Frederick's life, highly successful. He recalled: "Never having enjoyed, to any considerable extent, her soothing presence, her tender and watchful care, I received the tidings of her death with much the same emotions I should have probably felt at the death of a stranger."[4] In his third autobiography, Douglass wrote of a lasting contribution from his mother his life.

I have since learned that she was the only one of all the colored people of Tuckahoe who could read. How she acquired this knowledge I do not know. . . . I can therefore fondly and proudly ascribe to her an earnest love of knowledge. . . . The achievement of my mother, considering the place and circumstances, was very extraordinary. In view of this fact, I am happy to attribute any love of letters I may have, not to my presumed Anglo-Saxon paternity, but to the native genius of my sable, unprotected, and uncultivated mother—a woman who belonged to a race whose mental endowments are still disparaged and despised.[5]

For the first twenty-one years of his life, Frederick Bailey was a slave. During those years, his experiences were wide and varied. He labored on a big and beautiful plantation, on a small farm, in the village and large city. His duties ranged from domestic servant, to field hand, to skilled laborer. He had masters who were relatively lenient, and others who nearly killed his spirit through degradations, beatings, and imprisonment. But, as it has been with some others, it was in Douglass' unpromising beginnings that the seeds of his greatness were sown. Douglass became the eloquent orator and powerful writer that he was, not in spite of, but because of those things he learned, observed, and experienced during the first impoverished and degrading years of his life. James M'Cune Smith, a black doctor and abolitionist, wrote in 1855, that "for his special mission," Douglass's slavery education "was better than he could have acquired in any lettered school."[6]

Douglass was endowed with the gift of high intelligence, a gift that enabled him to take advantage of the few opportunities that came his way during his years of bondage. It was a gift, Douglass acknowledged, he had inherited from his mother who had "an earnest love of knowledge," so he came naturally to his own "love of letters." An early aspect of that intelligence was Douglass's keen powers of observation, the ability to take in what he saw, to remember it, and to later describe to others, in picturesque detail, what he had observed. A significant element that contributed importance and power to his later oratory, was Douglass's ability to look back on his days in slavery, and vividly relate what he had observed. In an 1845 address, about seven years after his flight from slavery, Douglass, before the eleventh annual convention of the American Anti-Slavery Society, held in the Broadway Tabernacle in New York City, described a particular instance he had observed as a slave. It stands as one example of the orator's ability to observe, to recall, and describe.

We had on the plantation an overseer, by the name of Austin Gore, a man who was highly respected as an overseer—proud, ambitious, cruel, artful, obdurate. Nearly every slave stood in the utmost dread and horror of that man. His eye flashed confusion amongst them. He never spoke but to command, nor commanded but to be obeyed. He was lavish with the whip, sparing with his word. I have seen that man tie up men by the two hands, and for two hours, at intervals, ply the lash. I have seen women stretched upon on the limbs of trees, and their bare backs made bloody with the lash. One slave refused to be whipped by him—I need not tell you that he was a man, though black his features, degraded his condition. He had committed some trifling offence—for they whip for trifling offenses—the slave refused to be whipped, and ran—he did not stand to and fight his master as I did once, and might do again—though I hope I shall not have occasion to do so—he ran and stood in a creek, and refused to come out. At length his master told him he would shoot him if he did not come out. Three calls were to be given him. The first, second, and third, were given, at each of which the slave stood his ground. Gore, equally determined and firm, raised his musket, and in an instant poor Derby was no more. He sank beneath the waves, and naught but the crimsoned waters marked the spot.[7]

When he was about six years of age, Frederick first began to understand some of the dreaded meanings of slavery. He was, he learned, owned by a white master whom his grandmother referred to with some dread as the "Old Master." His grandmother was also owned by this same mysterious person. In fact, all the black people he knew were owned by Master Aaron Anthony. The lad was also made to understand that one day soon he would have to leave his grandmother's cabin and go to live on Master Anthony's plantation. While in his sixth year the dreaded day came. One summer day, Frederick and his grandmother walked several miles to Aaron Anthony's plantation, where, for the first time, he met several of his cousins, two sisters, and a brother. As Frederick played with the children, Grandma Betsey left and returned to her home. When informed that his grandmother had gone, the youngster rushed to the road to join her. She was nowhere to be seen. Frightened and deserted, the little boy "threw himself on the ground, and crying, pummeled the dry dust." Later, he was taken to a bed "and cried himself to sleep. And he never fully trusted anyone again."[8]

Frederick was at this plantation for only two years, but those two years left vivid and never to be forgotten impressions as to the savagery of slavery. The treatment he personally received was relatively tolerable. There was an occasional whipping, but his greatest suffering was due to hunger and cold. "These were my two great physical troubles. I could neither get a sufficiency of food nor of clothing; but I suffered less from hunger than from cold."[9] His most terrible memories of plantation life were of the savage beatings and whippings administered to adults, especially women. The screams for mercy, the shrieks of agony, the sound of the lash upon bare flesh, and the gory sight of flowing blood, all became grist for future writings and speeches—accounts filled with burning indignation.

His eighth year marked the first major positive break in the young slave's life. Frederick was sent to live in Baltimore where his new owners would be Hugh Auld, Anthony's brother, and his wife, Sophia. The thought of living in a big city, of new owners, filled Frederick with excitement and hopeful anticipation. Anything would be better than life on the plantation. Furthermore, at a time of life when most slaves began the dreaded rigors of field work, his life was taking a different turn. Frederick's hopes, for the most part, were more than fulfilled. He was placed largely under the control of Mrs. Auld, a kindly woman who demonstrated great kindness to the family's only slave. Frederick's primary task was to provide companionship for the Auld's son, Tommy, who was a few years younger than Frederick. At the Auld home, young Frederick not only lived in the same house with his owners, he ate at their table and of the same food, and enjoyed many of the family privileges.

Most important of all, Sophia Auld began Frederick on a program of self-education, a program that he would follow for the rest of his life. Part of the learning process included religious instruction, another element that would have great influence and impact on a future orator and writer. Frederick's introduction to the world of books began soon after his move to Baltimore when Mrs. Auld read to Tommy and him from the Bible. Intrigued, the youthful slave asked his mistress to teach him how to read the Bible for himself. Though such instruction to slaves was not encouraged in Maryland, Sophia Auld readily consented. Her pupil was a fast learner. In a short period of time, Frederick had learned the alphabet and how to spell words of three or four letters. When Mrs. Auld told her husband of Frederick's astounding progress, Hugh Auld was angry and gave orders that there must be no further instruction. Within Frederick's hearing, Auld informed Sophia as to why slaves must not be taught to read. "If you give a nigger an inch, he will take an ell. A nigger should know nothing but to obey his master. . . . Learning would spoil the best nigger in the world." Speaking specifically of Frederick, Auld warned: "If you teach that nigger . . . how to read, there would be no keeping him. It would forever unfit him to be a slave. He would at once become unmanageable." Frederick listened carefully to Auld's words of warning that learning and slavery were not compatible. He resolved to continue his education, even without Sophia Auld's aid.

Conscious of the difficulty of learning without a teacher, I set out with high hope, and a fixed purpose, at whatever cost of trouble, to learn how to read. The very decided manner with which he spoke . . . [of] the evil consequences of giving me instruction, served to convince me that he was deeply sensible of the truths he was uttering. . . . In learning to read, I owe almost as much to the bitter opposition of my master, as to the kindly aid of my mistress.[10]

Frederick next turned to the city streets to further his education. When sent out on errands, or during times of play, he asked schoolboys to instruct him. Some of the lads rendered their services for a slice of bread or a biscuit. Others simply "took pleasure in teaching me."[11] Frederick was able to secure an old spelling book that he assiduously studied at every opportunity. By the time he was twelve years of age, the young slave had become quite an accomplished reader. The schoolboys informed him of a popular school book, Caleb Bingham's *The Columbian Orator,* from which they were memorizing selections to be recited in a declamation exhibition. With fifty cents he had earned from blackening boots, the eager student purchased a copy for himself. What a treasure! Douglass called it "a noble acquisition." Within the book there were extracts from speeches by Lord Chatham, William Pitt, Charles James Fox, and Richard Sheridan. Douglass read the speeches over and over, memorized some and recited them. An orator was born.

The reading of these speeches added much to my limited stock of language, and enabled me to give tongue to many interesting thoughts, which had frequently flashed through my soul, and died away from lack of utterance . . . from the speeches of Sheridan, I got a bold and powerful denunciation of oppression, and a most brilliant vindication of the rights of man.[12]

The selection that most captivated Douglass's attention was one titled "Dialogue between a Master and Slave," in which a slave attempted to convince his master as to the injustice and brutality of slavery.

Mast. It is in the order of Providence that one man should become subservient to another. It ever has been so, and ever will be. I found the custom, and did not make it.

Slave. You cannot but be sensible, that the robber who puts a pistol to your breast may make just the same plea. Providence gives him a power over your life and property; it gave my enemies a power over my liberty. But it has also given me legs to escape with; and what should prevent me from using them? Nay, what should restrain me from retaliating the wrongs I have suffered, if a favorable occasion should offer?

Mast. Gratitude; I repeat, gratitude! Have I not endeavored ever since I possessed you to alleviate your misfortune by kind treatment; and does that confer no obligation? Consider how much worse your condition might have been under another master.

Slave. You have done nothing more for me than for your working cattle. Are they not well fed and tended? Do you work them harder than your slaves? Is not the rule for treating both designed only for your advantage? You treat both your men and beast slaves better than some of your neighbors, because you are more prudent and wealthy than they.

Mast. You might add, more humane too.

Slave. Humane! Does it deserve that appellation to keep your fellow-men in forced subjection, deprived of all exercise of their free will, liable to all the injuries that your own caprice, or the brutality of your overseers, may heap on them, and devoted, soul and body, only to your pleasure and emolument? Can gratitude take place between creatures in such a state, and the tyrant who holds them in it? Look at these limbs; are they not those of a man? Think that I have the spirit of a man too.[13]

Douglass recalled that the reading of this selection "powerfully affected me; and I could not help feeling that the day might come, when the well directed answers made by the slave to the master . . . would find their counterpart in myself."[14] Waldo E. Martin has noted that the *Columbian Orator* gave Douglass "his first formal introduction to rhetoric."

Even as a free man, he might return to the lessons he gathered from that text. Most likely, his critical decision to employ oratory as a strategy toward freedom, equality, and justice derived in part from the book's strong initial impact on him. The stress on a natural style, in addition to issues such as emancipation, temperance, and education, on one hand, and grand ides like liberty, courage, and patriotism, on the other, clearly made a lasting impression on him.[15]

At the same time Frederick was developing his ability to read and write, a religious interest was being awakened. Sophia Auld had read to him from the Bible, adding her own understanding to the written words. The teachings of a white Methodist minister and a few black lay preachers all made their impact. Most influential of all, however, was an elderly, partially literate, and intensely devout black man, whom Douglass would later refer to as "Uncle Lawson." "A more devout man than he, I never saw," Douglass recalled. It was Lawson who imparted to the impressionable young Frederick a strong sense of self-esteem, convincing the youth that he had an important mission to fulfill. Though Hugh Auld threatened to whip Frederick if he continued to see Lawson, the youth ignored the threat and saw his spiritual father at every opportunity. The old man told Frederick that the "Lord had a great work for me to do." When Frederick responded that he did not see how this was possible—he was after all a slave—Lawson responded, "the good Lord would bring it to pass in his own good time." As an adult, Frederick Douglass evaluated the effect of "Uncle Lawson" upon his life: "He threw my thoughts into a channel from which they have never entirely diverged. He fanned my already intense love of learning into a flame, by assuring me that I was to be a useful man in the world."[16]

Religion would play an important role in the life, orations, and writings of Frederick Douglass. In the early years it was a sustaining force that would motivate him to fulfill his mission. While still in slavery, Douglass came to see the hypocrisy of many religious expressions and convictions. He observed the use of religion to justify slavery, to support the doctrine of racial superiority and inferiority, and condone the use of the whip and other forms of brutality to keep the people of color in their "God–ordained places." His religious convictions would change over time from the religious orthodoxy he learned from Sophia Auld and "Uncle Lawson" to a liberal Christian humanism wherein human beings had to work out their own salvation. Nevertheless, the great speeches he would deliver in the future during his more than fifty-five years of freedom were saturated with religious references, concepts and metaphors—all used to support and illustrate his ideas and arguments.

During his years at Baltimore, Frederick developed yet another talent, the art of mimicry. His keen ear quickly picked up the differences in dialect, inflection, and manner of speech. He was soon able to replicate the speech patterns of his most cultured white masters. He was intrigued by the nuances of speech he heard from a Massachusetts visitor, and in a short time was able to speak as if from New England. As a boy, Frederick entertained his young friends my mimicking others. As a man, mimicry became a highly developed rhetorical tool. He would amuse and captivate his future audiences by mimicking southern preachers and slave auctioneers.

In 1833, when Frederick was about sixteen years old, he was returned to Talbot County where Thomas Auld would reassume the role of the boy's master. Frederick's memory was that "Master Thomas was a mean man. . . . I do not know of one single noble act ever performed by him." Though a prosperous man, Thomas Auld never gave his slaves enough to eat and they were continually hungry, forced to beg and steal in order to supplement the small rations allotted to them. Soon after Frederick's arrival, Thomas Auld experienced a religious conversion at a Methodist camp meeting. His slaves, including Frederick, had hopes that their master's conversion would translate into more humane treatment toward them. It did not happen. "Prior to his conversion, he relied upon his own depravity," asserted Douglass, "but after his conversion, he found religious sanction and support for his slaveholding cruelty."[17]

As an example, I will state one of many facts going to prove the charge. I have seen him tie up a lame young women, and whip her with a heavy cowskin upon her naked shoulders, causing the warm red blood to drip, and, in justification of the bloody deed, he would quote this passage of Scripture—"He that knoweth his master's will, and doeth it not, shall be beaten with many stripes."[18]

Frederick's experiences with Thomas Auld were but a few out of so many, many more as to the great gulf that existed between so much religious profession and daily practice. In later speeches he would refer to the anguishing paradox again and again. On one occasion, Auld and a few of his friends, with clubs in their hands, broke up a Sunday school class which was meeting in the home of a free Negro. Upon discovering that Frederick was a leader and teacher at the school, Auld administered several severe lashes to the teenaged boy.

After nine months of futile attempts to break his young slave's spirit, Auld decided to turn him over to one who specialized in slave breaking. On January 1, 1834, Frederick was sent to Edward Covey's farm where he was to remain until the following Christmas. From dawn until dusk, and sometimes until midnight, six days a week, the young slave labored in the fields. During hot temperatures and cold, under the scorching sun and during fierce storms, the boy, for whom life had been so promising just a short time ago, was subjected to hard labor. He was continually hungry, and at least once every week Covey contrived some reason for a harsh flogging of the young slave. Slowly, but most certainly, the labor, the hunger, and the beatings took their collective toll. "Mr. Covey succeeded in breaking me," Douglass wrote. "I was broken in body, soul, and spirit. . . . My intellect languished, the disposition to read departed. . . . The dark night of slavery closed in upon me; and behold a man transformed into a brute!" Sundays, his only day free from labor, were spent "in a sort of beast-like stupor, between sleep and wake." Moments of hope would sometimes arise within the young man, only to be quickly crushed, when "I sank down again, mourning over my wretched condition." Despair was so overwhelming that Douglass "was sometimes prompted to take my life, and that of Covey."[19]

Early one morning in mid-August, as Covey was preparing once again to whip his young slave, Frederick resolved to resist, regardless of the consequences. For two hours the adversaries fiercely fought each other. When the combat ceased due to mutual exhaustion, Frederick fully expected reprisals, perhaps death itself, but there were none. From that moment on, and for the remaining months with Covey, the slave breaker largely ignored Douglass. There were no more beatings. The only explanation Douglass could think of for the failure to retaliate—he could have been turned over to the authorities and hung—was that Covey who "enjoyed the . . . reputation of being a first rate overseer and negro breaker," was "probably, ashamed to have it known . . . that he had been mastered by a boy of sixteen."[20] The encounter with Covey was, according to Douglass

the turning-point in my career as a slave. It rekindled the few expiring embers of freedom, and revived within me a sense of my own manhood. . . . My long-crushed spirit rose, cowardice departed, bold defiance took its place; and I now resolved that, however long I might remain a slave in form, the day had passed forever when I could be a slave in fact.[21]

On January 1, 1835, Thomas Auld sold the services of Frederick Bailey to a neighboring slaveowner, William Friedland. Friedland was, said Douglass, "the best master I ever had, till I became my own master."[22] Working hours were reasonable and food was adequate.

Another advantage I gained in my new master was, he made no pretensions to, or profession of, religion; and this, in my opinion, was truly a great advantage. I assert most unhesitatingly, that the religion of the south is a mere covering for the most horrid crimes,—a justifier of the most appalling barbarity,—a sanctifier of the most hateful frauds,—and a dark shelter under which the darkest, foulest, grossest, and most infernal deeds of slaveholders find the strongest protection. Were I to be again reduced to the chains of slavery, next to that enslavement, I should regard being the slave of a religious master the greatest calamity that could befall me.[23]

To augment his argument, Douglass pointed to some clergymen and lay church leaders who lived near the Friedland farm, churchmen widely noted for their severe cruelty to their slaves.[24] During his stay at the Friedland farm, Frederick conducted a secret Sunday school for over forty slaves. Though life had greatly improved for Frederick under Friedland, and he found great satisfaction in conducting the Sunday school, he was "still restless and discontented." The youthful slave wanted freedom. "Give [a slave] a bad master," noted Douglass, "and he aspires to a good master; give him a good master, and he wishes to become his own master."[25] Thus, in 1836 Frederick and five other slaves made plans to escape to the freedom of the North. Elaborate preparations were made, and on the chosen day, just hours before the escape was to take place, constables appeared on the farm and arrested the would-be runaways. One of the conspirators, it seems, had lost his nerve and turned informer on the others. The five were put in chains and held in the Talbot County jail. It looked as though Frederick would be sent into the Deep South, and all chances of future escape would be remote. Once again, however, the young man averted dire consequences that could have precluded all possibilities of the great career that eventually came to pass.

Thomas Auld informed Frederick that he would be returned to Baltimore and placed once again under the supervision of his brother, Hugh Auld. Furthermore, Thomas told Frederick that he would be taught a trade, and upon good behavior would be emancipated on his twenty-fifth birthday. The motives of Thomas Auld for such a generous offer are impossible to discover. Perhaps it was kindness, or perhaps emancipation was offered to discourage any further attempts to escape. Hugh Auld found a job for Frederick as an apprentice caulker in a large shipyard. There were, however, racial tensions in the yard. White workers resented the presence of black workers. Threats turned to violence. After his fight with Covey, Frederick had vowed that he would never again be physically assaulted by white men without putting up a forceful resistance. He could and did hold his own when faced by one attacker, but one day in 1836 he was nearly killed when four white workers attacked him. It was one more incident, one more time, when the name of Frederick Douglass came ever so close to being relegated to obscurity.

After regaining his health, Frederick was given an apprenticeship in Price's Shipyard where his master, Hugh Auld, was a general foreman. In a short time Frederick became a skilled caulker, earning a dollar and a half a day, which had to be turned over to his master. In May 1838 Auld and his slave came to an agreement whereby Frederick would pay his master a fixed amount of three dollars a week and would be able to keep all above that for himself. With the money that Frederick kept for himself he was expected to pay for his own board and clothing, and purchase his own caulking tools.[26] After expenses, Frederick was still able to put some money away for a future escape.

During the evening hours, Frederick met with a group of free negroes who called themselves the East Baltimore Improvement Society, a gathering of young black men committed to mental growth. Frederick, as a slave, should have been excluded from the society, but an exception was made. Before this group "Frederick delivered his first public speeches and engaged in his first formal debate."[27] Years later Douglass wrote, "I owe much to the society of these young men."[28] Frederick also became associated with a congregation of black Methodists, and it is possible that he was provided opportunities to speak before this group. It was at one of these social gatherings of this Methodist congregation that Frederick met Anna Murray, a free black woman who worked as a domestic in Baltimore. Meeting Anna, and desiring to marry her, provided Frederick even further motivation for freedom.

In early August, one Saturday night, Frederick left Baltimore to attend a religious camp meeting some twelve miles away. He failed to notify Auld that he was leaving town. Furthermore, the three dollar payment was due on Saturday nights and thus would be delayed. When Frederick returned to Auld's home to make the payment, Frederick found a furious master. "You rascal," shouted Auld, "I have a great mind to give you a severe whipping. . . . You are bound to show yourself here every Saturday night." The agreement of the previous May whereby Frederick had obtained a small portion of freedom was revoked. "The next thing I shall hear of," snarled Auld, "will be your running away. Bring home your tools and your clothes, at once. I'll teach you how to go off in this way."[29]

Frederick complied, but not for long. On Monday, September 3, 1838, he made good on his long anticipated plans to escape. Borrowing a sailor's outfit (which would be returned by mail), and identification papers from a free black, Douglass boarded a train to Philadelphia. Throughout the journey the escapee feared discovery, and there were some anxious moments, but he safely arrived in Philadelphia that afternoon. When night came he took a train to New York City, arriving there on Tuesday morning.

Warned to trust no one, Douglass proceeded cautiously through the city. He made his way to the boarding house of David Ruggles, secretary of the New York Vigilance Committee, a group dedicated to the purpose of helping runaway slaves. Frederick remained with Ruggles until Anna could join him. On September 15 Frederick and Anna were married. James W. C. Pennington, who had himself escaped from a Maryland master in 1830, and was now a Presbyterian minister and abolitionist, officiated at the ceremony. Ruggles suggested that the couple move on to New Bedford, Massachusetts. It was a place that would provide a safer climate for fugitives, and with its shipbuilding industry would be able to provide Frederick an opportunity to employ his trade. Ruggles gave the newlyweds five dollars and sent them on their way with a letter of introduction to Nathan Johnson.

The Johnson family welcomed Frederick and Anna, providing them with food and shelter until Frederick could secure suitable employment. Nathan Johnson was also instrumental in giving the couple a new name. During his escape, Frederick had used several different surnames in order to avoid detection.

In New York he had chosen "Johnson" as a suitable and perhaps permanent name. Nathan Johnson, however, protested that there were already too many Johnsons in New Bedford. He had been reading Sir Walter Scott's *Lady of the Lake,* and from that source he suggested the name of "Douglass." Frederick readily agreed. All within a few days, a new freedom, a new wife, a new name, and, in the not too distant future, a new and grand career.

2

THE PREWAR YEARS OF FREEDOM (1838-1861)

The first twenty-three years of freedom for Douglass would bring radical changes to his life. The years began with Douglass as just one more unknown fugitive from slavery but would end with Douglass becoming a figure of national and international fame. The years began with Douglass being an echo of the thoughts and words of William Lloyd Garrison but would end with Douglass formulating and asserting his own thoughts, resulting in a break with Garrison. The years began with Douglass making his first attempts at public oratory—sometimes in a halting and insecure manner—but would culminate in the recognition of Douglass as one of the premier public speakers in the United States. In less than a quarter of a century, a slave, once owned and in bondage to another, became a free man who would make an enormous impact on his times.

THE LAUNCHING OF A CAREER (1838–1845)

In New Bedford, Douglass's sensitive sense of sound and observation were delightfully awakened. He became aware of a certain wonderful quietness.

Almost everybody seemed to be at work, but noiselessly so, compared to what I had been accustomed to in Baltimore. There were no loud songs heard from those engaged in loading and unloading ships. I heard no deep oaths or horrid curses on the laborer. I saw no whipping of men; but all seemed to go smoothly on. Every man appeared to understand his work, and went at it with a sober, yet cheerful earnestness, which betokened the deep interest which he felt in what he was doing, as well as a sense of his own dignity as a man.[1]

After three days in New Bedford, Douglass found employment for himself, "stowing a sloop with a load of oil." It was, remembered Douglass, "dirty, and hard work for me; but I went at it with a glad heart and willing hand. I was now my own master." Life was not perfect, however, in New Bedford. Douglass became aware, as he often would, of deep prejudices in the North. When he sought employment as a caulker, he discovered that white caulkers refused to work with a black caulker, and, thus, there were no jobs available in the trade for which he was highly qualified. Undaunted, Douglass found plenty of work to do. "There was no work too hard—none too dirty," Douglass would later write. "I was ready to saw wood, shovel coal, carry the hod, sweep the chimney, or roll oil casks,—all of which I did for nearly three years in New Bedford before I became known to the anti-slavery world."[2]

After disappointing experiences at a predominantly white Methodist Church in the community, where blacks had to sit in the gallery and were treated condescendingly by the pastor and members of the congregation, the Douglass family began attendance at New Bedford's Zion Chapel, a congregation in the African Methodist Episcopal Zion denomination. At Zion Chapel, Douglass was licensed as a lay preacher. He recounted "the days I spent in little Zion, New Bedford, in the several capacities of sexton, steward, class leader, clerk, and local preacher, . . . [as] among the happiest days of my life."[3] This small congregation provided one more training ground in the development of Douglass's oratorical skills. His duties as lay preacher gave him the opportunity to address a number of different issues and topics: biblical expositions, temperance, colonization, and most important, his experiences as a slave.

He had been in New Bedford for about four months when he was introduced to William Lloyd Garrison's abolitionist paper, *Liberator*. The paper's uncompromising and tenacious attacks on slavery were the words Douglass had been longing to read and hear.

The paper became my meat and my drink. My soul was set all on fire. Its sympathy for my brethren in bonds—its scathing denunciations of slaveholders—its faithful exposures of slavery—and its powerful attacks upon the upholders of the institution—sent a thrill of joy through my soul, such as I had never felt before.[4]

Douglass began to attend local abolitionist meetings where he soon was an active participant in the discussions that took place. These mixed meetings with both races in attendance were a new experience for Douglass. On March 29, 1839, Douglass's name appeared in print for the first time, as far as can be determined. The *Liberator* carried an account of a March 9 meeting of negro abolitionists in New Bedford. The article noted that Douglass was one of ten speakers who condemned the American Colonization Society and praised Garrison as "the uncompromising advocate of immediate and unconditional emancipation," a man who was "deserving of our confidence and support."[5] The tone of the article was a recognition of the division of aims and thought in the antislavery movement of the North, and that Douglass was unhesitatingly taking a stand on those issues. There were those who recommended the freeing of slaves and "colonizing" them in Africa. Douglass, like Garrison, would have none of it. There was also a division in thought over Garrison himself who represented the more "radical" wing of the antislavery movement. Those more moderate in the movement were embarrassed and repulsed by what they considered Garrison's abrasive speeches and writings. He attacked the churches for their failure to take a strong abolitionist stance. With equal denunciation, he scorned both political parties, the Democrats and the Whigs, declaring that both of them were tools of slavery interests. Garrison argued that true abolitionists should have no dealings in politics and must devote their energies to "moral suasion." Garrison also proclaimed that women should have equal opportunity with men in participation in the antislavery societies. Douglass, through actions and words, was a staunch supporter of Garrison. In the years to follow, Garrison and Douglass would differ significantly over several issues, but in his early years with the antislavery movement Douglass was uncompromising in his support of Garrisonianism.

Douglass was delivering speeches before antislavery gatherings as early as 1839. It was, however, on August 12, 1841, that he began his journey on the road to prominence. The Massachusetts Anti-Slavery Society was meeting in Nantucket and Douglass had been asked to speak before the assembly by William A. Coffin, a New Bedford abolitionist. A few years after that speech, Douglass recalled the event.

My speech on this occasion is about the only one I ever made of which I do not remember a single connected sentence. It was with the utmost difficulty that I could stand erect, or that I could command and articulate two words without hesitation and stammering. I trembled in every limb. I am not sure that my embarrassment was not the most effective part of my speech, if speech it could be called. At any rate, this is about the only part of my performance that I now distinctly remember.[6]

Those who heard Douglass that day were much more impressed with the speech than was the speaker. Dr. James M'Cune Smith, a black physician from New York City, recalled: "He [Douglass] was about the age when the younger Pitt entered the House of Commons; like Pitt, too, he stood up a born orator."[7] Four years after the Nantucket speech, Garrison's recollections were still vivid.

He came forward to the platform with a hesitancy and embarrassment, necessarily the attendants of a sensitive mind in such a novel position. After apologizing for his ignorance, and reminding the audience that slavery was a poor school for the human intellect and heart, he proceeded to narrate some of the facts in his own history as a slave, and in the course of his speech gave utterance to many noble thoughts and thrilling reflections.[8]

Garrison continued: "I think I never hated slavery so intensely as at that moment; certainly, my perception of the enormous outrage which is inflicted by it on the godlike nature of its victims, was rendered far more clearer than ever."

When Garrison followed Douglass to the platform to deliver his own speech, referring back to that oration that had just mesmerized the audience, Garrison declared that "Patrick Henry, of revolutionary fame, never made a speech more eloquent in the cause of liberty than the one we have just listened to from the lips of that hunted fugitive."[9]

A correspondent, who attended the event, reported: "One recently from the house of bondage, spoke with great power. Flinty hearts were pierced, and cold ones melted by its eloquence. Our best pleaders for the slave held their breath for fear of interrupting him."[10]

Douglass was asked by Garrison and others from the Massachusetts Anti-Slavery Society to travel about the country as a paid agent for the society. Doubting his own ability, Douglass at first refused, but after further deliberation agreed to try it for a three-month period. For the next three months he traveled about New England with John A. Collins, an officer of the society. The reception Douglass received was so positive that it erased most reservations the speaker had as to his skills. A reporter from a New Hampshire paper was exuberant after hearing Douglass. "As a speaker he [Douglass] has few equals. It is not declamation—but oratory, power of debate. He has wit, arguments, sarcasm, pathos—all that first rate men show in their master efforts."[11] The three-month trial period turned into twenty years of the most powerful and effective antislavery rhetoric the nation has ever experienced.

One of Douglass's early assignments was to deliver four speeches before the Old Colony Anti-Slavery Society in Hingham, Massachusetts, on November 4, 1841. In these speeches, Douglass's words demonstrated that he was a true Garrisonian. He strongly advocated "moral suasion" as opposed to political involvement.

We ought to do just what slaveholders don't want us to do; that is, use moral suasion. They care nothing about your political action; they don't dread the political movement; it is the moral movement, the appeal to men's sense of right, which makes them and all our opponents tremble. . . . One great recommendation of this power of moral suasion is, that every body may exercise it, women as well as men, children as well as adults. Slavery is at the North as well as at the South: it has interwoven itself in all departments of society but the antislavery department; and sometimes I think I see a little of it there. Hence again results the need of the power of moral suasion.[12]

As Garrison believed, so Douglass advocated, the Union must be dissolved. There should be no bonds with the practioneers of slavery. As long as the Union was intact, runaway slaves were, according to many in the North, bound to be returned. A dissolution of the Union would solve that problem.

I want to say a word about this Union. It is a fact that the northern people stand pledged by the Union to return runaway slaves, that constitutes the bulwark of slavery. The slaves are told that, if they escape to the North, they will be sent back; and this discourages very many from making any attempts to gain their freedom. This is the Union whose "desolation" we want to accomplish; and he is no true abolitionist, who does not go against this Union. The South care not how much you talk and act against slavery as an evil in the abstract; they will agree with you; yet they cling to it as to life; and it is this pledge binding the North to the South, on which they rely for its support.[13]

Douglass spoke of the futility of political petitions, and the false hopes such petitions raised in slaves, thus holding them "in check."

My first knowledge of the abolition movements was through the petitions for the abolition of slavery in the District of Columbia. These petitions delight the hearts of the slaves; they rejoice to know that something is going on in their favor. Waiters hear their masters talk at table, cursing the abolitionists, John Quincy Adams, etc. The masters imagine that their poor slaves are so ignorant that they don't know the meaning of the language they are using; for the slaves always pretend to be very stupid; they commit all sorts of foolery, and act like baboons and wild beasts in presence of their masters; but every word is noted in memory, and is told to their fellow-slaves; and when they get together, they talk over what they have heard—they talk about liberty, and about these petitions. They get a vague idea that somebody is doing something to ameliorate their condition. Thus these petitions hold the slave in check; thus they are good for the master as well as for the slave, for they have prevented many an assassination, many an insurrection. I was myself contemplating measures and making arrangements for my own emancipation, when hearing of these petitions stopped me. But, sir, the slaves are learning to read and write, and the time is fast coming when they will act in concert, and effect their own emancipation, if justice is not done by some other extraneous agency.[14]

Douglass then turned to the subject of the churches, and with biting sarcasm, and stinging wit, denounced the racial prejudice he had discovered in northern congregations.

At the South, I was a member of the Methodist church. When I came North, I thought one Sunday I would attend communion, at one of the churches of my denomination, in the town where I was staying. The white people gathered around the alter, the blacks clustered by the door. After the good minister had served out the bread and wine to one portion of those near him, he said, "These may withdraw, and others come forward"; thus he proceeded till all the white members had been served. Then he drew a long breath, and looking out toward the door, exclaimed, "Come up, colored friends, come up! for you know, God is no respecter of persons!" I haven't been there to see the sacrament taken since.

At New Bedford, where I live, there was a great revival of religion not long ago—many were converted, and "received," as they said, "into the kingdom of heaven." But it seems, the kingdom of heaven is like a net; at least so it was according the practice of these pious Christians; and when the net was drawn ashore, they had to sit down and cull out the fish. Well, it happened now that some of the fish had rather black scales; so these were sorted out and packed by themselves. But among those who experienced religion at this time was a colored girl; she was baptized in the same water as the rest; so she thought she might sit at the Lord's table, and partake of the same sacramental elements with the others. The deacon handed around the cup; and when he came to the black girl, he could not pass her, for there was the minister looking right at him, and as he was kind of an abolitionist, the deacon was rather afraid of giving him offence; so he handed the girl the cup, and she tasted. Now it so happened that next to her sat a young lady who had been converted at the same time, baptized in the same water, and put her hope in the same blessed Savior; yet when the cup containing the precious blood which had been shed for all, came to her, she rose in disdain, and walked out of the church. Such was the religion she had experienced!

Another young lady fell into a trance. When she awoke, she declared she had been to heaven. Her friends were all anxious to know what and whom she had seen there; so she told the whole story. But there was one good old lady whose curiosity went beyond that of all the others—and she inquired of the girl that had the vision, if she saw any black folks in heaven? After some hesitation, the reply was, "Oh! I didn't go into the kitchen!"

Thus you see, my hearers, this prejudice goes even into the church of God. And there are those who carry it so far that it is disagreeable to them even to think of going to heaven, if colored people are going there too![15]

He then spoke of southern clergymen who used religion to defend slavery, and this before the slaves themselves. Again, wit and sarcasm were masterfully used.

The slaveholding ministers preach up the divine right of slaveholders to property in their fellow men. The southern preachers say to the poor slave, "Oh! if you wish to be happy in time, happy in eternity, you must be obedient to your masters; their interest is yours. God made one portion of men to do the working, and another to do the thinking; how good God is! You have no trouble or anxiety; but ah! you can't imagine how perplexing it is to your masters and mistresses to have so much thinking to do in your behalf! You cannot appreciate your blessings; you know not how happy a thing it is for you that you were born of that portion of the human family which has the working instead of the thinking to do! Oh! how grateful and obedient you ought to be to your masters! How beautiful are the arrangements of Providence! Look at your hard, horny hands—see how nicely they are adapted to the labor you have to perform! Look at our delicate fingers, so exactly fitted for our station, and see how manifest it is that God designed us to be the thinkers and you the workers—oh! the wisdom of God![16]

Douglass's attacks on the churches and clergymen would be a theme to which he would return again and again during his years of antislavery rhetoric. The reaction to Douglass at Hingham was mostly that of high praise. Garrison, who followed one of Douglass's speeches, said, "I am almost afraid to speak now, lest I should undo the impression made by our friend Douglass—a noble man indeed! . . . he is a miracle! a proof of what man can do and be, in spite of station or condition."[17] The editor of the *Hingham Patriot* wrote that Douglass was "very fluent in the use of language, choice and appropriate language too; and talks as well for all that we could see, as men who have spent all their days over books."[18] A few nonabolitionists, however, were offended by what they considered the arrogance of Douglass, especially for his urging of the dissolution of the Union and his attacks on American churches.[19]

Douglass was just what the antislavery movement needed at that point in time. One of the criticisms that southerners were using against the abolitionists was that the abolitionists really knew nothing about slavery. They had not seen it, had not experienced it, and were only making charges based on hearsay and their own imaginations. Douglass became the unimpeachable response to such criticism. Early in 1842 Collins wrote to Garrison that "the public have itching ears to hear a colored man speak, and particularly a slave." In the same letter Collins described Douglass's particular role as an antislavery speaker.

Though he has never been favored with the advantages of an education, his style of speaking is chaste, free and forcible—his enunciation clear and distinct—his manner deliberate and energetic, alike free from tameness and ranting vehemence. His descriptions of slavery are most graphic, and his arguments are so lucid, and occasionally so spiced with pleasantry, and sometimes a little satire, that his addresses, though long, are seldom tedious, but are listened to with the most profound attention.[20]

As has been noted, the Garrisonian wing of the antislavery movement dismissed involvement in politics as a venture in futility and thus, a waste of energy and expenditures. Therefore, when the Liberty party was established—an antislavery party that arose as an alternative to the Whigs and Democrats—the Garrisonian abolitionists would not support it. In 1840 the Liberty party ran James G. Birney for the presidency, and he polled an insignificant 7,000 votes.[21] Undaunted, the party vowed to do better in the next presidential contest. They worked tirelessly to gain the support of the Garrisonians, whose growing numbers would greatly add to the party roles, but without success. In an address delivered on January 26, 1842, Douglass outlined the reasons for not supporting an antislavery political party. He began by affirming a basic Garrisonian tenet that a third party "disposes men to rely entirely on political, and not moral action." Though political action may alter laws, it fails to move hearts. "I ask," questioned Douglass, "was it political action that removed your prejudices, and raised in your minds a holy zeal for human rights? No one will say this." Douglass further raised questions about Birney and the Liberty party. "Why am I to suppose this man is an abolitionist, any more than the candidate of the other parties? Then, again, look at the root of this third party. Those who were active once in the cause, and began to find out that it led to more sacrifice than they wanted to make, got it up when they found their plans to put down the old Society failed."[22]

However, Douglass did become involved in actions that appeared very political in nature. In the fall of 1842 Douglass became involved in the George Latimer case. Latimer, a fugitive slave from Virginia, had, in October, been arrested in Boston and confined in jail there, without a warrant, to await the coming of his captors. An appeal to the Chief Justice of Massachusetts demanding a jury trial for Latimer was denied. In early November, abolitionists in the state, led by Douglass and another black orator, Charles Lenox Remond,[23] held a series of "Latimer meetings" in order to stir public opinion on Latimer's behalf. On November 8, Douglass, from Lynn, Massachusetts, wrote to Garrison about the Latimer case. The letter, reprinted in the *Liberator,* was Douglass's first public letter. In the latter half of the letter, Douglass condemned Boston for its part in the capture of a fugitive. The letter was, in all likelihood, a reflection of the speeches Douglass was making for Latimer.

Slavery, our enemy, has landed in our very midst, and commenced its bloody work. Just look at it; here is George Latimer, a man—a brother—a husband—a father, stamped with the likeness of the eternal God, and redeemed by the blood of Jesus Christ, outlawed, hunted down like a wild beast, and ferociously dragged through the streets of Boston, and incarcerated within the wall of Leverett—st. jail. And all this done in Boston—liberty-loving, slavery-hating Boston—intellectual, moral, and religious Boston. And why was this—what crime had George Latimer committed? He had committed the crime of availing himself of his natural rights, in defence of which the founders of this very Boston enveloped her in midnight darkness, with the smoke proceeding from their thundering artillery. What a horrible state of things is here presented. Boston has become the hunting-ground of merciless man-hunters and man-stealers. Henceforth we need not portray to the imagination of northern people, the flying slave making his way through thick and dark woods of the South, with white fanged blood-hounds yelping on his blood-stained track; but refer to the streets of Boston, made dark and dense by crowds of professed Christians. . . . We need not point to the sugar fields of Louisiana, or to the rice swamps of Alabama, for the bloody deeds of this soul-crushing system, but to the city of the pilgrims. . . . I say, turn your attention from all . . . cruelty abroad, look now at home—follow me to your courts of justice—mark him who sits upon the bench. He may, or he may not—God grant he may not—tear George Latimer from a beloved wife and tender infant.[24]

The editor of the *Salem Register* heard one of Douglass's speeches for Latimer and published his evaluation.

The most wonderful performance of the evening was the address of Frederick Douglass, himself a slave only four years ago! His remarks and his manner created the most indescribable sensations in the minds of those unaccustomed to hear freemen of color speak in public, much more to regard a slave as capable of such an effort. He was a living, speaking, startling proof of the folly, absurdity and inconsistency . . . of slavery. Fluent, graceful, eloquent, shrewd, sarcastic, he was without making any allowance, a fine specimen of an orator. He seemed to move the audience at his will, and they at times would hang upon his lips with staring eyes and open mouths, as eager to catch every word, as any "sea of upturned faces" that ever rolled at the feet of Everett or Webster, to revel in their classic eloquence.[25]

Douglass, Remond, and others were highly successful in their Latimer meetings. First of all, enough money was raised to purchase Latimer's freedom. An even broader victory was a petition, signed by 65,000 citizens, which was presented to the Massachusetts House of Representatives on February 9, 1843, asking for a state law to make it illegal for any official to arrest a fugitive and detain him in jail. Bowing to public pressure, the legislators passed such a law. The victory would only be temporary, however, for seven years later the national Congress would pass the Fugitive Slave Act which would supersede all state laws to the contrary.

On May 9, 1843, Douglass delivered a brief speech before the tenth anniversary meeting of the American Anti-Slavery Society in New York City. His remarks were in defense of a resolution, "the anti-slavery movement is the only earthly hope of the American slave." He began this speech, as he often did, with words of self-deprecation; a deliberate method of establishing his credibility and winning the sympathetic attention of his audience.

I have myself been a slave, and do not expect to awaken such an interest in the minds of this intelligent assembly as those have done who spoke before me. For I have never had the advantage of a single day's schooling in all my life, and such have been my habits of life as to instill into my heart a disposition I never can quite shake off, to cower before white men. But one thing I can do. I can represent here the slave,—the human chattel, the despised and oppressed, for whom you, my friends, are laboring in a good and holy cause.

Douglass acknowledged that there were those who thought and claimed that the antislavery movement was not an aid in accomplishing emancipation, but he affirmed, "this is a grievous error." The slaves, Douglass asserted, heard of the antislavery movement through the curses of their masters. "And in the curses of our masters against the abolitionists," he said, "did we not feel instinctively, that these same abolitionists were our friends? . . . Prior to this movement, Sir, the slave in chains had no hope of deliverance. . . . when he heard of this movement, hope sprang up in his mind." The antislavery movement was the slave's only hope, for

there was no hope for the slave in Church, or State, or in the working of society, framed as it now is: nothing whatever in any of the institutions of the day. But in the American Anti-Slavery Society, the slave sees an exposition of his true position in the scale of being. He finds that he is, indeed, a Man,—admitted, recognized as such as he is by them, and he goes on, calmly and quietly hoping in his chains, that the day may come, when by their aid, he shall be relieved from his thraldom! For this Society, Sir, is above either Church or State; it is moving both, daily, more and more.[26]

On August 15, 1843, Douglass and Remond were invited to be delegates to a national Negro convention in Buffalo. They were the only Garrisonians in attendance and it soon became evident that most at the convention took positions to which Douglass and Remond were opposed. The convention proposed a resolution in support of the Liberty party, and though Douglass vigorously spoke against it, the resolution was adopted by a substantial majority. At another session, Henry Highland Garnet, a Presbyterian minister who had been a slave in Maryland, gave an address in which he urged slaves to violently overthrow their masters.

In the name of God we ask, are you a man? Where is the blood of your fathers? Has it all run out of your veins? Awake, awake; millions of voices are calling you! Your dead fathers speak to you from the graves. Heaven, as with a voice of thunder, calls on you to arise from the dust.
    Let your motto be RESISTANCE! RESISTANCE! RESISTANCE! No oppressed people have ever secured their liberty without resistance. What kind of resistance you had better make, you must decide by the circumstances that surround you, and according to the suggestions of expediency. Brethren, adieu. Trust in the living God. Labor for the peace of the human race, and remember that you are four millions.[27]

    Garnet's speech caused great controversy at the convention. Douglass, a strong proponent of Garrisonian nonviolence, led the convention to vote down (by one vote) a watered-down approval of Garnet's speech. Before the commencement of the Civil War in 1861, Douglass would change his stance and come to support both involvement in politics and the use of force to overthrow slavery.
    Later that summer, Douglass and other abolitionists began a project known as the "Hundred Conventions," whereby teams of speakers would be sent into the western states to strengthen the antislavery movement. It was an ambitious assignment and over a period of several weeks Douglass and others would speak in western New York, Indiana, Ohio, and Pennsylvania. The most noted event of the project took place in Indiana. In September Douglass and his associates conducted a meeting in Richmond where a mob pelted the speakers with rotten eggs. On September 15 a meeting was held in Pendleton where the abolitionists were confronted by an intoxicated mob. Serious trouble was averted by a sudden cloud burst. Two days later, a morning meeting was conducted in the woods near Pendleton. "As soon as we began to speak," recalled Douglass, "a mob of about sixty of the roughest characters I have looked upon ordered us . . . to be silent, threatening us . . . with violence."[28] William A. White, with whom Douglass shared the platform that morning, was beaten. Douglass, "laying aside his non-resistance principles . . . seized a club, and went at the blood-thirsty monsters."[29] Outnumbered, Douglass was soon beaten into unconsciousness. White suffered the loss of several teeth and some severe gashes. In addition to numerous bruises, Douglass's right hand was broken. Both men were fortunate to have survived.
    In November Douglass journeyed to Pittsburgh where he joined with Remond to conduct a series of meeting. The *Pittsburgh Spirit of Liberty* described the efforts of the two black orators in glowing terms.

The two colored men, Douglass and Remond, have at least convinced most, if not all who heard them, that, in the language of one of the first speakers and the most talented man in our city, "there are few or none more eloquent in the Union."

The meetings have been full—many of them crowded—and the enthusiasm most grateful. We may say . . . that more has been done during the past week, and almost solely by Douglass and Remond . . . to push forward the great and glorious cause, than could have been hoped for in months, by any other instrumentality. We have heard of many, many converts already made.[30]

Over the next several months Douglass spoke throughout New England. Though each oration had its own unique stamp, in many ways the same basic themes were pronounced again and again: accounts of his experiences in slavery, told with humor and great indignation; a severe judgment on churches and clergymen, North and South, for their complicity in slavery; a denunciation of the present political parties; and always an appeal to join with him and others in the antislavery cause. One newspaper sample gives some idea of Douglass' effectiveness. From the *Herald of Freedom,* in Concord, New Hampshire, on February 16, 1844, N. P. Rogers wrote:

He was advertised as a "fugitive from slavery." He said he was not a fugitive from slavery—but a fugitive slave. . . . There was great oratory in his speech—but more of dignity and earnestness than what we call eloquence. . . . He is one of the most impressive and majestic speakers I have ever heard. . . . I have never seen a man leave the platform, or close a speech with more real dignity and eloquent majesty.[31]

In the fall of 1844 Douglass, Anna, and what would be four children by year's end, moved to Lynn, Massachusetts, a place where there was strong support for Garrisonian abolitionism. During that fall and into the following spring, Douglass labored on his first autobiography, *Narrative of the Life of Frederick Douglass, An American Slave.* The biography was written because there were those who doubted he had ever been a slave. He was too eloquent, too learned, too polished, too sophisticated, to have ever been an uneducated slave. These doubters charged that he was a fraud. In his second biography, Douglass wrote:

People doubted if I had ever been a slave. They said I did not talk like a slave, look like a slave, nor act like a slave, and that they believed I had never been south of Mason and Dixon's line. "He don't tell us where he came from—what his master's name was—how he got away—nor the story of his experience. Besides, he is educated, and is, in this, a contradiction of all the facts we have concerning the ignorance of the slaves." Thus, I was in a pretty fair way to be denounced as an imposter.[32]

The *Narrative* was written to answer such doubts and accusations. Names of former masters, that had not been formerly divulged for Douglass's own protection, would now be disclosed. Detailed information, specific names, and people—all of which could be corroborated—would be written in the *Narrative.* On May 6, 1845, just days before the publication of the *Narrative,* Douglass delivered an address before the Twelfth Annual Convention of the American Anti-Slavery Society in New York City's spacious Broadway Tabernacle. For the first time in a public address, Douglass specified the names of former masters and overseers, and called the audience's attention to the various cruelties these slave owners had committed. Douglass was very much aware that in reciting these names he placed himself in grave danger.

I mention the name of this man, and also of the persons who perpetrated the deeds which I am about to recite, running the risk of being hurled back into interminable bondage—for I am yet a slave;—yet for the sake of the cause—for the sake of humanity, I will mention the names, and glory in running the risk. I have the gratification to know that if I fall by the utterance of truth in this matter, that if I shall be hurled back into bondage to gratify the slaveholder—to be killed by inches—that every drop of blood which I shall shed, every groan which I shall utter, every pain which shall rack my frame, every sob in which I shall indulge, shall be the instrument, under God, of tearing down the bloody pillar of Slavery, and of hastening the day of deliverance for three millions of my brethren in bondage.[33]

When the *Narrative* was published in May 1845, it not only helped to verify Douglass's story, but it placed him in the danger of reenslavement. His master, who still legally owned him, now knew who and where his "property" was. At the suggestion of Wendell Philips, Douglass planned a lecture tour of the British Isles. With funds from the sale of his autobiography, along with $250 raised by his abolitionist friends, Douglass set sail for England in August 1845. Traveling with him were James N. Buffum, a fellow Garrisonian, and the Hutchinsons, a musical family who would sing antislavery songs at some of the meetings where Douglass would speak. Douglass's family remained in America.

Because of his color, Douglass was compelled to travel steerage on the trip across the Atlantic. Nevertheless, he and the captain become good friends, and near the end of the voyage the captain invited Douglass to give a lecture on slavery. Southern passengers were offended and attempted to mob Douglass, but after the captain threatened to put the protestors in irons, Douglass delivered his speech without interference.

EXILE IN THE BRITISH ISLES (1845–1847)

On August 28, 1845, the ship carrying Douglass and the other passengers docked at Liverpool, England. Two days later Douglass and Buffum began a four-month tour of Ireland. Douglass was warmly received throughout the Emerald Isle. Mayors and other dignitaries often shared the platform at the antislavery meetings. The press was generous in its praise of Douglass, and the sale of his autobiography was very successful.

He spoke at several temperance meetings where his addresses combined attacks on liquor and slavery. On October 20, in a speech at Cork, Ireland, Douglass bitterly described what the consumption of alcohol (intemperance) had done to the free blacks in the northern portion of the United States.

Teetotalism has been an interesting subject to me. We have a large class of free people of color in America; that class has, through the influence of intemperance, done much to retard the progress of the anti-slavery movement—that is, they have furnished arguments to the oppressors for oppressing us; they have pointed to the drunkards among the free colored population, and asked us the question, tauntingly—"What better would you be if you were in their situation?" This of course was a great grievance to me. I set my voice against intemperance. I lectured against it, and talked against it, in the street, in the wayside, at the fire-side; wherever I went during the last seven years, my voice has been against intemperance. But notwithstanding my efforts, and those of others, intemperance stalks abroad among the colored people of my country. Still I am pleased to be able to say, that the change in their situation, with regard to intemperance, has been great in the last seven years.[34]

An often repeated theme in Ireland, as it would be throughout the British Isles, as it had been in the United States, was the one Douglass knew best: the brutality of slavery. In a speech delivered on October 14, Douglass noted the number of lashes prescribed for various slave offenses.

If more than seven slaves are found together in any road, without a white person—twenty lashes a piece. For visiting a plantation without a written pass—ten lashes. For letting loose a boat from where it is made fast—thirty-nine lashes; and for a second offence, shall have his ear cut off. For having an article for sale without a ticket from his master—ten lashes. For being on horseback without the written permission of his master—twenty-five lashes.[35]

A theme that quickly followed Douglass's accounts of the cruelty of slavery was the moral impotency of the United States to deal with such cruelty. In Ireland, as in America, Douglass laid much of the blame for the nation's moral laxity on its churches and clergy. He urged the religious institutions of Ireland to exert moral pressure on their counterparts in America.

Let the Methodist minister, the Presbyterian minister, the Baptist minister, the Unitarian minister, the Catholic clergyman, and the Protestant clergyman—let the Society of Friends—let all, of every denomination in Ireland, be faithful to their Saviour, and slavery in America will soon fall to the ground. For they are all in connection with churches in America, to whom they can send out faithful remonstrances.... While our people claim to be the most enlightened and the most civilized, and the freest upon the earth; and while they are vain of their institutions, they are sensitive in the extreme to the opinions entertained of them in European countries, particularly in England and Scotland and Ireland.[36]

There were criticisms of Douglass in Ireland for his harsh denunciations of the American churches. Early in his tour, Douglass attempted to make clear that it was not religion to which he was opposed, but the prevarication of it.

I love religion—I love the religion of Jesus, which is pure and peaceable, and easy to be entreated. I ask you all to love this religion; but I hate a religion which, in the name of the Saviour . . . prostitutes his blessed precepts to the vile purposes of slavery, ruthlessly sunders all the ties of nature, which tears the wife from the husband—which separates the child from the parent—which covers the backs of men and women with bloody scars—which promotes all manner of licentiousness. I hate such a religion as this, for it is not Christianity—it is of the devil.—I ask you to hate it too, and to assist me in putting in its place the religion of Jesus.[37]

Yet another theme addressed by Douglass in Ireland had to do with the claim made by those who justified slavery, that black people were inferior to whites. In one sense it was an unnecessary theme in the British Isles, for, as Douglass discovered, people in Ireland, Scotland, and England were, when contrasted to most Americans, relatively free of racial prejudice and discrimination. Douglass soon experienced in Great Britain that he was treated as a man without reference to his color. Though he was a curiosity as an ex-slave, for the first time in his life, everything that was available to white people was also available to him. Citizens in Great Britain had traveled much farther along the road of racial equality and fairness than their counterparts across the Atlantic.

It was in Cork, the place of Douglass's first speaking assignment in Ireland, that he addressed the subject of racial inferiority. "There is perhaps," he spoke, "no argument more frequently resorted to by the slaveholder, in support of the slave system, than the inferiority of the slave. This is the burden of all their defence of the institution of Slavery, 'the negro is degraded—he is ignorant, he is inferior—and therefore 'tis right to enslave him.'" Attempting to turn the argument against itself, Douglass asked, "What if we are inferior? Is it a valid reason for making slaves of us, for robbing us of our dearest rights?" Continuing, Douglass emphasized, "If we search the words of inspired wisdom, we shall find that the strong are to bear the infirmities of the weak." Attacking the question in a different manner, Douglass noted, "I will grant frankly . . . that the negroes in America are inferior to the whites." But that is because, Douglass affirmed, "the people of America deprive us of every privilege," then they "turn around and taunt us with our inferiority. They stand upon our necks . . . and ask the question why we don't stand erect? They tie our feet and ask us why we don't run." Douglass quoted laws from South Carolina, Georgia, Virginia, and Louisiana that made it illegal to teach slaves how to read and write and learn. Then, because slaves are illiterate, they are charged with being inferior, "hence, 'tis right to enslave us." Douglass then informed his audience that slaves and black people in America were not only said to be "of intellectual inferiority, but of want and affection for each other." To answer such an accusation, Douglass shared touching examples of love and sacrifice that slaves gave to each other and told how difficult it was to establish natural affections when instant separation from a loved one was a continual possibility, even probability.[38]

Douglass delivered more that fifty addresses during his four-month stay in Ireland. Thousands had heard him speak. He had become "a national celebrity."

Sales of the *Narrative* had gone well. The press "unstintingly praised his speaking; and for the first time in his life he had been free of all the influences of racial prejudice—even members of the upper class had frequented his meetings and solicited his presence at their tables."[39] As the crusade in Ireland drew to a close, a correspondent of the *London Inquirer* made the following observation:

He is, in truth, a wonderful man. A man of colour, born in slavery, and an oppressed slave till within the last few years, without instruction or the means of self-improvement in his youth, now attracting to the halls in which he lectures, assemblies large and respectable, assemblies which are drawn around him, perhaps, in the first instance, by the novelty of the matter, but which cannot fail to be delighted and electrified by the addresses of the lecturer.[40]

In early January 1846 Douglass left Ireland to begin a series of lectures in Scotland. There, an emotional and divisive issue, directly related to American slavery, was in process, an issue that provided a ready-made vehicle through which Douglass could transport his antislavery message. In May 1843 Thomas Chalmers, perhaps the Church of Scotland's greatest and most noted preacher, led a group of 450 ministers out of the established church to form the Free Church of Scotland. The schism, known as "The Disruption," had to do with state control of the church, and the ministers who seceded represented about 40 percent of all the clergymen in the established church. Though glad to be free of various state controls, the seceders found themselves to be without church buildings, without homes for their clergy, without schools to train their clergy, and without funds to remedy these and other pressing problems. The leaders of the Free Church sought relief by appealing for financial aid from Presbyterians in other countries, including the United States. In the spring of 1844 a five-man deputation from the Free Church arrived in the United States seeking funds. The American and Foreign Anti-Slavery Society warned the group not to solicit funds from churches in the South, lest it appear they approved of slaveholders and slavery. The warning was ignored, and the deputation collected $15,000 from southern churches, four-fifths of all the money collected in America.

Various abolitionist groups in the British Isles sought to pressure the Free Church into returning the "blood money." After some initial successes, the campaign weakened, and by the time Douglass arrived in January 1846, it was all but dead. After being informed of the situation, Douglass vowed to revive the controversy and to be an instrument in shaming the Free Church to return the money. In speech after speech throughout Scotland, Douglass spoke of the cruelty of slavery, of its endorsement by the southern churches, and emphasized there must be no cooperation or fellowship with the devil by Christians in Scotland. He was responsible for developing a slogan, "Send Back the Money!" that was chanted over and over at the meetings where Douglass spoke. He urged the children to write the slogan wherever they could find a place to do so, and they did. Throughout Scotland, the cry was everywhere heard, "Send back the money!"

In his addresses, Douglass made it clear that he had no quarrel with the Free Church as a denomination, its theology, or the fact that it had broken from the Church of Scotland. Some in the Free Church had charged that he was a paid agent of the established church and Douglass wanted it known that this was not so. His problem with the Free Church, the only problem, was that it had accepted money from the voices and practioners of slavery in the United States. In a speech on January 30, in Dundee, Douglass spoke with contempt about those agents from the Free Church who "go to the United States, and strike hands in good Christian fellowship with men whose hands are full of blood—the coats, the boots, the watches, the houses, and all they posses, are the result of the unpaid toil of the poor fettered, stricken, and branded slave."[41]

In a speech at Arbroath on February 12, Douglass began by emphasizing, "I have no war with the Free Church as such. I am not here to offer one word as to the right or wrong of the organization of that body." However, Douglass stressed, I am "maintaining to the last that man-stealing is incompatible with Christianity—that slaveholding and true religion are at war with each other—and that a Free Church should have no fellowship with a slave church." Douglass spoke of that delegation from the Free Church that went to the United States in search of funds. "They were," he said, "beseeched in the name of the perishing slave not to go to the slave-holding churches of the south; that as sure as they went they would contaminate their own cause, as well as stab the cause of the slave."

But reason gave way to avarice, purity yielded to temptation, and the result is, the Free Church is now wallowing in the filth and mire of slavery, possessing the bad pre-eminence at this time of being the only church in Scotland that makes it a religious duty to fellowship men-stealers as the followers of Jesus Christ. Now, you have the case before you.

As Douglass drew his words to a conclusion, he acclaimed: "I now propose three cheers, which shall be given in the following words—Send back that money." The audience joined the speaker, shouting three times, "Send back that money."[42] It is said the building shook because of the noise.

Douglass believed the work in Scotland was effective. He wrote to Garrison that "Scotland is in a blaze of anti-slavery agitation. The Free Church and Slavery are the all-engrossing topics. . . . The Free Church is in a terrible stew. . . . Its members are leaving it, like rats escaping from a sinking ship."[43] The victory, however, was never complete. The Free Church's General Assembly met in Edinburgh, beginning on April 27. The pressures on the assembly to return the money were great. Other denominations implored the delegates to "send back the money." In all probability the majority of Scottish people agreed. The assembly, however, would not be pressured or persuaded by public opinion.

A substantial majority of the assembly delegates accepted a report that condemned slavery but denied the concept that slaveholding was inherently sinful. The report also condemned the abolitionists for their intemperate words and actions. Though Douglass would continue to press the issue until he left the British Isles in the spring of 1847, the Free Church never altered its position and never sent back the money.

Douglass's participation in the Free Church controversy proved to be a personal victory. It greatly enhanced his standing in England, but even more so in the United States. His activities were widely reported in the American press and his stature grew immeasurably. He was no longer viewed as a beginner or as a stand-in for Garrison. He was his own man, a leader, a professional, the most effective orator in the antislavery movement.

In early August 1846 William Lloyd Garrison arrived in England. As in the United States, the British antislavery movement was divided between those who followed the ways of Garrison and those who, though they mostly agreed on objectives, disagreed on Garrisonian means. English Garrisonians had invited the leader himself to cross the Atlantic to help bolster their position. On August 10 Douglass joined Garrison and aided in the formation of a national Garrisonian society, the Anti-Slavery League. Seven days later the league held its first public meeting with Henry C. Wright, Garrison, and Douglass featured as the main speakers. As usual Douglass outshone all others on the platform. Garrison himself recognized that fact. In a letter to his wife, Helen, he noted that Wright's opening speech was "a scorcher." Of the response to Douglass's words, Garrison recorded, "I never saw an audience more delighted."[44] Two weeks later, in yet another letter to Helen, Garrison acknowledged, that wherever Douglass went he was "the lion of the occasion."[45] Garrison, along with other antislavery speakers, had been relegated to a supporting cast role to the one who had emerged as the star, Frederick Douglass.

As the Free Church controversy provided an attention-getting issue for Douglass in Scotland, the Evangelical Alliance furnished a similar platform in England. In the summer of 1846 London hosted the first international convention of evangelical church bodies called the Evangelical Alliance. The sessions began on August 19. Twelve hundred delegates attended, including sixty Americans, many of those Americans being supporters of slavery. Slavery soon became an issue of contention. A weak antislavery resolution was passed as a compromise between the antislavery British delegates and the proslavery Americans. The Americans then threatened to withdraw from the alliance unless the compromise was rescinded and all references to slavery be deleted from the minutes. The alliance gave in to the American demands. English abolitionists were furious. On September 14 6,000 people attended a public meeting, sponsored by the Anti-Slavery League and other abolitionists, to protest the acquiescence of the Evangelical Alliance to slavery. The main speakers were Douglass, Garrison, and George Thompson, an eloquent English reformer and a close friend of Garrison. Douglass was the last to speak and began with an attack on American churches.

You will observe, that during the speeches of Mr. Garrison and Mr. Thompson, special reference has been made to the church in America. Why, Sir, do we so often allude to this, and make special attacks on the American church and clergy? It is not because we have any war with them as a body of Christians, not because we have any war with the ministers in America, as such,—not at all; but they have thrown themselves across the pathway of emancipation, and made it our duty to make war upon them, or desert the cause of the slave. Why, Sir, the political parties in the United States that uphold the sin of slavery dwindle into insignificance, when compared with the power exercised by the church to uphold and sustain that system.[46]

Douglass then referred to his own experiences wherein he had observed religious support of slavery.

I have heard sermon after sermon, when a slave, intended to make me satisfied with my condition, telling me that it is the position God intended me to occupy; that if I offend against my master, I offend against God; that my happiness in time and eternity depends on my entire obedience to my master. Those are the doctrines taught among the slaves, and the slave-holders themselves have become conscious about holding slaves in bondage, and their consciences have been lulled to sleep by the preaching and teaching of the Southern American pulpits. "There is no place," said an Abolitionist in the United States, "where slavery finds a more secure abode than under the shadow of the sanctuary." The simple fact in itself, that three millions of slaves exist in a land where there are more than two millions of Evangelical Christians, ought to be sufficient to show that Christianity, that Evangelical religion, is not what it ought to be—(cheers).[47]

Douglass went on to scold the Alliance for allowing slaveholders to attend their convention and denounced the hypocrisy of the religious slaveholders and slave sympathizers.

Only think of a religion under which the handcuffs, the fetters, the whip, the gag, the thumbscrew, blood-hounds, cat-o'-nine-tails, branding-irons, all these implements, can be undisturbed. Only think of a body of men thanking God every Sabbath-day that they live in a country where there is civil and religious freedom, when there are three millions of people herded together in a state of concubinage, denied the right to learn to read the name of the God that made them—where there are laws that doom the black man to death for offenses which, if committed by white men, would pass unpunished. Think of a man standing up among such a people, and never raising a whisper in condemnation of such a state of things, denouncing the slaveholders, or speaking a word of pity or sympathy with the poor slave. This in itself should have been sufficient to have led the Evangelical Alliance to have barred and bolted its gateways, to keep out from them the persons who have been here, such as Dr. Smyth, of Charleston, South Carolina. I happen to know something of him. Sir, that man stands charged, and justly charged, with performing mock marriages, in the city of Charleston, among the slaves, leaving out the most important part of the ceremony, "What God has bound together, let no man put asunder." When marriages are performed among slaves, this is left out, and for the best of reasons,—when they marry them with the understanding that their masters have the right and power of tearing asunder those they have pretended to join together—(cries of "Shame, shame"). I do believe the Evangelical Alliance was hoodwinked, that they were misled; I do not think they really understood the matter. . . .[48]

I know the prayers of slaveholders. I have been the slave of religious and irreligious slaveholders, and I bear testimony, that next to being a slave at all, I regard the greatest calamity to be that of belonging to a religious slaveholder. (Cries of hear, and cheers.) I have found them the most mean, the most exacting, the most cruel. This is a startling position, but it is true as far as my experience is concerned. I know not how to explain it, but such is the fact. The religious slaveholders are the most tenacious of slavery.[49]

For the next several weeks, Douglass and Garrison, sometimes assisted by others, conducted a speaking tour in the major cities of Ireland, Scotland, and England. Their speeches focused on the Free Church, the Evangelical Alliance, and recruiting members for the Anti-Slavery League. At Edinburgh, on October 29, Ellen and Anna Richardson, from Newcastle, publicly announced the beginning of a fund drive to purchase Douglass's freedom. Though the sisters were not in the Garrison camp of the antislavery movement, Garrison approved the project and made a small contribution.

Before Garrison left to sail back across the Atlantic, he asked Douglass to remain in Great Britain for a few more months in order to strengthen the Anti-Slavery League. Douglass agreed, and for the next four months he would speak almost every night to a total of about 60,000 people. On December 28 the Richardson sisters presented Douglass with his papers of freedom. Hugh Auld had signed the papers on December 5 for a payment of $750. Frederick Douglass, at the age of twenty-eight, was, for the first time in his life, a legally free man. There would be one more gift for Douglass. The Richardsons informed him of plans to raise further funds that would be invested to provide Douglass with an annual income. Douglass suggested an alternative. He pointed out that there was no printing press in the United States under the control of blacks. There had been previous failed attempts. The time had come, Douglass asserted, when a black paper or journal could survive and would be an important tool in the fight against slavery and prejudice. His British friends agreed to raise funds for the purchase of a printing press.

By the end of March 1847, an exhausted and weakened Douglass prepared to leave for home. On March 30 he gathered strength to deliver another address at the London Tavern where an elaborate soiree was held in his honor. Seven hundred admirers came to bid him a fond and grateful farewell. Douglass's address that evening was long and eloquent. He began with his often used technique of self-deprecation. After thanking his listeners for the eulogies bestowed, Douglass noted, "I am conscious of possessing very little just right to them; for I am but a plain, blunt man—a poor slave, or rather, one who has been a slave. (Cheers.) Never had I a day's schooling in my life; all that I have of education I have stolen. (Laughter.)" He was vehement in his denunciation of America. "I am not here," he emphasized, "to make any profession whatever of respect for that country, of attachment to its politicians, or love for its churches or national institutions. . . . The entire network of American society, is one great falsehood, from beginning to end." He condemned the American Constitution for its defense of slavery. Nevertheless, he was returning to America, because there was work to be done.

No, my friends, I am going back, determined to be honest with America. I am going to the United States in a few days, but I go there to do, as I have done here, to unmask her pretensions to republicanism, and expose her hypercritical professions of Christianity; to denounce her high claims to civilization, and proclaim in her ears the wrongs of those who cry day and night to Heaven, "How long! How long! O Lord God of Sabaoth!" (Loud cheers.)

He praised the abolitionists. "When the history of the emancipation movement shall have been fairly written, it will be found that the abolitionists of the nineteenth century were the only men who dared to defend the Bible from the blasphemous charge of sanctioning and sanctifying negro slavery. (Loud cheers.)" He extolled William Lloyd Garrison, declaring that because he had so "fearlessly unmasked hypocrisy" he had "brought down upon himself the fierce execrations of a religious party in the land." He firmly denounced the Evangelical Alliance and declared that "British Christians" had "suffered themselves to be sadly hoodwinked upon this point."

He thanked the British for the purchase of his freedom. Because some abolitionists had criticized this purchase as participating in the buying and selling of human beings, Douglass felt the need to respond.

As to the kind friends who have made the purchase of my freedom, I am deeply grateful to them. I would never have solicited them to have done so, or have asked them for money for such a purpose. I never could have suggested to them the propriety of such an act. It was done from the prompting or suggestion of their own hearts, entirely independent of myself. While I entertain the deepest gratitude to them for what they have done, I do not feel like shouldering the responsibility of the act. I do, however, believe that there has been no right or noble principle sacrificed in the transaction. Had I thought otherwise, I would have been willingly "a stranger and a foreigner, as all my fathers were," through my life, in a strange land, supported by those dear friends who I love in this country.

Douglass recalled how well he, a black man, had been treated in the British Isles. "In none of these various conveyances, or in any class of society, have I found any curled lip of scorn, or an expression that I could torture into a word of disrespect of me on account of my complexion; not one." Though he was grateful for invitations to make England his permanent home, he affirmed, "I prefer living a life of activity in the service of my brethren. I choose rather to go home; to return to America. I glory in the conflict, that I may hereafter exult in the victory. I know that victory is certain. (Cheers.)"[50]

Those few in Great Britain who did not appreciate Douglass the man or the message he delivered were, for the most part, conservative churchmen. Encouraged by some of their counterparts in America, these British clergy charged Douglass with infidelity and immorality. The infidelity charges, of course, had their roots in Douglass's bitter attacks on the American churches. The insinuations of immorality arose because of Douglass's popularity with British women. The fact that Douglass was a handsome man, blessed with a powerful body and a deep, sensuous voice, certainly drew the attention of the opposite sex. There was never any evidence, however, of impropriety. Such negative evaluations were shared by only a small minority.

Douglass's exile in the British Isles had lasted only nineteenth months, but those few months were an important milestone in his life and career. He began the exile, still legally a slave, still owned by another; he concluded the exile a legally free man. He had come to England known only to a few but left a famous and venerated man. He had earned the praise of some of the most distinguished men in the British Isles—Richard Cobden, John Bright, Benjamin Disraeli, Robert Peel, Lord John Russell, Lord Broughham, and Daniel O'Connell.[51] When he left the United States he was a subordinate to Garrison in the American antislavery movement; he returned a leader in his own right, subordinate to no one. From 1847 to the beginning of the Civil War, Frederick Douglass became increasingly independent. Though he and Garrison would continue to agree on ends, they would separate over significant differences as to how those ends could best be achieved.

AN INDEPENDENT AND DIVERGENT PATH (1847–1861)

Douglass returned to the United States in the spring of 1847. It would be fourteen years before the sectional dispute over slavery would erupt into a civil war. As these years were ones of great crisis for the nation, so, too, they would be for Frederick Douglass. These were the years when Douglass emerged as an independent leader in the antislavery movement. He began to speak and act in ways that differed from Garrison until the break between the two was unbridgeable. They were both strong-willed men, too much so for either to be subservient to the other. They were both leaders, incapable of being followers. The independence that Douglass discovered in Great Britain solidified in the fourteen years before the Civil War.

Soon after his return home Douglass approached Garrison with his plans for a journalistic venture, using money from English friends to purchase a press. To Douglass's dismay and deep disappointment, Garrison and Wendell Phillips declared his plans a serious mistake. They pointed out the probabilities of financial disaster. Douglass's talents, they insisted, could be far better used in public speaking, a known quality, than through journalism, an unknown quality. It is difficult to judge whether this is what Garrison really thought or whether he feared a potential rival in antislavery journalism. Douglass submitted to

Garrison's argument and allowed Garrison to write in the June 25 issue of *Liberator:* "Mr. Douglass . . . has deemed it both prudent and proper to suggest to his British friends the inexpediency of sending over to him the noble gift which they contemplate bestowing upon him."[52]

Douglass's acquiescence was only temporary. Before the year was over, he and his family moved to Rochester, New York, where Douglass soon announced his intention to publish the *North Star*. The press, set up in the basement of a black church, came out with its first issue on December 3, 1847. In that first edition, Douglass wrote that the purpose of the *North Star* was "to attack slavery in all its forms and aspects; advocate Universal Emancipation; exact the standard of public morality; promote the moral and intellectual improvement of colored people; and to hasten the day of freedom to our three million enslaved fellow-countrymen."[53] Garrison had heard of Douglass' plans in October and was predictably disturbed. From a sickbed in Cleveland, in a letter to his wife, dated October 20, Garrison noted that Douglass's decision to publish would "greatly surprise our friends in Boston . . . that, in regard to his project for establishing a paper . . . he never opened to me his lips on the subject, nor asked my advice in any particular whatever. Such conduct grieves me to the heart. This conduct about the paper has been impulsive, inconsiderate, and highly inconsistent with his decision in Boston."[54]

Douglass now had two careers, public speaking and journalism. He was already eminently successful in one and would become so in the other. One mode would supplement the other. The public lectures rendered financial aid to the press. The press would enable Douglass a wider dissemination of his views. Journalism, however, would never eclipse the importance of his public speeches. Several months after the publication of the first edition of the *North Star,* Douglass, in the midst of a speaking tour, wrote to his readers:

Speech! speech! the live, calm, grave, clear, pointed, warm, sweet, melodious, and powerful human voice, is its chosen instrument. The pen is not to be despised, but who that knows anything of the might and electricity of speech as it bursts from hearts of fire, glowing with light and life, will not acknowledge . . . [its] superiority over the pen for immediate effect. Astronomy, Zoology, Botany, Conchology, Chemistry, and Geology, are fit subjects for the pen; but humanity, justice and liberty, demand the service of the living human voice, and the power of exalted eloquence, as their exponent.[55]

Douglass would speak to all the issues he had addressed in the past, and added others. When the historic women's rights convention met in Seneca Falls, New York, in July 1848, Douglass was the only man to play a significant role. Forty years later, recalling that convention, Douglass told the International Council of Women: "When I ran away from slavery, it was for myself; when I advocated emancipation, it was for my people; but when I stood up for the rights of women, self was out of the question, and I found a little nobility in the act."[56] Until the day he died—he attended a women's rights rally on the day of his death—Douglass was an active voice in the support of women's rights. He and various leaders of the women's movement did not always agree on some matters, but mutual support was largely consistent. Douglass addressed the first National Woman's Rights Convention on October 24, 1850, and urged the women to be bold and seize their rights.

Seize hold of those which are most strongly contested. You have already free access to the paths of literature; women may write books of poetry, travels, etc., and they will be read with avidity. Let them strike out in some other path where they are not now allowed to go. If there is some kind of business from which they are excluded, let some heroic Woman enter upon that business, as some of these noble Women have entered upon the practice of medicine. Let Woman take her rights, and then she shall be free.[57]

In 1849 the colonization movement, a plan that would release slaves and return them to Africa, was being revived. Leadership for such an effort was provided by the American Colonization Society and its president, Henry Clay. On May 31, Douglass addressed an audience of about 5,000 people in Boston's historic Faneuil Hall. In the address he bitterly criticized the idea of colonization, the American Colonization Society, and Henry Clay. "The American Colonization Society," charged Douglass, "cherishes and fosters this feeling of hatred against the black man." He asked, "if this is not mean and impudent in the extreme, for one class of Americans to ask for the removal of another class?" Douglass asserted, "for my part, I mean, for one, to stay in this country; I have made up my mind to live among you." He noted that the Colonization Society had claimed that "prejudice can never be overcome—that it is natural—God has implanted it." Douglass refuted such a claim by relating several examples of progress that had taken place in the North over the past few years. "Prejudice against color is not invincible," he emphasized.[58]

In early May 1850 Douglass went to New York City in order to participate in the sixteenth annual convention of the American Anti-Slavery Society. Much of the New York press was hostile to the convention in general and to Douglass in particular, an indication that abolitionism was still unpopular in parts of the North. One paper referred to the abolitionists as "traitors"; another suggested that Douglass be assassinated.[59] The first session of the convention was held on May 7 in the Broadway Tabernacle. The session had just begun when a mob, led by Isaiah Rynders, a New York City gang leader and Tammany Hall boss, disrupted the meeting. Seizing the platform, a Dr. Grant delivered a speech in which he claimed that blacks had descended from monkeys, were less than human, and had no rightful claims to equal treatment. When Grant concluded, the delegates shouted for Douglass to respond. His response was indicative of Douglass's ability to think and speak with great quickness. Referring to Grant's speech, Douglass retorted, "Look at me. . . . I invite you to the examination. . . . Am I a man?" The audience enthusiastically assented. When they had quieted, Rynders, standing within three feet of Douglass, exclaimed, "You are not a black man; you are only half a nigger." Douglass quickly replied, "He is correct; I am, indeed, only half a negro, a half-brother to Mr. Rynders." The Tabernacle reverberated with laughter. Douglass, knowing that he had touched a responsive chord with his audience, returned again to the idea that Rynders was his half brother. After Rynders charged that blacks were incapable of handling freedom, that they would die off if granted such a privilege, Douglass, again showing his talent to think quickly, responded:

It is said that in a state of slavery we increase, and in freedom we decrease. Up in Rochester, they say, the negroes are most shockingly on the increase. If it be true that we are decreasing, why then be uneasy about us? Let us die without the aid of oppression; let us die a natural death. I have heard something about the descent of the negro. I care not whether I am descended from a man or a monkey. One thing, I have a head to think, and know that God meant I should exercise the right to think—that I have a heart to feel, and a tongue to speak whatever that heart listeth, and God meant that I should use that tongue in behalf of humanity and justice for every man.[60]

On October 14, 1850, Douglass was back at Faneuil Hall in Boston to protest the Fugitive Slave Law that has passed Congress less than a month before. The four-hour meeting at Boston heard speeches by Charles Francis Adams, who presided over the affair, Wendell Philips, Theodore Parker, Charles Remond, James A. Briggs, William B. Spooner, and Frederick Douglass. The meeting attracted a capacity crowd of 5,000 people with hundreds turned away because there was no more room available. Douglass, who followed Adams, delivered the second speech of the evening, a speech of about one hour's duration. He emphasized the terror that a fugitive experienced when captured and returned to slavery.

This every slave well understands; and he knows that if he returns to bondage, he returns not merely to Slavery, not merely to labor for his master, but to gratify a deep-seated, malignant and deadly revenge. He who has once tasted the sweets of freedom, that man can never more be made a profitable slave, and his master will have a harder task to keep him than he would to whip him. (Cheers and laughter.) . . . They therefore pursue the slaves in order to make examples of them; and the slave knows that, if returned, he will have to submit to excruciating torture.[61]

The meeting concluded with the appointment of a fifty-member Committee of Vigilance and Safety to operate in Boston, which would "take all measures which they shall deem expedient to protect the colored people of this city in the enjoyment of their lives and liberties."[62]

Douglass was also an active participant in the Underground Railroad. Rochester was one of the last stops on the Underground Railroad before a fugitive reached the freedom and safety of Canada. It has been estimated that over a ten-year period, Douglass assisted about 400 fugitives in their quest for freedom.[63] Because of his involvement in the Railroad, Douglass met Harriet

Tubman, also an escaped slave from Maryland, but one who courageously returned into the South again and again to lead other slaves to freedom. Douglass, comparing their respective contributions, once told her:

Most that I have done has been in public, and I have received much encouragement. . . . You on the other hand have labored in a private way. . . . I have had the applause of the crowd . . . while the most that you have done has been witnessed by a few trembling, scared and footsore bondsmen.[64]

In addition to his venture into journalism, there were two even more significant ways that Douglass deviated from the ideas and wishes of Garrison in the years prior to the Civil War.

Political Involvement

Because Garrison viewed the Constitution as a proslavery document, he concluded that the entire political foundation of the United States was corrupt and, as presently constituted, beyond redemption. Therefore, abolitionists should not be involved in the political process. Such involvement was not only a waste of time but also a consorting with evil. The only tactic the abolitionists could rightfully use, according to Garrison, was that of moral suasion. Within months after his return from England, Douglass began to have reservations about these basic Garrisonian doctrines: that the Constitution was a proslavery document and that moral suasion was the abolitionists' only legitimate weapon. The change was gradual, but long before 1860 the two men were diametrically opposed on these issues.

Upon moving to Rochester, Douglass's repeated exposure to political abolitionists—those who advocated political action as a means to bring about emancipation—began to cause him to reevaluate his previous stance against politics and the Constitution. He read the writings of Lysander Spooner, Gerrit Smith, and William Goodell, all of whom thought that the Constitution was not a proslavery document and advocated political involvement. One of the first indications that Douglass was departing from Garrisonian ideology on these subjects was announced in the February 9, 1849, issue of the *North Star*. "On a close examination of the Constitution," he wrote, "I am satisfied that if strictly 'construed according to its reading,' it is not a pro-slavery instrument." However, to assure his readers that his change was only a small one, he went on to declare that "the original intent and meaning of the Constitution (the one given to it by the men who framed it, those who adopted it, and the one given to it by the Supreme Court of the United States) makes it a pro-slavery instrument—such a one as I cannot bring myself to vote under, or swear to support."[65]

In early May Douglass attended the annual meeting of the American Anti-Slavery Society at the Broadway Tabernacle in New York. On May 9, Douglass delivered an address in which he returned to an old theme—the guilt of

American churches in supporting and/or condoning slavery. Excerpts reveal that Douglass still felt great indignation on the subject. After singling out the Methodist Episcopal Church, the Presbyterian Church, and the Protestant Episcopal Church for special attention, Douglass continued:

Now I have taken these three Christian Churches and they are for samples of the rest. The Baptists are no better than the Methodists and Presbyterians, and the Episcopalians are as bad as either. They are all as pro-slavery as they can be. It is because these churches have passed resolutions favoring Slavery, and have in other cases resolved to have nothing to do with the matter, that we are compelled to attack them if we would be faithful to Anti-Slavery. . . .[66]

I believe the grand reason why we have Slavery in this land at the present moment is that we are too religious as a nation, in other words, that we have substituted religion for humanity—we have substituted a form of Godliness, an outside show for the real thing itself. We have houses built for the worship of God, which are regarded as too sacred to plead the cause of the down-trodden millions in them. They will tell you in these churches that they are willing to receive you to talk to them about the sins of the Scribes and Pharisees, or on the subject of the heathenism of the South Sea Islands, or on any of the subjects connected with missions, the Tract Society, the Bible Society, and other Societies connected with the Church, but the very moment you ask them to open their mouths for the liberation of the Southern slaves, they tell you, that is a subject with which they have nothing to do, and which they do not wish to have introduced into the Church; it is foreign to the object for which churches in this country were formed, and houses built.[67]

Two days later Douglass and Samuel Ringgold Ward engaged in a public debate as to whether the Constitution was an antislavery document. Ward, himself a fugitive slave, insisted that it was; Douglass, still considering himself a loyal Garrisonian, declared that it was not. The debate, though vigorous on both sides, was conducted with great amicability. When the debate was over, Douglass wrote as to how much he enjoyed the encounter, and with great respect for his opponent, added, "If Mr. Ward was not victorious in this argument, it was . . . solely owing to the unsoundness of the cause which he undertook to defend."[68] The debate had an even wider significance, for it caused Douglass to continue more deeply into his study as to the constitutionality of slavery. Urging him to leave his old views was Gerrit Smith, a wealthy New Yorker and a leader among political abolitionists. An exchange of letters developed between the two men, who would soon become the closest of friends. Julia Griffiths, a young English abolitionist, who had come to America to help Douglass with the publication of the *North Star* and was strongly anti-Garrison in her perspective, was another important influence in Douglass's eventual conversion to political abolitionism.[69]

In the meantime, Douglass continued his heavy speaking schedule. In comments in the *North Star* during the fall of 1849, Douglass wrote of the importance and influence of public address in combatting slavery, and called for more orators to join in the task.

From the experience of the last four weeks, and the general aspect of the public mind in this region [western New York], I am satisfied there never was a time that afforded a better opportunity of doing good by Anti-Slavery lectures than now. The field may be properly said to be white for the harvest. A general disposition to hear the subject discussed is manifested in all quarters; and I am persuaded that if one or two devoted and earnest laborers could be secured to lecture in the field, they would not only greatly advance the common cause, but secure the prompt aid and warm sympathy of great numbers of the Abolitionists.

From every view of the present state of feeling I have been able to take, I am persuaded that now is the time for anti-slavery lectures in New York. We want laborers, and we ought to have them; but alas! they are few in number, and are closely occupied in quarters where they reside. Single handed and alone, I shall go forth during the remainder of the autumn and winter, speaking to the best of my ability, and doing all within my power to cultivate this section of the anti-slavery field.[70]

In January 1850 an antislavery convention was held in Syracuse, New York, in an attempt to reconcile differences between anticonstitutional Garrisonians and proconstitutional elements in the antislavery movement. It would be the first and last large scale attempt to reconcile the two points of view. Highlighting the convention was a debate; with Gerrit Smith, Samuel R. Ward, and Stephen Foster arguing that the Constitution was not a proslavery document, and Charles C. Burleigh, Parker Pillsbury, and Frederick Douglass saying that it was.[71] It was one of the last times that Douglass publicly took such a position. A few days later, he editorialized that the meeting accomplished little.

We may be asked our opinion as to what especial good this long looked for meeting has accomplished! and we are sorry to say that we believe that no especial good has resulted from it. . . . The most that has been accomplished, has been a meeting of the two wings of the anti-slavery movement. We have seen each other face to face, and parted with no other ties to bind us to each other than those of affinity, which before existed.[72]

One year later, on January 21, 1851, Douglass wrote to Gerrit Smith of a changing point of view. "I have already ceased to affirm," he announced, "the proslavery character of the Constitution."[73] In the spring, Smith wrote to Douglass with a surprising offer. Smith had been publishing and financing the *Liberty Party,* a political abolitionist paper in danger of collapse. Smith suggested to Douglass the merger of their two papers, with Douglass assuming the role of editor. Smith promised financial assistance for at least two years and then suggested that the combined paper assume the name of its editor. On May 1, Douglass wrote to Smith and accepted the offer. He also assured Smith that his conversion to an antislavery interpretation of the Constitution was complete.

I am prepared to contend for those rules of interpretation which when applied to the Constitution make its details harmonize with its declared objects in its preamble. I am satisfied on those points, and my heart is strong. The change in my views on this question has not been sudden, nor brought about with reference to any emergency. I have arrived at my present position after months of thought and investigation.[74]

Thus, *Frederick Douglass' Paper* was born. The next step was for Douglass to make public what he had privately affirmed in his letter to Smith. The following week, the annual meeting of the American Anti-Slavery Society was held in Syracuse. On the morning of May 9, with Garrison and other like-minded colleagues in attendance, Douglass announced his "heresy." Garrison was shocked, angered, and hurt. In the afternoon session a lively debate ensued on the constitutionality of slavery, with Garrison and William H. Burleigh on one side, and Douglass and William Goodell on the other. Even though Douglass and Garrison would agree on many other issues, most especially on the termination of slavery, the Syracuse convention resulted in a severe rupture of relations between the two committed and strong-willed men. With determined inflexibility, over the next few years, each would hurl bitter verbal and written attacks against the other.

At the 1852 convention of the Free Soil party, Douglass was called on to deliver an impromptu speech. He reminded the delegates that "the object of this Convention is to organize a party not merely for the present, but a party identified with eternal principles and therefore permanent." The speech further demonstrated that Douglass was departing from Garrison on yet another fundamental issue. Garrison strongly advocated that emancipation must be accomplished through nonviolent means, and Douglass had supported that conviction. However, in this speech, Douglass showed that even as he had come to believe that moral suasion must be accompanied by political involvement, so nonviolence may not always be the most effective way to accomplish certain goals. Douglass would take further steps away from nonviolence in the future, but this speech at the Free Soil Convention was an indication of where he was heading.

Slavery has no rightful existence anywhere. The slaveholders not only forfeit their right to liberty, but to life itself. (Applause.) . . . The only way to make the Fugitive Slave Law a dead letter is to make half a dozen or more dead kidnappers. (Laughter and applause.) A half dozen more dead kidnappers carried down South would cool the ardor of Southern gentlemen, and keep their rapacity in check. . . . I believe that the lines of eternal justice are sometimes so obliterated by a course of long continued oppression that it is necessary to revive them by deepening their traces with the blood of the tyrant. (Much applause.)[75]

John P. Hale of New Hampshire and George W. Julian of Indiana were nominated by the Free Soil party as candidates for president and vice president respectively. Douglass approved the selections and would urge delegates of the Liberty party, soon to assemble at Canastoga, New York, to back the Free Soil candidates. Most did. Hale and Julian did not do well in the national election, garnering only 5 percent of the votes cast. If Douglass was disappointed over the results of the national election, he was elated by the fact that his friend, Gerrit Smith, was elected to Congress from the twenty-second district of New

York on the Liberty ticket. In a letter of congratulations to Smith, he wrote:

The cup of my joy is full. If my humble labors have in any measure contributed . . . to your election, I am most amply rewarded. . . . Your election forms an era in the history of the great antislavery struggle. . . . You go to Congress, not by the grace of a party caucus, bestowed as a reward for party services; not by concealment, bargain, or compromise, but by the unbought suffrages of your fellow citizens, acting independently, and in defiance of party.[76]

Four years later, when it was time for another presidential election, there was a new political party on the American scene. Largely as a response to the Kansas-Nebraska Act (1854) and disenchantment with the Whigs' seeming inability to stop the spread of slavery into the territories, the Republican party was inaugurated. This new political party was not committed to ending slavery but to the principle that slavery must not spread beyond the southern states where it already existed. Douglass was skeptical about the Republicans. On the evening of May 28, 1856, he was given the opportunity to address an audience of Republican State Convention delegates meeting in Syracuse. He did not hide his skepticism. Some critics of the new alliance referred to them as the Black Republicans, a great misnomer according to Douglass. He pointed out that the party had some very good men, namely William Seward and Charles Sumner, but he doubted if the new party had the courage or insight to nominate either of them.

You are called Black Republicans. What right have you to that name? Among all the candidates you have selected, or talked of, I have not seen or heard of a single black one. (Laughter.) Nor have I seen one mentioned with any prospect of success, who is friendly to the black man in his sympathies, or an advocate of the restoration of his rights. The men mentioned in connection with your presidential nomination, are Col. Fremont, Judge McLean, Francis Blair, the latter of whom only owns twenty slaves (laughter), and T. H. Benton, who owns, I know not how many. I have heard your own great Senator Seward mentioned; but nobody expects that he will receive the nomination. He, though acting with the Whig party so long as there was a Whig party—and though he has never identified himself with any Abolition Society, still has succeeded in saying such words for freedom, and, at times, in evincing such a spirit of liberty, that the Republicans shrink back from urging his nomination, because of his radical anti-slavery sentiments. And then there is the man who was struck down in the Senate; and he is the man you would be the first to elevate, if acting on the tactics of Napoleon. He laid down a rule never to occupy a position which the enemy desired him to occupy. That Charles Sumner is at this time the special object of hatred in the South, no one doubts. If you want to give us an example of your Black Republicanism—of your determination to resist and defy the Slave power, take Charles Sumner, and make him master at Washington.[77]

Also meeting in Syracuse on the same date was the Radical Abolitionist Convention, which on the morning of May 29 nominated Douglass's good friend, Gerrit Smith, for the presidency and Samuel McFarland for the vice presidency.

Douglass pledged his support. When the Republican party nominated John C. Fremont and William L. Dayton as the new party's first candidates for the nation's highest offices, Douglass reaffirmed his support of the Radical Abolitionists, rightly declaring that they were the only political party dedicated to the eradication of slavery. On August 15, in *Frederick Douglass' Paper,* the editor announced he had changed his position and would support the candidates of the Republican party. "We deem it proper frankly to announce our purpose to support . . . John C. Fremont and William L. Dayton . . . in the present political canvass." Douglass noted that his new position was not "hastily or inconsiderably taken," but after much thought and examination he believed the election of the Republicans would result in "the severest, deadliest blow upon Slavery that can be given at this particular time." He was not surrendering for a moment his previous beliefs in the complete eradication of slavery, but he urged abolitionists to make their presence and influence known in this new political alliance. In a note of political realism, Douglass continued:

We shall support (the Republicans) because they are the most numerous Anti-Slavery Party, and, therefore, the most powerful to inflict a blow upon, and the most likely to achieve a valuable victory over, the Slave Oligarchy. . . . Whereas, on the other hand, the moral effect of the Radical Abolition vote, separated as it must be from the great Anti-Slavery body of the North, must, from the very nature of the case, be very limited for the good, and only powerful for mischief, where its effect would be to weaken the Republican Party. We shall support Fremont and Dayton, because there is no chance whatever in the present contest of electing better men than they. And we are the more reconciled to accepting them, by the fact they are surrounded by a Party of progressive men. Take them, therefore, not merely for what they are, but for what we have good reason to believe they will become when they have lived for a time in the element of Anti-Slavery discussion.[78]

Some abolitionists understood and agreed with Douglass' reasoning. Even Gerrit Smith, though at first hurt by his friend's announcement, realized that every effort needed to be made to prevent the election of the Democrat, James Buchanan. Other abolitionists, however, were furious with Douglass and felt betrayed. As would be expected, Garrison led the criticism and called Douglass "a selfish adventurer, a mere trickster in morals, whose object is his own advancement, and on whom no reliance can be placed, except that he will prove treacherous to every party that fails to gratify his acquisitiveness or ambition."[79]

Douglass's motive did seem to be pragmatic. There was no chance for a Radical Abolitionist victory, and though the Republicans represented only a partial victory in the fight for emancipation, they represented the most realistic hope the antislavery forces had. Fremont, though he did not win, made a strong showing, receiving 33 percent of the popular vote and 114 electoral votes from eleven free states.[80] The future of the Republican party appeared promising. Douglass, even though he had supported Fremont, did not yet consider himself a Republican, and continued to call himself a Radical Abolitionist.

National politics and Douglass's role in such, would reappear four years later. In 1860 *Frederick Douglass' Paper* became *Douglass' Monthly*. In May of that year the Republicans nominated Abraham Lincoln as their candidate for the presidency. Though Douglass would have preferred Seward as the Republican standard bearer, he was not displeased with Lincoln. In June he wrote of the nominee: "Mr. Lincoln is a man of unblemished private character; a lawyer, standing near the front rank of the bar of his own state, has a cool, well-balanced head; great firmness of will, is pervasively industrious; and one of the most frank, honest men in political life."[81]

In August Douglass attended the Radical Abolitionist Convention in Syracuse which once again nominated Gerrit Smith. The convention also chose Douglass as a presidential elector-at-large, the first time in American history that a black man had been chosen for such a position. The abolitionists, as always, took an uncompromising antislavery position, whereas the Republicans, as in 1856, announced that slavery must not spread beyond the states where it already existed. Douglass declared his support for the Radical Abolitionists but, realizing they could not win, hoped for a Republican victory. "Abolitionist though I am, and resolved to cast my vote for an Abolitionist," he announced, "I sincerely hope for the triumph of [the Republican party] over all the odds and ends of slavery combined against it."[82] In the last weeks of the campaign, Douglass's pragmatic nature, once again, took over, and he actively campaigned for the election of Lincoln.

After Lincoln's victory, Douglass was cautiously optimistic. Lincoln's election, he said, had ended the "haughty and imperious slave oligarchy" that for fifty years had been the "Presidential makers of the Republic." He continued: "Mr. Lincoln's election breaks this enchantment, dispels the terrible nightmare, and awakes the nation to the consciousness of new powers, and the possibility of higher destiny than the perpetual bondage to an ignoble fear."[83]

In those years after his return from England to the election of Lincoln, though Douglass became increasingly involved in the nation's political process, the majority of his speeches addressed other concerns. New developments demanded oratorical attention. On July 5, 1852, Douglass delivered his most famous and in all probability the best antislavery speech in history, "What to the Slave Is the Fourth of July?" He had been invited to deliver this address at Corinthian Hall in Rochester by the Rochester Ladies Anti-Slavery Society. Through most of Douglass's speeches were extemporaneous, and many impromptu, this speech was the result of three weeks of preparation. A week before the speech, Douglas wrote to Samuel D. Porter, declaring that he was "quite anxious that the proceedings shall be worthy of the day."[84] The speech was constructed around the basic irony that Douglass perceived in America. How was it that a nation which boasted of its democracy, its freedom and liberty, could tolerate an institution of bondage within its borders? Neil Leroux has noted that this speech is a prime example of "attention-shifting," wherein Douglass, "by shifting attention from a day of national celebration to a case for national mourning," was able to focus the attention of his listeners on "the plight of the slaves."[85] In the address, after paying the expected respect to the Declaration of Independence and the Founding Fathers, Douglass asked what this annual celebration of independence meant to the slaves. His answer became a summary statement of the entire speech.

> What, to the American slave, is your 4th of July? I answer: a day that reveals to him, more than all other days in the year, the gross injustice and cruelty to which he is the constant victim. To him, your celebration is a sham; your boasted liberty, an unholy license; your national greatness, swelling vanity; your sounds of rejoicing are empty and heartless; your denunciations of tyrants, brass fronted impudence; your shouts of liberty and equality, hollow mockery; your prayers and hymns, your sermons and thanksgivings, with all your religious parade, and solemnity, are, to him, mere bombast, fraud, deception, impiety, and hypocrisy—a thin veil to cover up crimes which would disgrace a nation of savages. There is not a nation on the earth guilty of practices, more shocking and bloody, than are the people of these United States, at this very hour.[86]

Further attention to this vital speech is given in Part II, accompanied by a printing of the address in its entirety.

Two years later, in 1854, Douglass delivered two important and unique addresses. Early in the year the literary societies at Ohio's Western Reserve College invited Douglass to deliver an address during commencement week in July. The college administrators were appalled. An uneducated ex-slave, they assumed, would be unable to deliver an address worthy of academia. Pressure was exerted upon the students to withdraw the invitation, but the students would not comply. Douglass accepted the invitation. Dr. Henry Wayland, a member of the Rochester faculty, provided Douglass with information and books for the speech, over which Douglass labored for "many days and nights." It would be another address that was the culmination of extensive preparation and written in manuscript form before delivery. On July 12, before a crowd of nearly 3,000 people, Douglass delivered his speech, "The Claims of the Negro Ethnologically Considered." In learned terms, the speaker demolished the arguments that alleged blacks were inferior to whites. The speech was a triumph, in itself an irrefutable demonstration against charges of black inferiority. The Worcester, Massachusetts, paper, *Spy,* expressed the general reaction to the speech, declaring that Douglass "showed he was familiar with the general and natural history of man. His language was chaste, and his reasoning strong, able and logical."

Douglass began the two-hour address with a recognition of the uniqueness of the occasion, "in selecting me as your speaker . . . as it is novel in the history of American Collegiate or Literary Institutions." He acknowledged "the moral courage displayed by the gentlemen at whose call I am here." It was for Douglass, "the first time," he had been a part "of any College Commencement." The remainder of the speech was a scholarly, well-researched discourse. Douglass quoted from the leading scholars of the era. It was a very different kind of speech for Douglass. There were few personal references. For the most part it was not a speech aimed at stirring the emotions. It was a speech for scholars in an academic environment. Once again Douglass demonstrated his ability to adapt his speech to a particular kind of audience.[87]

On October 30 Douglass delivered an address in response to a particular national crisis. Five months earlier, the Congress had passed the Kansas-Nebraska Act, which declared that the question of slavery in those territories would be settled by a vote of the people living there—popular sovereignty. The act nullified the Missouri Compromise of 1820, which called for no slavery in the territories north of Missouri's southern border. The bill's sponsor, Stephen A. Douglas, senator from Illinois, became an object of scorn from those who viewed the new bill as one more opportunity for the extension of slavery. Douglass and other abolitionists traveled to Illinois to speak against the bill and its author. One of Douglass's addresses was delivered in Chicago's Metropolitan Hall. In response to those who were critical of him coming to the Senator's home state in order to speak against him, Douglass replied: "If Hon. S. A. Douglas, your beloved and highly gifted Senator, has designedly, or through mistaken notions of public policy ranged himself, on the side of oppressors and the deadliest enemies of liberty, I know of no reason . . . which should prevent me, or prevent anyone else, from thinking so, or from saying so." The speaker castigated both the Democrats and Whigs for their roles in the passage of the bill, but his strongest denunciations were reserved for Stephen Douglas.

But again: This bill, this Nebraska bill, gives to the people of the territories the right to hold slaves. Where did this bill get this right, which it so generously gives away? Did it get it from Hon. Stephen A. Douglass? Then I demand to know where he got that right? Who gave it to him? Was he born with it? Or has he acquired it by some noble action? I repeat, how came he by it, or with it, or to have it? Did the people of this State, from whom he derived his political and legislative life, give him this right, the right to makes slaves of men? Had he any such right?

The answer is, he had not. He is in the condition of a man who has given away that which is not his own.

Freedom, according to Douglass, was a God-given, fundamental right, and a nation that denies such a right to any of it citizens, does so at its peril.

Such a truth is man's right to freedom. He was born with it. It was his before he comprehended it. The title deed to it is written by the Almighty on his heart, and the record of it is in the bosom of the eternal—and never can Stephen A. Douglas efface it unless he can tear from the great heart of God this truth. And this mighty government of ours will never be at peace with God until it shall, practically and universally, embrace this great truth as the foundation of all its institutions, and the rule of its entire administration.[88]

In August 1855 Douglass's second autobiography, *My Bondage and My Freedom,* was published. Five thousand copies were sold in two days, and thousands more would follow. Most consider it the best of his three life stories. William McFeely has appraised that "if in Douglass' time readers distorted the book into just another runaway's tale, it stands today as one of the most suggestive inquiries into the heart of slavery that we have."[89]

The *Dred Scott* decision rendered by a seven-to-two Supreme Court vote on March 6, 1857, was another momentous national event that drew biting oratory from Douglass. In May, in New York City, Douglass explained just what the Court's decision meant. Then, as he had in his speech on the Kansas-Nebraska Act, declared that a higher moral law, God's law, had been violated by Roger Taney's Court. The Court's ruling must and would eventually fail.

This infamous decision of the Slaveholding wing of the Supreme Court maintains that slaves are, within the contemplation of the Constitution of the United States, property; that slaves are property in the same sense that horses, sheep, and swine are property; that the old doctrine that slavery is a creature of local law is false; that the right of the slaveholder to his slave does not depend upon the local law, but is secured wherever the Constitution of the United States extends; that Congress has no right to prohibit slavery anywhere; that slavery may go in safety anywhere under the star-spangled banner; that colored persons of African descent have no rights that white men are bound to respect; that colored men of African descent are not and cannot be citizens of the United States. . . .[90]

The Supreme Court of the United States is not the only power in this world. It is very great, but the Supreme Court of the Almighty is greater. Judge Taney can do many things, but he cannot perform impossibilities. He cannot bale out the oceans, annihilate this firm old earth, or pluck the silvery star of liberty from our Northern sky. He may decide, and decide again; but he cannot reverse the decision of the Most High. He cannot change the essential nature of things—making evil good, and good, evil.[91]

Douglass's involvement in the reform movement covered a wide range of issues. In addition to his denunciations of slavery, discrimination and prejudice, he also spoke in favor of temperance and suffrage for women. On October 7, 1858, a rally was held at Rochester's City Hall, where Douglass spoke against capital punishment as "a mockery of justice." The occasion was the impending execution of Ira Stout, a convicted murderer scheduled to be hanged on October 22. Though the rally had been called by those who opposed capital punishment, advocates on both sides of the controversy appeared. The meeting was boisterous and it was difficult for the speakers to be heard. Susan B. Anthony, one of the chief organizers of the rally, was greeted with hisses and insults. Douglass received a chorus of racial taunts. Nevertheless, he spoke his mind. He charged that capital punishment was something that belonged only to a dim and unenlightened past. "Murder is not the cure for murder—lying and stealing will not cure lying and stealing. The old doctrine was: 'An eye for an eye—a tooth for a tooth'—but that was the doctrine of a by-gone age and generation, and not for this one of light, intelligence and reason." The safety of society was secure with the accused murderer in prison, affirmed Douglass. "Who is afraid that Ira Stout can do mischief to life and property while confined in chains in yonder lonely jail! He is just as secure as if he were dead." Executions, charged Douglass, corrupt the society that administers them.

And the whole history of executions in England and in this country, plainly teaches this lesson that the gallows blunt all the better feelings of human nature, and stimulates all the bad. The hanging day is the high day for gamblers, thieves, robbers and murderers, and they do not hesitate to improve the opportunity even while the convict is dangling on the gallows in the agonies of death![92]

During the fall of 1860, at the same time he was campaigning for the election of Lincoln, Douglass was also directing his energies toward the repeal of a New York State law that required blacks to own real estate valued at a minimum of $250 as a condition for voting. Douglass was annoyed when he observed that it was an issue the New York Republicans were ignoring. On election day, though Lincoln carried New York by 60,000 votes, the suffrage issue lost by 140,000 votes.[93] Douglass knew where to place the blame. "Had the Republican party," he charged, "been as true to the sacred cause of liberty and equality, as the Democratic party always proves itself to slavery and oppression, the invidious and odious discrimination against our equal citizenship would have been blotted out, and the colored voters of the State would have had some reason for the enthusiasm with which they have shouted their praises of the Republican party."[94] Blacks in New York would not be given equal voting rights until the ratification of the Fifteenth Amendment in 1870.

Support of Violence

Perhaps the most significant way in which Douglass departed from Garrison in the years prior to the Civil War was in the use of violence to overthrow the institution of slavery. Garrison declared that no matter how great the evil, violence must never be used a means to destroy it. It was wrong to do evil that good might come. In 1837 Garrison went so far as to denounce American government because the nation had gained its independence through the use of physical force and continued to use it in the cause of national defense: "The nation is destined to perish because in wading through blood and carnage to independence, it at the outset discarded the Prince of Peace, and elected George Washington to be its Savior; and it is now confidently relying upon its naval ships, its strong fortifications, its military prowess, for security."[95]

In his early years as a part of the abolitionist movement, Douglass leaned toward the Garrisonian doctrine of nonresistance, but never completely so. In 1834, while still a slave, Douglass had physically resisted Edward Covey, and later wrote, "It rekindled . . . within me a sense of my own manhood."[96] Nine years later, at an abolitionist meeting in Pendelton, Indiana, Douglass seized a club and attacked a mob that was threatening him and a fellow speaker, William A. White. In 1847 Douglass spoke against slave insurrections. His point was not that such rebellions were wrong but rather that they were futile: "The slave is in the minority, a small minority, the oppressors are an overwhelming majority." Such insurrections, noted Douglass, were "the perfection of folly, suicidal in the extreme."[97]   Douglass's argument was based on pragmatic foundations, not moral ones. It has been noted that in an 1852 speech, Douglass had moved a long way from nonviolence when he spoke of an effective way to fight the Fugitive Slave Act was "to make a half dozen or more dead kidnappers."[98]

It was his involvement with John Brown, a militant white visionary, that demonstrated Douglass was abandoning nonviolence as a means of combatting slavery. Moral suasion has failed to move the nation. More radical means were necessary if slavery was ever to be abolished. As nearly as can be determined, Douglass first came into contact with Brown in 1847. At that time Brown was a merchant in Springfield, Massachusetts, and Douglass was on a speaking tour of New England. Douglass was intrigued with Brown's concept that slavery was in essence a state of war against black people.   From 1847 on the two men visited in each other's homes, with Douglass stopping over in Springfield at various intervals and Brown visiting in Rochester. In February 1850 Brown was a guest in Douglass's home for at least two and possibly three weeks. During those visits, Brown described to Douglass a plan "for destroying the value of slave property" by helping slaves to escape into the mountains of the border states. Douglass recalled:

That plan . . . was to take twenty or twenty-five discreet and trustworthy men into the mountains of Virginia and Maryland, and station them in squads of five, about five miles apart, on a line of twenty-five miles. . . . They were to have selected for them, secure and comfortable retreats in the vastness of the mountains, where they could easily defend themselves in case of attack. They were to subsist upon the country roundabout. They were to be well armed, but were to avoid battle or violence, unless compelled by pursuit or in self-defense. . . . The work of going into the mountains was to be committed to the most courageous and judicious man connected with each squad.[99]

Douglass perceived merit in the plan, writing that slave owners would begin to feel apprehensive about owning property that they were constantly in danger of losing. "Men do not like to buy runaway horses," Douglass argued, "nor to invest their money in a species of property likely to take legs and walk off with itself."[100] Douglass was also aware of problems in the plan. There was the danger that slave owners would become more vigilant and more oppressive, and there was the problem of providing adequate supplies to those isolated in the mountains.

After Brown returned from Kansas in 1859, where he had participated in a bloody territorial civil war over the extension of slavery, he rented property about five miles from Harpers Ferry, Virginia. There, he began to collect arms and men for the seizing of that community where he planned to take some of the leading citizens hostage while his group spirited area slaves into the nearby mountains. On August 20 Douglass was informed of the plan and apparently counseled against the attack on Harpers Ferry, but he was willing to help with the original plan of helping slaves to escape into the mountains.

On October 16, 1859, Brown and his "army" of eighteen took possession of the U.S. armory in Harpers Ferry. The following morning, a company of U.S. Marines, under the command of Colonel Robert E. Lee, overpowered Brown's group. Ten of Brown's men, including two of his sons, were killed in the skirmish. Brown was captured, tried for treason, and hanged on December 2 at Charlestown. There were those who were ready to implicate Douglass in the raid. He fled to Canada and then to England where he would spend the next six months. As he had some twelve years before, Douglass received a warm welcome in England. The English stay was shortened when Douglass received news of the death of his youngest daughter, Annie, in March 1860. It was safe to return, for by that time Douglass had been cleared of any involvement in what happened at Harpers Ferry.

After Harpers Ferry, however, the militancy in Douglass—apparently always there, but usually suppressed—was openly expressed. In a newspaper editorial during the summer of 1860, he lamented:

I have little hope of the freedom of the slave by peaceful means. A long course of peaceful slaveholding has placed the slaveholders beyond the reach of moral and humane considerations. They have neither ears nor hearts for the appeals of justice and humanity. While the slave will tamely submit his neck to the yoke, his back to the lash, and his ankle to the fetter and chain, the Bible will be quoted, and learning invoked to justify slavery. The only penetrable point of a tyrant is the fear of death.[101]

In a speech on August 1, 1860, Douglass praised the memory and deeds of John Brown. Through most abolitionists in the North admired the goals of Brown, they questioned his means and even his sanity. Douglass exalted Brown without reservations.

His behavior was so unusual that men did not know what to make of him. It was thought the race of such men had become extinct. . . . We have not yet recovered from the wonder with which this man's deeds filled us. . . . He was as a comet, whose brightness overspread half the sky. . . . with John Brown and his associates, the NEGRO IS A MAN. . . . Brave and glorious old man! Yours was the life of a true friend of humanity, and the triumphant death of a hero. The friends of freedom shall be nerved to the glorious struggle with slavery by your example, the hopes of the slave shall not die while your name shall live, and after ages shall rejoice to do justice to your great history.[102]

On December 3, 1860, a meeting was held in Boston to commemorate the death of John Brown. A mob broke into the meeting place and threw Douglass down a staircase. Blacks in the audience were assaulted as they fled from the building. It all substantiated Douglass's now consistent militancy. There would be no defeat of slavery without violence. When the Civil War began in the spring of 1861, Douglass was more than ready for the fight.

3

THE WAR YEARS (1861–1865)

During the four years of civil war, Douglass's writings and speeches continually emphasized two themes: the war must be fought to end slavery, and blacks must become a part of the military force that would be necessary to defeat the southern rebels. One month after the surrender of Fort Sumter, Douglass, then forty-three years of age, wrote of these twin goals. "The simple way, then, to put an end to the savage and desolating war now waged by the slaveholders," instructed Douglass, "is to strike down slavery itself, the primal cause of the war." Furthermore, he announced, "let the slaves and free colored people be called into service, and formed into a liberating army, to march into the South and raise the banner of Emancipation among the slaves."[1]

In the first weeks and months of the war, Douglass reiterated these two themes again and again. In a speech on April 28, two weeks after Sumter, Douglass affirmed his allegiance to the nation. "All that I have and am," he declared, "are bound up with the destiny of this country. When she is successful, I rejoice . . . and when she is afflicted, I mourn with her, as sincerely as any other citizen, for though not yet taken into full communion with her, I still feel that she is my country, and that I must fall or flourish with her." It was not a difficult choice, noted Douglass, for "we all know what the rebels and traitors mean. They mean the perpetuity and supremacy of slavery." Douglass chided the North for its failure to use blacks in the armed services. "The South are wiser in their generation than the North," he emphasized. "Black people are being made soldiers at Montgomery. They piled the sand-bags and raised the batteries which drove Major Anderson from Sumter; but you Northerners are too aristocratic to march by the side of a 'nigger.'" Yet, Douglass was hopeful of a change. "The time may yet come," he offered, "when the President shall proclaim liberty through all the land."[2]

The following week, Douglass, in a speech at Rochester, urged the North not to succumb to any temptation to compromise a brief end to the war. Though the Lincoln government, and most of the North, perceived the war as a conflict to preserve the Union, Douglass believed the war would bring an end to slavery. Thus, the war must be fought to a decisive conclusion.

I am quite free to say, aside from any direct influence this war is to have towards liberating my enslaved fellow countrymen, I should regret the sudden and peaceful termination of this conflict.

The mission of the revolution would be a failure were it to stop now. It would, in that case, only have lived long enough to do harm, and not long enough to do any good.

One important element of this war on the part of the North is to teach the South a lesson which it has been slow to learn.[3]

Douglass was persistent in his demands that the U.S. government proclaim the war as primarily a battle to end slavery. In a June 30 speech, the war two and a half months in duration, the orator reminded his listeners that the abolition of slavery must be the focus of the conflict.

Thus far our Government has done nothing against the alleged compromises of the Constitution of the United States. . . . It has taken up no hostile attitude against slavery itself, and thus has left the door of compromise wide open. . . .

The great and grand mistake of the conduct of the war thus far, is the attitude of our army and Government towards slavery. That attitude deprives us of the moral support of the world. It degrades the war into a war of sections, and robs it of the dignity of being a mighty effort of a great people to vanquish and destroy a huge system of cruelty and barbarism. It gives to the contest the appearance of a struggle for power, rather than a struggle for the advancement and disenthrallment of a nation. It cools the ardor of our troops, and disappoints the hopes of the friends of humanity.

Now, evade and equivocate as we may, slavery is not only the cause of the beginning of this war, but slavery is the sole support of the rebel cause. It is, so to speak, the very stomach of this rebellion.[4]

In the fall of 1861 the Boston Emancipation League was formed to promote a series of lectures that would arouse public opinion in support of emancipation. The formation of the league resulted in a renewed friendship between Douglass and William Lloyd Garrison. Past differences were put behind them and they reunited in a new mission. Douglass and the league would rebuke Lincoln and the Union government for their failures to proclaim emancipation as a goal of the war and for what they perceived as immoral policies.

One of Douglass's best known war addresses, "Fighting the Rebels with One Hand," was delivered on January 14, 1862, at the National Hall in Philadelphia. At the time, the war, which had been going on for nine months, was not proceeding well for the North. A reporter for the Philadelphia *Christian Recorder* had come to hear Douglass wondering if the orator still maintained the "magnetism and melody of his wonderfully elastic voice." The journalist was not disappointed and wrote that "the Frederick Douglass before us was the Frederick Douglass of former days—and even more: his majestic bearing and dignity were not gone—the power and influence of his voice, the cutting logic and lofty eloquence of other days, were not diminished." The reporter reminded his readers that great oratory, such as Douglass rendered, must be seen and heard, rather than read. "No printed sentences," he noted, "can convey any adequate idea of the manner, the tone of voice, the gesticulation, the action, the round, soft, swelling pronunciation with which Frederick Douglass spoke, and which no orator we have ever heard can use with such grace, eloquence and effect as he."[5]

He began the speech by affirming black loyalty to the Union cause. "No man, however malignant," Douglass said, "has been able to cast the shadow of a doubt upon the loyalty and patriotism of the free colored people in this the hour of the nation's trial and danger. . . . There are no black rebels." Douglass asserted that Abraham Lincoln could not be blamed for the war, because "this rebellion was planned and prepared long before the name of Abraham Lincoln was mentioned in connection with the office he now holds." Neither, as many were accusing, could the abolitionists be blamed: "A very large class of persons charge all our national calamities upon the busy tongues and pens of the Abolitionists. Thus we accord to a handful of men and women everywhere despised, a power superior to all other classes in the country. Absurd and ridiculous as this is, its adherents are hoary headed and bearded men." The cause of the war could be found in the nation's futile attempt "to maintain our Union in utter defiance of the moral Chemistry of the universe. We have endeavored to join together things which in their nature stand eternally asunder. We have sought to bind the chains of slavery on the limbs of the black man, without thinking that at last we should find the other end of that hateful chain about our own necks."

Douglass then went to the heart of his speech. The North needed to apply more vigor to the fight: "The only road to national honor and permanent peace for us, is to meet, fight, dislodge, drive back, conquer and subdue the rebels." The North, however, was engaged in a limited fight: "We are fighting the rebels with only one hand, when we ought to be fighting them with both." The North had failed to press the great moral issue of slavery and had neglected to recruit blacks: "We are striking the guilty rebels with our soft, white hand, when we should be striking with the iron hand of the black man, which we keep chained behind us." Douglass prophesied, "that if this nation is destroyed . . . it will be solely owing to the want of moral courage and wise statesmanship in dealing with slavery, the cause and motive of the rebellion."

During the speech, Douglass took the opportunity to denounce one of Lincoln's recent policies. General John C. Fremont had declared martial law in Missouri and declared the slaves of those in rebellion to be free. President Lincoln condemned Fremont's declarations, noting that they were not the policies of the government. Douglass looked upon Fremont's words as something "strong enough to vibrate the heart of a continent." He angrily rejected Lincoln's response as "weakness and imbecility." In Lincoln's letter to Fremont, Douglass asserted, "we have the secret of all our misfortune in connection with this rebellion." Before the issuance of the Emancipation Proclamation, there would be other governmental policies over which Douglass was equally bitter. He pleaded once again with the government to make emancipation the primary purpose of the war: "To let this occasion pass unimproved, for getting rid of slavery, would be a sin against unborn generations." In mid-January 1862, though there were very few indications that the war would end slavery, the speaker was not completely discouraged. "I am still hopeful," he announced, "that the Government will take direct and powerful abolition measures. That hope is founded on the fact that the Government has already traveled further in that direction than it promised."[6] Before the year would end, Douglass would see the fulfillment of his hopes.

Criticism of the administration temporarily came to a halt in September of 1862 when President Lincoln announced the Emancipation Proclamation, which stated that after January 1, 1863, all slaves in rebellious states would be declared free. Douglass was ecstatic over what the president "in his own peculiar, cautious, forebearing and hesitating way, slow, but we hope sure" had proclaimed. To those who feared that Lincoln might reconsider, Douglass assured: "Not a word of it. Abraham Lincoln may be slow, Abraham Lincoln may desire peace even at the price of leaving our terrible national sore untouched, to fester on for generations, but Abraham Lincoln is not a man to reconsider, retract or contradict words and purposes solemnly proclaimed over his official signature."[7] Though there were those who faulted the proclamation as being limited in its scope (applying only to those states in rebellion), Douglass perceived a wider application. In a later autobiography, he recalled: "For my part, I took the proclamation, first and last, for a little more than it purported; and saw in its spirit, a life and power far beyond its letter."[8]

After the Emancipation Proclamation became official on January 1, 1863, Douglass delivered several speeches praising the document and extolling its possibilities. One of those speeches was delivered on February 6 at the Cooper Institute in New York City. Just to read the speech is to sense Douglass's euphoria. "I hail it [the proclamation] as the doom of Slavery in all the States," Douglass exalted. "I hail it as the end of all that miserable statesmanship, which has for sixty years juggled and deceived the people, by professing to reconcile what is irreconcilable." The proclamation ranked as one of the great events in the nation's history. "There are certain great national acts," Douglass noted, "which by their relation to universal principles, properly belong to the whole human family, and Abraham Lincoln's Proclamation . . . is one of these acts. . . . It will stand with every distinguished event which marks any advance made by mankind from thraldom and darkness of error to the glorious liberty of truth." Douglass's optimism for the future knew no bounds. "I believe in the millennium—the final perfection of the race," he exclaimed, "and hail this Proclamation, though wrung out under the goading lash of a stern military necessity, as one reason of the hope that is in me."

He reminded his audience of John Brown and observed that many had come around to the martyr's point of view. "Good old John Brown was a madman at

Harper's Ferry. Two years pass away, and the nation is as mad as he. (Great cheering.) Every General and every soldier that now goes in good faith to Old Virginia, goes there for the very purpose that sent honest John Brown to Harper's Ferry." (Renewed Cheers.)

Douglass was not much disturbed that the proclamation abolished slavery only in those states in rebellion. He was certain of a broader application.

It is objected to the Proclamation of Freedom, that it only abolishes Slavery in the Rebel States. To me it seems a blunder that Slavery was not declared abolished everywhere in the Republic. Slavery anywhere endangers the National cause, and should perish everywhere. (Loud applause.) But even in this omission of the Proclamation the evil is more seeming than real. When Virginia is a free State, Maryland cannot be a slave State. When Missouri is a free State, Kentucky cannot be a slave State. (Cheers.) Slavery must stand or fall together. Strike it at either extreme—either on the head or at the heel, and it dies. A brick knocked down at either end of the row brings every brick in it to the ground. (Applause.)

Douglass concluded the speech by urging the Union to use black troops in its fight against the South. After the proclamation, no one could be more highly motivated to fight than black men.

I hold that the Proclamation, good as it is, will be worthless—a miserable mockery—unless the nation shall so far conquer its prejudice as to welcome into the army full-grown black men to help fight the battles of the Republic. . . . The colored man only waits for honorable admission into the service of the country. They know that who would be free, themselves must strike the blow, and they long for the opportunity to strike that blow. . . . I know the colored men of the North; I know the colored men of the South. They are ready to rally under the stars and stripes at the first tap of the drum.[9]

In the same month the Emancipation Proclamation became official, Governor John Andrew of Massachusetts authorized the organization of the Fifty-fourth Massachusetts Regiment, the first black regiment of the Civil War. Because Massachusetts had a comparatively small black population, recruits needed to be enlisted from other states, and Douglass became an official agent for the recruitment of black men. No one in the North was more important, more persuasive, or more successful in black recruitment than Douglass. Two of his sons, Charles and Lewis, enlisted. He published in pamphlet form and in various newspapers a condensation of his recruitment speeches titled "Men of Color, to Arms!" Douglass reminded those who heard or read his speeches that he had been urging the recruitment of black troops since the beginning of the war: "When first the rebel cannon shattered the walls of Sumter . . . I predicted that the war, then and there inaugurated would not be fought out entirely by white men. . . . With every reverse to the National arms, with every exulting shout of victory by the slaveholding rebels, I have implored the imperilled nation to unchain against her foes her powerful black hand." Douglass recognized that blacks had good reasons not to risk their lives for a nation that had treated them so badly. However, this was not the time to question, but to act: "This is not the time to discuss. . . . Leave it to the future. . . . Action! action! not criticism, is the plain duty of this hour." He reminded his brothers that they had a big stake in the war: "Liberty won by white men would lose half its luster. Who would be free themselves must strike the blow."

Massachusetts had provided the long-awaited opportunity: "Massachusetts now welcomes you to arms as her soldiers. She has but a small colored population from which to recruit. She has full leave of the General Government to send one regiment to the war, and she has undertaken to do it. Go quickly and help fill up this first colored regiment from the North." Douglass then assured the potential recruits of a promise the Government had made to him, but a promise that would not be kept. It was in good faith that Douglass declared, "I am authorized to assure you that you will receive the same wages, the same rations, the same equipment, the same protection, the same treatment and the same bounty secured by white soldiers."[10]

But Douglass had been misled, and his task of recruiting black men for the army was a difficult one. It soon became known that whereas white soldiers received $13 a month and a $3.50 clothing allowance, black soldiers received $7 a month and a $3 clothing allowance.[11] Douglass urged young black men to enlist despite unequal and unjust treatment.

Colored men going into the army and navy must expect annoyance. They will be severely criticized and even insulted—but let no man hold back on this account. We shall be fighting a double battle, against slavery in the South and against prejudice and pro-scription in the North—and the case presents the very best assurances of success.[12]

In a July 6, 1863, recruitment speech in Philadelphia, Douglass told potential soldiers that serving in the military was an opportunity to prove themselves, and thus bring an end to discrimination.

The opportunity is given to us to be men. With courageous resolution we may blot out the hand-wringing of ages against us. Once let the black man get upon his person the brass letters U.S.; let him get an eagle on his button, and a musket on his shoulder, and bullets in his pocket, and there is no power on the earth or under the earth which can deny that he has earned the right of citizenship in the United States. (Laughter and ap-plause.) I say again, this is our chance, and woe betide us if we fail to embrace it.[13]

Blacks did indeed distinguish themselves on the battlefield, drawing praise from Union officers and suffering high casualty rates. Their most renowned battle occurred in July 1863, when the Fifty-fourth Massachusetts Regiment stormed Fort Wagner. Though the mission failed, the black regiment, suffering 42 percent casualties, earned rave acclamations for great courage under a barrage of bullets and mortar shells. Even Fort Wagner, however, did not bring about better treatment for black soldiers. The disparity in pay and equipment continued. There were no opportunities for blacks to become officers. Black soldiers were sometimes sent into battle without adequate preparation. Worst of all, Jefferson Davis announced that captured black soldiers would not be treated as prisoners of war, but would be dealt with according to Southern slave codes. This often meant execution for captured black soldiers. Douglass, in an open letter to President Lincoln, protested against the government's failure to retaliate. "What has Mr. Lincoln to say about this slavery and murder?" asked Douglass. "What has he said?—Not one word. In the hearing of the nation he is as silent as any oyster on the whole subject." Douglass's letter announced that at least for the time being he would no longer be involved in recruiting. "When I plead for recruits I want to do it with all my heart," he emphasized. "I must for the present leave to others the work of persuading colored men to join the Union Army. I owe it to my long abused people, and especially of them already in the army, to expose their wrongs and plead their cause."[14]

In late July 1863 Douglass asked for and was granted an audience with Lincoln in order to discuss the problems faced by black recruits. When Douglass recounted the event, he wrote of his first impressions of the president. "There was no vain pomp and ceremony about him. I was never more quickly or more completely put at ease in the presence of a great man than in that of Abraham Lincoln." Douglass recalled that the president "appeared to be much overworked and tired. Long lines of care were already deeply written on Mr. Lincoln's brow, and his strong face, full of earnestness, lighted up as soon as my name was mentioned." Douglass remembered that "I at once felt myself in the presence of an honest man—one whom I could love, honor, and trust without reserve or doubt." When Douglass attempted to introduce himself, the president stopped him, saying, "I know who you are Mr. Douglass; Mr. Seward has told me about you. Sit down. I am glad to see you."

Douglass soon told the president that the purpose of his visit was to inform him that many black recruits did not feel the government was fair in its dealings with them. Douglass spoke of unequal pay; of the treatment suffered by black soldiers when captured by the Confederates and how the Union government had a responsibility to retaliate in kind; and the need for reward and promotion for distinguished service on the battlefield. Douglass noted that "Mr. Lincoln listened with patience and silence to all I had to say. . . . By his silent listening not less than by his earnest reply to my words, impressed me with the solid gravity of his character."

The president told Douglass that unequal pay "seemed a necessary condition to smooth the way to their employment at all as soldiers, but that ultimately they would receive the same." As regards retaliation, Lincoln thought it "a terrible remedy . . . if once begun, there was no telling where it would end." As far as promotions were concerned, Lincoln promised to "sign any commission to colored soldiers whom his Secretary of War should commend to him." In his evaluation of his session with the president, Douglass wrote: "Though I was not entirely satisfied with his views, I was so well satisfied with the man and with the educating tendency of the conflict that I determined to go on with the recruiting."[15]

After his interview with Lincoln, Douglass met with Secretary Stanton who offered him a commission as an "assistant adjutant to General Thomas." However, Douglass wrote, "my commission never came. The government, I fear, was still clinging to the idea that positions of honor in the service should be occupied by white men, and that it would not do to inaugurate just then the policy of perfect equality." Summarizing his visit to the nation's capital, Douglass recalled: "My interviews with President Lincoln and his able Secretary . . . greatly increased my confidence in the antislavery integrity of the government."[16]

The following month, Douglass ceased the publication of his paper and would devote the remainder of the war to public lectures. On January 13, 1864, at New York City's Cooper Institute, Douglass delivered one of his more memorable addresses of the war. The speech, "The Mission of the War," had been delivered previously in Rochester, Philadelphia, Boston, and other northern cities. Though the Emancipation Proclamation had been in effect for a year, Douglass thought it increasingly necessary to emphasize that the war must be fought for the abolition of slavery. Such a goal, unmistakably reiterated, would have worldwide implications. "The blow we strike," declared the orator, "is not merely to free a country or continent—but the whole world from Slavery—for when Slavery falls here—it will fall everywhere. We have no business to mourn over our mission. We are writing the statutes of eternal justice and liberty in the blood of the worst tyrants as a warning to all after-comers."

Douglass expressed his ambivalence as to the depth of President Lincoln's antislavery commitment.

It is true we have the Proclamation of January, 1863. It was a vast and glorious step in the right direction. But unhappily, excellent as that paper is—and much as it has accomplished temporarily—it settles nothing. It is still open to decision by courts, canons and Congresses. I have applauded that paper and do now applaud it, as a wise measure—while I detest the motive and principle upon which it is based. By it the holding and flogging of negroes is the exclusive luxury of loyal men.

Our chief danger lies in the absence of all moral feeling in the utterances of our rulers. In his letter to Mr. Greeley the President told the country virtually that the abolition or non-abolition of Slavery was a matter of indifference to him. He would save the Union with Slavery or without Slavery. In his last Message he shows the same moral indifference, by saying as he does say that he had hoped that the Rebellion could be put down without the abolition of Slavery.

The speaker concluded his address with the same plea he had offered again and again since the guns from Charleston fired on Fort Sumter.

I end where I began—no war but an Abolition war; no peace but an Abolition peace; liberty for all, chains for none; the black man a soldier in war, a laborer in peace; a voter at the South as well as at the North; America his permanent home, and all Americans his fellow-countrymen. Such, fellow-citizens, is my idea of the mission of the war. If accomplished, our glory as a nation will be complete, our peace will flow like a river, and our foundations will be the everlasting rocks.[17]

As Douglass pondered the war, he became concerned not just with the abolition of slavery but also with what would happen to former slaves after their emancipation. What would be the place of freed blacks in American society? Black suffrage was of paramount importance. On the evening of April 12, 1864, Douglass attended a dinner at the Parker House in Boston honoring two representatives of the free black population of New Orleans who had recently been in Washington lobbying for suffrage and other political rights. Douglass was called on to deliver some impromptu remarks. He began with words of caution, declaring that "I am not quite as sanguine as some are as to the death of slavery in this country by this war." Douglass cited other events in American history that were thought to have ended slavery, but did not. He then spoke to the importance of black suffrage, saying that he joined with the representatives from Louisiana "in asking you, gentlemen of Massachusetts and of Boston, to exert your influence, not so much for the abolition of slavery (the greater includes the lesser) but for the complete, absolute, unqualified enfranchisement of the colored people of the South, so that they shall not only be permitted to vote, but to be voted for, eligible to any office."[18]

In June 1864 the Republican party nominated Lincoln for a second term. In late August, the president requested an interview with Douglass. Lincoln feared that with the continuation of the war, accompanied by its mounting casualties, he might be forced to accept a negotiated peace with the South. Such a peace would mean the slave states were no longer in rebellion and thus the peculiar institution would not end. Lincoln inquired of Douglass as to the best way to induce slaves to cross over into federal lines before such a limited and compromising peace would take place. Douglass later recalled the conversation.

What he [Lincoln] said on this day showed a deeper moral conviction against slavery then I had ever seen before in anything spoken or written by him. I listened with the deepest interest and profoundest satisfaction, and, at his suggestion, agreed to undertake the organizing a band of scouts, composed of colored men, whose business should be somewhat after the original plan of John Brown, to go into the rebel States, beyond the line of our armies, and carry the news of emancipation, and urge the slaves to come within our boundaries.[19]

The plan became unnecessary as Union victories—such as the fall of Atlanta to Sherman's troops—assured a northern triumph in the near future. Douglass announced his support for the reelection of the president, offering to make speeches on Lincoln's behalf. Republican leaders, fearing that Douglass might turn moderate voters away from the party, were cool to the black orator's offer. After Lincoln's victory at the polls, Douglass was invited to attend an evening reception at the White House on the occasion of Lincoln's second inaugural. When policemen prevented him from entering the White House, informing him that negroes were not invited, Douglass got word to Lincoln who personally welcomed him and proceeded to ask Douglass's opinion of the inaugural address.

One month later, Douglass was in Rochester at the time Lincoln was assassinated. In midafternoon of April 15—Lincoln had died earlier that morning—a public memorial service was held at City Hall. When it was noticed that Douglass was in attendance, he was asked to speak.

This call to address you on this occasion was quite unexpected to me, and one to which I find it almost impossible to respond. If you have deep grief in the death of Abraham Lincoln, and feel in it a severe stab at republican institutions, I feel it on all these accounts and more. I feel it as a personal as well as national calamity, on account of the race to which I belong and the deep interest which that good man ever took in its elevation. This is not an occasion for speech making, but for silence. I have scarcely been able to say a word to any of those friends who have taken my hand and looked sadly in my eyes to-day. A dreadful disaster has befallen the nation. It is a day for silence and meditation; for grief and tears. . . .

How I have to-day mourned for our noble President, I dare not attempt to tell. It was only a few weeks ago that I shook his brave, honest hand, and looked into his gentle eye and heard his kindly voice uttering those memorable words—words which will live immortal in history, and be read with increasing admiration from age to age. . . .

To-day, to-day, as never before, the American people, although they know they cannot have indemnity for the past—for the countless treasure and the precious blood—yet they resolve to-day that they will exact ample security for the future! And if it teaches us this lesson, it may be that the blood of our beloved martyred President will be the salvation of our country. Good man we call him; good man he was. If "an honest man is the noblest work of God," we need have no fear for the soul of Abraham Lincoln.

Douglass placed the blame for Lincoln's death, as did many in the North, on the South, and he warned of too quickly welcoming rebels back into the national family: "This new demonstration of the guilt of slavery, teaches another lesson. Hereafter we must not despise any hand or any arm that has been uplifted in defence of the Nation's life. Let us not be in too much haste in the work of restoration. Let us not be in a hurry to clasp to our bosom that spirit which gave birth to Booth." Someone who was there that day, made the following observation of Douglass's impromptu remarks: "I have heard Webster and Clay in their best moments, Channing and Beecher in their highest inspiration; I have never heard truer eloquence; I never saw profounder impressions. When he finished, the meeting was done."[20]

The war years added further dimensions to Douglass as an orator and a man. From the beginning of the conflict he urged that the war be one for emancipation, and the proclamation of 1863 fulfilled his hopes. He also labored tirelessly to persuade the government to recruit black troops and use them in the fight against the forces of slavery. This too came to pass, though with some serious disappointments. The war years brought to Douglass invitations to the White

House to meet with the president of the United States. Though Douglass had some significant reservations about some of Lincoln's policies, there can be no doubt as to his admiration for and fondness of the man. Finally, the war years forged a strong bond between Douglass and the Republican party, a bond that in future years, though sometimes severely strained, would remain intact.

4

The Postwar Years (1865–1895)

Frederick Douglass was forty-seven years old when the Civil War came to an end. His life and work would continue for another thirty years. As with all his previous years, these postwar years, were years of continued development, expanding influence, and extraordinary oratory. In these three decades Douglass would meet with each of the nation's presidents who served during this period, including a very acrimonious meeting with Andrew Johnson. Douglass would vigorously support every Republican candidate for the presidency and be rewarded with political appointments. He would move from Rochester to the nation's capital where he would live comfortably for the rest of his life. Douglass's first wife, Anna, died, and within two years Douglass married a white woman, Helen Pitts, twenty years younger than himself—an act that brought strong criticisms from many sources. He would continue his oratory, sometimes on the lyceum circuit, consistently on behalf of Republican candidates, often in behalf of the plight of the freedmen in the South, and frequently to further the cause of both black and woman suffrage.

If by the time of his second meeting with Abraham Lincoln, Douglass had developed a particular fondness and admiration for the president, no similar feelings or estimation was ever directed toward Lincoln's successor, Andrew Johnson. Douglass's first impression of Johnson was in March 1865 at Lincoln's second inauguration ceremony. On that day, Douglass notes, "I caught a glimpse of the real nature of this man, which all subsequent developments proved true." It seems that Lincoln turned to Johnson and pointed out Douglass who was standing in the crowd. Douglass recalled that "the first expression which came to his [Johnson's] face, and which I think was the true index of his heart, was one of bitter contempt and aversion." When Johnson observed that Douglass was looking at him, "he tried to assume a more friendly appearance, but it was too late; it is useless to close the door when all within has been seen." At that moment Douglass turned to a friend and remarked, "Whatever Andrew Johnson may be, he certainly is no friend of our race." As Douglass recalled that day he drew a contrast between Lincoln and Johnson. "Mr. Lincoln was like one who was treading the hard and thorny path of duty and self-denial. Mr. Johnson was like one just from a drunken debauch. The face of one was of manly humility, although at the topmost heights of power and pride; that of the other was full of pomp and swaggering vanity."[1]

On February 7, 1866, President Johnson received a delegation of thirteen men—including Douglass and his son Lewis—who represented the National Convention of Colored Men. The delegation had come to express their concerns on the enforcement of the Thirteenth Amendment and the question of black suffrage in the South. Citing the example of Lincoln, Douglass informed Johnson: "Your noble and humane predecessor placed in our hands the sword to assist in saving the nation, and we do hope that you, his able successor, will favorably regard the placing in our hands the ballot with which to save ourselves." Johnson replied that he would not enforce black suffrage upon the South, fearing that it would only further strain the relations between the races. "It would be tyrannical in me to attempt to force such upon them without their will," Johnson emphasized. "It is a fundamental tenet in my creed that the people must be obeyed. Is there anything wrong or unfair in that?" Douglass quickly retorted, "A great deal wrong, Mr. President, with all respect." Johnson restated his position. "It is the people of the States that must for themselves determine this thing. I do not want to be engaged in a work that will commence a war of the races." Johnson went on to suggest that if blacks were unhappy in the southern states they should emigrate to other sections in the country. The delegates left the meeting acknowledging that the president had been courteous but was obviously attempting to conceal "a repressed anger."[2] Years later Douglass recalled that Johnson "occupied at least three-quarters of an hour in what seemed a set speech, and refused to listen to any reply on our part, although solicited to grant a few moments for that purpose."[3]

It was not merely political or social matters that occupied Douglass during these postwar years. He devoted much of his time as a lyceum lecturer, speaking on a variety of topics. The most widely requested lecture, "Self-Made Men," was one he first wrote and delivered in 1855, and had repeated for many years into the future, undergoing several revisions. In reading the speech, there would seem to be little doubt that it was Douglass himself who was the "self-made man."

[Self-made men] are the men who owe nothing to birth, relationship, friendly surroundings, wealth inherited, or to early and approved means of education; who are what they are, without any of the conditions by which other men usually achieve the same results. . . . In a peculiar sense they are indebted to themselves for themselves. . . . Every instance of this type is an example and a help to the race. It assures us of the latent powers and resources of simple and unaided manhood. . . .

When we find a man who has ascended high beyond ourselves, who has a broader range of vision than we, and a horizon with many more stars in it than we have, we may know that he has worked harder, better, and more wisely than we have. He was awake while we slept, was busy while we were idle, and wisely improved his time while we wasted ours. . . .

America, not without reason, is said to be pre-eminently the home and patron of self-made men. . . . The principle of measuring and valuing men, according to their respective merits, is better established and more generally enforced and observed here than in any other country. . . .

It must be admitted that self-made men are not generally over-modest or self-forgetful men. . . . The very energies employed, the obstacles overcome, the heights to which some men rise, and the broad contrasts which life forces upon them at every step tend to make them egotistical.[4]

One of the postwar issues that occupied much of Douglass's time and attention was his quest to attain black suffrage. In doing so, he alienated, for a time, another group who also wanted the vote—women. When the American Equal Rights Association was founded in 1866 to gain the right to vote for black men and all women, Douglass was chosen one of the three vice presidents. It was not long, however, before Susan B. Anthony, Elizabeth Cady Stanton, and other suffragists began to accuse that Douglass, in his arduous efforts for black suffrage, was neglecting the issue of woman suffrage. In several speeches Douglass explained that he was an ardent proponent of woman suffrage but that black suffrage must take priority, because the abuse of blacks was so much greater. At a meeting of the Equal Rights Association on May 14, 1868, Douglass declared:

I have always championed woman's rights, but it will seem that the present claim of the negro is one of the most urgent necessity. The assertion of the right of women to vote has never met anything worse than mere ridicule, but the public are tolerant; no deep-seated malignity is in the breasts of the people against them; but name the right of the negro to vote, and all hell is turned loose in the breasts of the people, and Ku-Klux Klans and Regulators commence to hunt and slay the unoffending black. It is easily to be seen that this is an urgent question. The Government of this country loves women. They are the sisters, mothers, wives, and daughters of our rulers; but the negro is loathed.[5]

At the Equal Rights Convention the following year, Douglass stressed a similar theme.

When women, because they are women, are dragged from their homes and hung upon lamp-posts; when their children are torn from their arms and their brains dashed upon the pavement; when they are objects of insults and outrage at every turn; when they are in danger of having their homes burnt down over their heads; when their children are not allowed to enter schools, then they will have an urgency to obtain the ballot.[6]

Shortly after this convention, the Equal Rights Association disbanded, and women formed the National Woman Suffrage Association, separating themselves from the issue of black suffrage.

In 1870 Douglass and a few others began publication of a newspaper, *New*

Era. Within six months the paper encountered serious financial problems. Some stockholders withdrew their commitments. Douglass temporarily left the lecture circuit, moved to Washington, at first purchased one-half interest in the paper and then the remaining half. The paper was renamed *New National Era,* and Douglass proclaimed that the paper's position would be: "Free men, free soil, free speech, a free press, everywhere in the land. The ballot for all, education for all, fair wages for all."[7]

Douglass continued as an avid supporter of and spokesman for the Republican party. In 1868 he campaigned for Ulysses S. Grant in the old soldier's successful run for the presidency. In early November 1870 Douglass returned to Rochester in order to vote. On election-day eve he attended a Republican party rally held at City Hall. Called on to speak at the rally, Douglass told the audience why it was important to support Republicans: "The greatness of this government has been enhanced by the Republican administration. If our flag is loved at home and honored abroad, it is because of the efforts of the Republican party to make it honorable. It is for the character which this party has given it." He warned of what the South would do to the negro if the Democrats gained control: "The transfer of power from the Republican to the Democratic party would be the signal for an attempt all over the South to undo all that has been done and reduce the negro to a condition as near his former servitude as possible." Douglass then challenged his audience: "Because I wish to see this great nation grow greater, more glorious and free, I shall vote as I wish you all to vote—for the whole Republican ticket."[8]

As 1872 drew near, the year when Grant would run for reelection, a division began to evolve in the Republican party. A liberal wing, lead by Carl Schurz and B. Gratz Brown, posed a serious threat to Grant's renomination. The movement believed it was time for Radical Reconstruction to come to an end and for a general amnesty to be granted to former Confederates. Douglass was disappointed to observe that Charles Sumner, who had been a consistent friend to black people and a champion for their rights, had become a part of this faction. At a convention in Cincinnati, on May 1, 1872, the Liberal Republicans nominated Horace Greeley for president and B. Gratz Brown for vice president. The Democrats endorsed the ticket. Though Sumner tried to assure Douglass and others that the Democrats had adopted Republican policies, Douglass refused to support Greeley and worked tirelessly for Grant's reelection. On July 24, Douglass delivered a campaign speech in Richmond, Virginia, wherein he stated his objections to Greeley. "My objection to Mr. Greeley," noted Douglass, "is that he is an uncertain man; that he is a vacillating man; that he is at the present moment in doubtful company, to say the least." He accused Greeley of being "a sort of amphibious animal, living on neither land nor water, neither a Republican nor a Democrat; neither a protectionist nor a free-trader; in favor of centralization and against it; in favor of Ku-Klux laws and against them; opposed to Tammany and with it." Douglass warned, "I regard the election of Horace Greeley as one of the most calamitous that could possibly befall this Republic."[9]

The following day, in Raleigh, North Carolina, Douglass urged his audience to vote for the regular Republican ticket. He attempted to persuade the white people in the audience that he held no animosity toward them. "I am not," he insisted, "an enemy of any class of American citizens. God forbid. The truth in regard to the matter is just this: I always hated slavery, but never the slave-holder. Read over thirty years of my utterances and you will find nothing like malice toward the slave-holder." Douglass must have hoped that no one would accept that challenge. After granting Greeley faint praise, Douglass again accused the newspaper editor of inconsistency: "I should like to vote for Mr. Greeley—want to vote for him, if I only knew which Greeley my vote might help elect." Douglass then urged the reelection of Grant.

I know Ulysses S. Grant. It may seem to you a boast on my part that I, a negro—that I, with flat nose, distended nostrils—should be an acquaintance of the President of the United States. Yet I am. And let me tell you another thing: I never was received by any gentleman in the United States with more kindness and cordiality. I may say with more confidence—never felt more at home in the presence of any gentleman—than I have in the presence of Ulysses S. Grant. He is a good man, a true man, a steady man. You know what he is to-day, what he was yesterday, and what he will be to-morrow, for he does not turn with every wind of doctrine, and for that reason we want him.[10]

On June 2, 1872, Douglass's house in Rochester burned to the ground. Though no one was harmed, the contents of the house, including irreplaceable papers and documents, were destroyed. The fire was the work of an arsonist who was never identified. Friends in Rochester urged Douglass to rebuild in the city, but Douglass moved his family to Washington where he had been residing for much of the time over the past two years. Later in the year Grant was reelected, garnering 55.6 percent of the vote. Greeley carried only six states.

The year 1874 witnessed two financial failures associated with Douglass. In March Douglass was appointed the president of the Freedmen's Savings and Trust Company, usually referred to as the Freedmen's Bank. The bank had been created in 1865 for the purpose of aiding freedmen to improve their economic position. By the time of Douglass's appointment the bank was in financial trouble. He had been asked to take the job with the thought that his prestige might give stability to the institution. It was, however, too late. Douglass loaned the bank $10,000 of his own money, but the doors closed on June 24, 1874. Later, Douglass would recall that the bank was doomed to failure before he became its president. He sensed that he had been used. "I found that those trustees who wished to issue cards and publish addresses professing the utmost confidence in the Bank, had themselves not one dollar deposited there. Some of them, while strongly assuring me of its soundness, had withdrawn their money and opened accounts elsewhere."[11]

Three months after the bank failure, *New National Era* folded. A national economic panic which began in 1873 contributed to the demise of both the bank and the paper. Douglass relied on the lecture circuit for a major portion of his income. His fee was $100 per lecture and $500 for a series of two or three lectures. In one three-month period, he earned $3,700.[12] Lecturing on a wide variety of subjects (inspirational addresses, a recital of various events from his life, ethical challenges, partisan politics, and strong pleas for a fair and just treatment of the negro), Douglass drew large audiences. For the most part these audiences were friendly and appreciative, but on those occasions when Douglass uncompromisingly addressed political issues and matters pertaining to civil rights, there would be some boos and hisses.

Douglass experienced yet another loss in 1874, but one of a very different kind than the economic ones just related. On March 11 Senator Charles Sumner of Massachusetts died. Five days later, black citizens gathered at the Sumner School in the nation's capital to honor the memory of one who had been such an effective and uncompromising voice against slavery before the war and a champion of black rights after the war. Douglass, in moving eloquence, eulogized the Senator.

Charles Sumner had a deeper sense of our wrongs and a purer appreciation of our rights than we could have. Frequently has he stood in the Senate and demanded rights for us which we said we were not ready to accept. . . . The more Charles Sumner got for us the more he wanted for us. Each higher level he brought us to only prepared us for another still higher. . . .

Let us go home and teach our children the name of Charles Sumner; tell them his utterances, and teach them that they, like him, can make their lives sublime by clinging to principles. While stars were falling all around us Charles Sumner shone brightly, untainted by corruption—pure, spotless, stainless.[13]

Meanwhile, in the South, blacks were being terrorized. Unable to legally impose slavery, white supremacist groups wrecked their vengeance on the helpless freedmen. When Douglass and others in the North spoke against such lawless brutality, these protests, for the most part, fell upon unresponsive ears. People complained, "We have done enough for the negro." In a speech on April 14, 1875, in Philadelphia, Douglass answered those who claimed they had done enough and reminded his audience as to what life was like for the freedmen in the South.

It is said by some: "We have done enough for the negro." Yes, you have done a great deal for the negro, and, for one, I am deeply sensible of it, and grateful for it. But after all, what have you done? We were slaves—and you have made us free—and given us the ballot. But the world has never seen any people turned loose to such destitution as were the four million slaves in the South. The old roof was pulled down over their heads before they could make for themselves a shelter. They were free! free to hunger; free to the winds and rains of heaven; free to the pitiless wrath of enraged masters, who, since they could no longer control them, were willing to see them starve. They were free, without roofs to cover them or bread to eat, or land to cultivate, and as a consequence died in such numbers as to awaken the hope of their enemies that they should soon disappear. We gave them freedom and famine at the same time. The marvel is that they still live. What the negro wants is, first, protection to the rights already conceded by law, and secondly, education. Talk of having done enough for these people after two hundred years of enforced ignorance and stripes is absurd, cruel and heartless. . . . To-day, in the South, the school-house is burned. To-day, in Tennessee, Lucy Haydon is called from an inner room at midnight and shot down because she teaches colored children to read. To-day, in New Orleans and in Louisiana, and in parts of Alabama, the black man scarcely dares to deposit the votes which you gave him a right to deposit for fear of his life. We want your voices again.[14]

On April 14, 1876, the eleventh anniversary of Lincoln's assassination, the Freedmen's Memorial Monument to the slain president was unveiled in Washington's Lincoln Park. National leaders from every branch of government were in attendance, including President Grant, who was accorded the honor of officially unveiling the monument. Douglass delivered the principal address, of which Senator George S. Boutwell from Massachusetts said, was "the best contribution made to the department of literature in which it takes place, since the time of Mr. Webster." The speech was indicative that Douglass still held to a mixed appraisal of the sixteenth president. Lincoln was, said the speaker, "in his interests, in his associations, in his habits of thought, and in his prejudices . . . a white man." Black people were at best only "his step children, children by adoption, children by force of circumstances and necessity." Lincoln, Douglass reminded, was slow in announcing emancipation, but "whether he was slow or swift in his movements; it was enough for us that Abraham Lincoln was at the head of a great movement, and was in living and earnest sympathy with that movement, which, in the nature of things, must go on till slavery should be utterly and forever abolished in the United States." Douglass continued, "though Mr. Lincoln shared the prejudices of his white fellow-countrymen against the negro, it is hardly necessary to say that in his heart of hearts he loathed and hated slavery." The monument, Douglass attested, was not only a tribute to Lincoln, but to the black man as well. "When now it shall be said that the colored man is soulless, that he has no appreciation of benefits or benefactors; when the first reproach of ingratitude is hurled at us, and it is attempted to scourge us beyond the range of human brotherhood, we may calmly point to the monument we have this day erected to the memory of Abraham Lincoln."[15]

The presidential election of 1876 between Republican Rutherford B. Hayes and Democrat Samuel J. Tilden was decided by the House of Representatives in 1877 because neither candidate secured a majority of the electoral votes. In the House, Democrats from the South threw their support to the Republican Hayes in exchange for a promise that he would withdraw all remaining federal troops from the South and allow that region to conduct its own affairs. Reconstruction was over. Strangely enough, one looks in vain for Douglass's immediate comments on the Compromise of 1877, sometimes referred to as "the betrayal of the negro." When Hayes assumed the presidential office he appointed Douglass as the U.S. Marshall of the District of Columbia. Some accused that Douglass's "silence" had been obtained by the promise of federal office. This would seem doubtful. It would not be in harmony with what is known of Douglass's character, and, as a U.S. Marshall, he continued to lash out at racial injustice wherever he perceived it. He severely criticized the Jim Crow restrictions in the nation's capital. In a speech at Madison Square Garden in New York, on May 30, 1878, Douglass spoke of rampant injustices in the South. Recognizing that Hayes had extended a hand of conciliation toward the South, Douglass asked for reciprocation.

I do not say that Hon. Rutherford B. Hayes, the lawful and rightful President of the United States, was not justified in stepping to the verge of his constitutional powers to conciliate and pacify the old master class of the South; but I do say that some steps by way of conciliation should come from the other side, The prodigal son should at least turn his back upon the field of swine, and his face toward home, before we make haste to fall upon his neck and kill the fatted calf. He must not glory in his shame, and boast his non-repentance.[16]

In 1877 Douglass took a nostalgic trip down memory lane when he returned to Maryland and met with his old master, Thomas Auld, then a dying man. It was an emotional meeting for both persons. Douglass recalled: "We shook hands cordially, and in the act of doing so, he, having been long stricken with palsy, shed tears as men thus afflicted will do when excited by any deep emotion. . . . The circumstances of his condition affected me deeply, and for a time choked my voice and made me speechless." After both men had composed themselves, Douglass asked Auld's opinion of his former slave's escape to the North. Auld replied, "Frederick, I always knew you were too smart to be a slave and had I been in your place, I should have done as you did." To this, Douglass responded, "Capt. Auld, I am glad to hear you say this. I did not run away from you, but from slavery; it was not that I loved Caesar less, but Rome more." Auld also informed Douglass that he was born in 1818, and not in 1817 as Douglass had thought. "This date made me one year younger than I had supposed myself."[17]

By 1878 Douglass's finances had, for the first time in his life, stabilized. He was able to cut back on his exhausting speaking tours, which were exacting a physical toll. He purchased a home at the summit of a hill in the District of Columbia, an integrated area known as Uniontown in Anacostia. With the house came a barn and nine acres, plenty of room for the gardening which Douglass so much enjoyed. He purchased an additional fifteen adjacent acres the following year. The large house, built in the 1850s, had a library to house its owner's many books, and a music room where Douglass's violin rested on the piano. Cedar Hill, as the home was called, would be the Douglass family residence for the remainder of his years.

In 1879 Douglass became embroiled in a unique controversy, for in this dispute, as he would later admit, Douglass was on the wrong side. Black people in the South, frustrated by oppression, discrimination, and violence, were leaving the region and migrating to Kansas and other midwestern areas; hoping in the process to establish a new and more promising future. The move of the "Exodusters" was applauded by most prominent black leaders and by several of the old abolitionists such as Garrison and Phillips. Douglass found himself in sharp disagreement with those who had been former allies. He strongly opposed the exodus, believing that black labor was essential to the Southern economy. All blacks needed to do was withhold their labor for a time and they could bargain for better conditions. Douglass, it seems, had temporarily lost touch as to how miserable and degrading life had become for blacks in the South. He also failed to recognize that if blacks withheld their labor they would starve.

The American Social Science Association offered Douglass the opportunity to explain his position at their annual meeting on September 12, 1879, in Saratoga, New York. The opposing side would be given a similar opportunity. Douglass accepted, but three days before the meeting he canceled his agreement citing the press of other responsibilities. He agreed, however, to send his manuscript for someone else to read. The lengthy manuscript portrays how passionately Douglass believed in his stance.

It cannot be doubted, that in so far as this Exodus tends to promote restlessness in the colored people of the South, to unsettle their feelings of home and to sacrifice positive advantages where they are, for fancied ones in Kansas or elsewhere, it is an evil. . . . Not only is the South the best locality for the negro on the ground of his political powers and possibilities, but it is best for him as a field of labor. He is there, as he is nowhere else, an absolute necessity. . . . With a moderate degree of intelligent leadership among the laboring class in the South, properly handling the justice of their cause, using the Exodus example, they can easily exact better terms for their labor than ever before.[18]

Douglass's opposition to the exodus, McFeely notes, demonstrated that "he refused to see that something had changed—for the worse."

Black workers, in the wake of a ruined Reconstruction, needed his help, but Douglass could not give it. . . . The image of his people as miserable refugees was more than Douglass could face. For the first time in his life, he found himself hissed and booed by black audiences. . . . Those with their eyes open to the oppression of black laborers in Mississippi and Louisiana in 1879 saw Douglass as simply wrong when he claimed that "the conditions . . . in the Southern States are steadily improving."[19]

Ten years later Douglass toured South Carolina and Georgia. What he observed caused him to modify his views on the exodus. The Exodusters received his blessing and he pledged himself to greater efforts on behalf of those who stayed in the South. A few days after his return from the South, Douglass delivered a speech on the twenty-sixth anniversary of emancipation in the District of Columbia. He spoke, uncompromisingly, about the economic exploitation of blacks in the South. He began, "I have recently been in two of the southern states—South Carolina and Georgia, and my impression from what I saw, heard, and learned there is not favorable to my hopes for the race." Douglass continued:

Do you ask me why the negro of the plantation has made so little progress, why his cupboard is empty, why he flutters in rags, why his children run naked, and why his wife hides herself behind the hut when a stranger is passing? I will tell you. It is because he is systematically and universally cheated out of his hard earnings. The same class that once extorted his labor under the lash now gets his labor by a mean, sneaking, and fraudulent device. That device is a trucking system which never permits him to see or to save a dollar of his hard earnings. He struggles and struggles, but, like a man in a morass, the more he struggles the deeper he sinks. The highest wages paid him is $8 a month, and this he receives only in orders on the store, which, in many cases, is owned by his employer. The script has purchasing power on that one store, and that one only. . . . The only security the wretched negro has under this arrangement is the conscience of the storekeeper—a conscience educated in the school of slavery, where the idea prevailed in theory and practice that the negro had no rights which white men are bound to respect, an arrangement in which everything in the way of food or clothing, whether tainted meat or damaged cloth, is deemed good enough for the negro. For these he is often made to pay a double price.

Douglass railed against the injustices of tenant farming. Drawing his speech to a conclusion, he denounced the federal government for abandoning the negro and his rights under the Constitution.

Thus is the negro citizen swindled. The government professes to give him citizenship and silently permits him to be divested of every attribute of citizenship. It demands allegiance, but denies protection. It taxes him as a citizen in peace, and compels him to bear arms and meet bullets in war. It imposes upon him all the burdens of citizenship and withholds from him all its benefits.[20]

In December 1880 Douglass wrote to President-elect James Garfield requesting reappointment to the position of marshall. His request was supported by Mark Twain, who, in a letter to Garfield the following month, wrote, "I beg permission to hope that you will retain Mr. Douglass in his present office of Marshall of the District of Columbia. . . . He is a personal friend of mine, but that is nothing to the point, his history would move me to say these things without that, and I feel them too."[21] Douglass was not appointed to that post, but Garfield did appoint him Recorder of Deeds for the District, a position Douglass held through the Arthur administration, who assumed office after Garfield's assassination.

Douglass's third and most comprehensive autobiography, *Life and Times of Frederick Douglass,* was published in 1881 and suffered disappointing sales. The Park Publishing Company of Boston made a first printing of 200,000 copies. In spite of aggressive promotion, the book sold only 362 copies in the next seven years. DeWolfe, Fisk, and Company republished an extended version of the book in 1892, thinking that Douglass's appointment as Minister to Haiti would arouse new interest. Once again sales were distressing. Over a two-year period,

399 copies of the new version were sold.[22] Though the sales of Douglass's first two autobiographies were impressive, the failure of the third may have indicated that Douglass and/or the views he represented were no longer important to most Americans.

In August of the following year, Douglass's wife, Anna, died. About a year and a half later, in January 1884, he married Helen Pitts, a college-educated woman and active participant in the woman suffrage movement who had been Douglass's secretary in the recorder's office. She was twenty years younger than Douglass and she was white. The mixed marriage brought a storm of criticism from many quarters. Some blacks accused Douglass of showing "contempt for the women of his own race," and some whites looked upon him as "a lecherous old African Solomon."[23] Douglass's offspring would never become comfortable with the marriage. Douglass dismissed the controversy by noting that his second marriage demonstrated his impartiality; his first wife, he emphasized, "was the color of my mother, and the second the color of my father." Elizabeth Cady Stanton wrote to Douglass and denounced "the clamor" raised against the marriage. In a return letter to Stanton, Douglass wrote: "I could never have been at peace with my own soul or held up my head among men had I allowed the fear of popular clamor to deter me from following my convictions as to this marriage. I should have gone to my grave a self-accused and a self-convicted moral coward." A correspondent from the *Detroit Free Press,* who visited Cedar Hill several months after the marriage and heard Douglass play the violin to Helen's piano accompaniment, concluded that "it is not strange that Douglass should have wished to marry this woman somewhat his equal intellectually. Mrs. Douglass is very much in love with her husband. That she admires and is proud of him is plain to see."[24]

Grover Cleveland was elected to the presidency in 1884, the first Democrat to hold that office since before the Civil War. Douglass continued to hold his office as recorder during the first year of the new administration. During that time, Douglass and Helen attended presidential receptions and other functions, an honor never accorded under the Garfield and Arthur administrations. Early in 1886, at the president's request, Douglass offered his resignation. When various Republicans urged Douglass to make an issue over the resignation, he would not, and offered an explanation.

I am a Republican, and did all I could to defeat the election of Mr. Cleveland. He was under no political obligation to me whatever; yet I held the office of Recorder nearly a whole year under his administration. . . . While in office, President Cleveland treated me as he treated other office-holders in the District. He was brave enough to invite Mrs. Douglass and myself to all his grand receptions, thus rebuking the timidity—I need not say cowardice or prejudice—of his predecessor. I am a Republican, and if living shall do all I can to elect a Republican in 1888; but I know manliness wherever I find it; and I have found it in President Cleveland, and should despise myself if I should let any one think otherwise. Whatever else he may be, he is not a snob; and he is not a coward.[25]

In the fall of 1886 Frederick and Helen began a tour of Europe, during which the couple visited the grave of Theodore Parker in Florence, Italy. Standing by the headstone, Douglass recalled "the many services rendered the cause of human freedom by him [Parker], freedom not only from physical chains but the chains of superstition, those which not only galled the limbs and tore the flesh, but those which marred and wounded the human soul." Douglass remembered that Parker "had a voice for the slave when nearly all the pulpits in the land were dumb."[26] Shortly after the visit in Florence, the couple boarded ship for the return home.

In 1888 Douglass, having no income from a federal office, returned to the lecture circuit. He spoke that year at many places on a variety of topics. On February 12 the Republican National League, meeting in Washington, honored the birthday of Abraham Lincoln. Douglass's speech on that occasion was filled with unqualified praise for the former president. The speech was a contrast to other addresses he had given on Lincoln wherein he mixed bold criticism of the sixteenth president along with his praise. The determining factor for this different approach on that day was the audience Douglass was addressing. (It is noted in Part II that Douglass was highly skilled in adopting particular speeches to particular audiences.) On this day the audience consisted of Republican dignitaries, mostly white, for whom Lincoln was a national icon. Abraham Lincoln was, affirmed Douglass, on this occasion, "one of the greatest and best men ever produced by this country, if not ever produced by the world at large." Lincoln was, extolled the orator, a "glorious man! He was a man so broad in his character, so just in his action, so free from narrow prejudice; he touched the world completely at all sides that all classes, conditions, all nations, kindred, tongues, and people could hail him as a countryman, a clansman, a kinsman, a brother beloved, a benefactor." With great fondness Douglass recalled his meetings with the president. Even Mary Lincoln was mentioned with loving adulation. "Some people have said hard things about Mrs. Lincoln," Douglass admitted. "For my part I take no stock in them. I loved Mrs. Lincoln. I loved her because Abraham Lincoln loved her. That was enough for me." Douglass informed his audience that after Lincoln's death Mary Lincoln gave Douglass her husband's favorite cane. "She caused it to be sent to me at Rochester, N.Y., where I then lived; and I am the owner of this cane . . . and I mean to hold it and keep [it] in sacred remembrance of Abraham Lincoln, who once leaned upon it."[27]

In the same year Douglass delivered speeches on behalf of woman suffrage. On March 31, at the International Council of Women in Washington, Douglass spoke before an audience that included Susan B. Anthony, Elizabeth Cady Stanton, Lucy Stone, and several other international notables who were leading the battle for women's rights. Douglass began by acknowledging that as a man he should not be speaking to the delegates. "Men have very little business here as speakers," he observed, "if they come here at all they should take back benches and wrap them-selves in silence." Douglass continued: "No man, however gifted with thought and speech, can voice the wrongs and present the demands of women with skill and effect, with the power and authority of woman herself." He was proud, nevertheless, of the role he had played in the struggle. "There are few facts in my humble history," he noted, "to which I look back with more satisfaction than to the fact . . . that I was sufficiently enlightened at that early day, and when only a few years from slavery, to support your resolution for woman suffrage." A belief in the concept of male superiority was nearly universal, according to Douglass, but that didn't make it right. "Though the fallacy of this reasoning is too transparent to need refutation," he admitted, "it still exerts a powerful influence." Yet, Douglass was optimistic about the future. "When a great truth once gets abroad in the world, no power on earth can imprison it, or prescribe its limits, or suppress it. It is bound to go on till it becomes the thought of the world. Such a truth is woman's right to equal liberty with man."[28]

Though just beginning his seventh decade, Douglass campaigned vigorously for Benjamin Harrison during the 1888 presidential contest. On October 25 he delivered a major campaign address before a great crowd at the Hyperion Theater in New Haven, Connecticut. The speaker began by noting that at first his age had caused him to hesitate about being involved once again in political battles. "I am not as young as I once was, and it requires strength to travel and speak every night in the week, and then partake of a collation at midnight." Yet, it was important to Douglass that the Democrat Cleveland be defeated in his bid for a second term. For Douglass, the main issue was the return of a Republican to the White House after a brief interruption by Cleveland. Memories from antebellum and Civil War days still haunted Douglass. "The democratic party," he pronounced, "has always been on the wrong side of everything. That party said that the negro could not be civilized and made men of in God's world. Well, we have made men of them in this world and we are proud of them." On the other hand, "all that this country is, is due to the republican party."[29]

Harrison won the election and on July 1, 1889, the new president announced the appointment of Douglass as Minister-Resident and Consul-General to the Republic of Haiti. In late September Harrison added the post of Charge d'Affaires for Santo Domingo. There were objections to the appointment. White businessmen feared that a black man could not wrest enough economic concessions from Haiti. Even certain friends objected. Some thought the post not big enough for a man of Douglass's talents. Others worried about the affect of the Haitian climate on Douglass's health. Some blacks complained that his services and influence were needed in the United States. Suffragist Lucy Stone wrote to Douglass: "I am not sure we are glad to have you go. We need you here." Douglass, however, relished the opportunity. In a letter, he wrote, "President Harrison has done more and better for me than I asked—and has done it without my asking."[30] Haitian president Hyppolite acknowledged Douglass as "the illustrious champion of all men sprung from the African race, himself one of the most remarkable products of that race which we represent with pride on the American continent."[31]

Douglass did not retain his position for long. When the United States attempted to negotiate a lease of the port at Mole St. Nicholas in Haiti, Douglass refused to get involved in "underhand methods" against Haitian officials. He resigned his post in July of 1891. When some Americans accused him of failing to represent American interests, Douglass responded that he "had served the interests of the United States by refusing to ignore the interests of a million Haitians."[32]

Haitian officials honored Douglass by naming him cocommissioner of the Haitian Pavilion at the 1893 World's Columbian Exposition in Chicago. Douglass persuaded poet Paul Lawrence Dunbar to be his assistant. On January 2, 1893, Douglass delivered a speech, "Haiti and the Haitian People," at the Quinn Chapel in Chicago in connection with the opening of the exposition. The lengthy speech attracted about 1,500 "of the best citizens of Chicago." It was a brilliant defense of Haiti and its future possibilities, without ignoring the grave problems faced by the young republic. Haiti was, noted Douglass, "the one country to which we [United States] turn the cold shoulder." The reason for America's attitude, Douglass attested, was because "Haiti is black, and we have never forgiven Haiti for being black or forgiven the Almighty for making her black." To those who faulted Haiti for not allowing the United States to lease Mole St. Nicholas, Douglass retorted, "There was no insult or broken faith in the case. Haiti has the same right to refuse that we had to ask." The speaker acknowledged that there were warring factions in Haiti, but observed that America was not guiltless in this regard. "We have men in this country," accused Douglass, "who, to accomplish their personal and selfish ends, will fan the flame of passion between the factions in Haiti and will otherwise assist in setting revolutions afoot." Haiti could boast many "firsts," assured Douglass. After counter arguing many of the accusations made against Haiti and Haitians, Douglass concluded his speech by asking his audience to remember that Haiti was still an infant among the nations.

Though she is still an infant, she is out of the arms of her mother. Though she creeps, rather than walks; stumbles often and sometimes falls, her head is not broken, and she still lives and grows, and I predict, will yet be tall and strong. . . . In the face of the fact that Haiti still lives, after being boycotted by all the Christian world; in the face of the fact that she has attached herself to the car of the world's civilization, I will not, I cannot believe that her star is to go out in darkness, but I will rather believe that whatever may happen of peace or war Haiti will remain in the firmament of nations, and, like the star of the north, will shine on and shine on for-ever.[33]

As plans for the World's Columbian Exposition developed, it became obvious that blacks were being excluded from the planning and that their contributions to America would be ignored in the exposition itself. To counter this discrimination, Douglass began to work with Ida B. Wells, a southern black woman who by the 1890s was well known as an outspoken proponent for racial justice in America. Wells and Douglass collaborated in the publishing of a pamphlet *Why the Colored American Is Not in the World's Columbian Exposition.* Wells wrote the text and Douglass the introduction of this essay which enumerated the oppressive inequalities experienced by blacks in democratic America. The pamphlet was distributed from the Haitian Pavilion to both domestic and foreign visitors at the exposition.

August 25 was designated as Colored People's Day at the exposition. The day was, for the most part, a joke. Vendors distributed watermelons. The serious moment came in the afternoon when Douglass delivered an address. As he began, white men, standing near the rear of the crowd, began to jeer and poke fun. Douglass put down his manuscript and briefly surveyed the crowd. His eyes flashed with the vigor and indignation of old, and he began to speak in a thundering and outraged voice that soon quieted the hecklers. "Men talk of the Negro problem," the speaker boomed. "There is no Negro problem. The problem is whether the American people have loyalty enough, honor enough, patriotism enough, to live up to their own Constitution." For an hour, Douglass's words poured forth, interrupted only by applause and shouts of approval. Ida Wells, who had urged black people to boycott Colored People's Day, read about Douglass's speech in the newspaper. She rushed to see the renown orator, and told him that his speech "had done more to bring our cause to the attention of the American people than anything else which had happened during the fair."[34]

On the afternoon of February 20, 1895, Douglass attended a women's rights rally at Metzerott Hall in Washington. As he entered the hall, business was suspended, and Susan B. Anthony and Anna Shaw escorted him to the platform. The old veteran of civil rights was warmly received by an appreciative audience. He returned to Cedar Hill for supper. While waiting for a carriage to take Helen and him to a meeting at a nearby church, Douglass, in conversation with Helen, began to imitate and mimic one of the speakers he had heard at the afternoon rally. Suddenly, Douglass fell to his knees and then on his face. At the moment the carriage had come to take him to yet another speaking engagement, death determined that there would be no more oratory from Frederick Douglass. The lips of the seventy-seven-year-old orator were forever sealed. The next day Elizabeth Cady Stanton recalled in her diary the first time she ever saw Frederick Douglass. He was speaking at an antislavery rally in Boston.

He stood there like an African prince, majestic in his wrath, as with wit, satire, and indignation he graphically described the bitterness of slavery and the humiliation of subjection to those who, in all human virtues and powers, were inferior to himself. Thus it was that I first saw Frederick Douglass, and wondered that any mortal man should have ever tried to subjugate a being with such talents, intensified with the love of liberty. Around him sat the great antislavery orators of the day, earnestly watching the effect of his eloquence on that immense audience, that laughed and wept by turns, completely carried away by the wondrous gifts of his pathos and humor. On this occasion, all the other speakers seemed tame after Frederick Douglass.[35]

II

RHETORICAL TECHNIQUES AND SPEECHES

5

RHETORICAL TECHNIQUES

Frederick Douglass employed a wide variety of rhetorical techniques, strategies that can be organized under three general headings: ethos, pathos, and parallelism.

ETHOS

Persuasion was the primary purpose of Douglass's rhetoric. He needed to persuade his listeners as to the evil of slavery and the need for its abolishment; to vote for candidates that would speed the work of emancipation; to make the Civil War a war to end slavery; to allow African American men the right to fight for the Union and convince young black men that it was in their best interest to do so; and to bring about just and fair treatment for the freedmen after the war. Douglass's task was to persuade, sometimes in the face of what seemed to be impossible odds.

Essential to persuasion is the credibility of the speaker. Speakers must demonstrate to their audience that they have a right to speak and a right to be heard. It is imperative that speakers establish both their competence and his integrity. Aristotle wrote that the speaker's "character is the most potent of all the means of persuasion."[1] Ethos is the process whereby the speaker establishes credibility with the audience. In his earliest speeches it was important for the unknown Douglass to establish his credibility. He often did this through endearing self-deprecation, noting that he was an uneducated slave, unworthy that others should listen to him. The tactic caught the attention of his audiences and evoked sympathy for the speaker. In one of his very early speeches, delivered in October 1841, in Lynn, Massachusetts, Douglass began:

I feel greatly embarrassed when I attempt to address an audience of white people. I am not used to speaking to them, and it makes me tremble when I do so, because I have always looked up to them in fear. My friends, I have come to tell you something about slavery—what I know of it, as I have felt it.[2]

Eleven years later, after his reputation had been well established, Douglass continued to employ self-deprecation as a rhetorical tool. In his well-prepared and most famous address, "What to the Slave Is the Fourth of July?" delivered in 1852, Douglass began:

He who could address this audience without a quailing sensation, has stronger nerves than I have. I do not remember ever to have appeared as a speaker before any assembly more shrinkingly, nor with greater distrust of my ability, than I do this day. . . . Should I seem at ease, my appearance would much misrepresent me. The little experience I have had in addressing public meetings, in country school houses, avails me nothing on the present occasion.[3]

By this time in his career, Douglass had given speeches before very large audiences (not just "in country school houses"), but the orator was returning to a technique that had been so effective in prior years. After this particular use of self-deprecation, Douglass went on to deliver one of the great speeches in American rhetorical history.

Yet another means used by Douglass to affirm his ethos was by establishing his competence to speak on a given subject. He was an authority on slavery because he had been a slave. In an 1862 speech he informed his audience that because he had spent half of his life in slavery and the other half in freedom, he was qualified to speak on both subjects.

I take the stand tonight more as an humble witness than as advocate. I have studied slavery and freedom on both sides of Mason and Dixon's line. Nearly twenty-two years of my life were spent in slavery, and more than twenty-three have been spent in freedom. I am of age in both conditions and there seems an eminent fitness in allowing me to speak for myself and my race.[4]

It was important to Douglass to establish his competence not only through experience but also by the fact that though he had no formal education he was a learned and well-read man. Thus, his speeches abound with quotations from and references to literary passages. His interest in such sources began with *The Columbian Orator* that he read as a young slave. His orations are generously sprinkled with lines from Scott, Thackery, Pope, Shakespeare, and Emerson, along with references to various characters in *Uncle Tom's Cabin*. George L. Ruffin, who heard so many of Douglass's speeches, wrote in 1882 of Douglass's eloquence, observing that "the true source is his clear mind which is well stored by a close acquaintance with the best authors." Ruffin further noted that Douglass, then in his midsixties, continued to read and learn. "Douglass never made the great mistake (a common one) of considering that his education was finished. He has continued to study, he studies now, and is a growing man, and at this present moment he is a stronger man intellectually than ever before."[5]

The literary source most often alluded to or directly quoted by Douglass was William Shakespeare. Shakespearean quotes, allusions, and references are widely dispersed throughout Douglass's speeches. In an 1863 recruitment speech in Philadelphia, Douglass told young black men that it was important for them to register in the Union army. "This is our chance," he implored, "and woe betide us if we fail to embrace it! The immortal bard told us:

'There is a tide in the affairs of men,
Which taken at the flood, leads on to fortune,
Omitted, all the voyage of their life
Is bound in shallows and in miseries.
We must take the current when it serves,
Or lose our ventures.'"[6]

On April 16, 1885, at a celebration of the twenty-third anniversary of the emancipation of slaves in the District of Columbia, Douglass delivered an address that contained two Shakespearean references. Remembering the role of the Republican and Democratic parties in the years prior to the Civil War, Douglass noted that "the colored man . . . can see naught but ill in the ascendancy of the Democratic party." He addressed the situation much as Hamlet addressed his father's ghost.

Tell me why thy canonized bones, hearsed in death,
Have burst their cerements; why the sepulcher,
Wherein we saw thee quietly inurn'd,
Hath opened his ponderous and marble jaws to cast thee up again.
What may this mean, that thou, dead corpse,
Again in complete steel, revisit'st thus the glimpses of the moon,
Making night hideous, and we, poor fools of nature,
So horridly to shake our disposition
With thoughts beyond the reaches of our souls?[7]

Later in the speech, Douglass referred to a recent Supreme Court ruling that was a denial of black civil rights. Using a Shakespearean analogy and a biblical quotation, Douglass elaborated on his opinion of the decision.

Portia strictly construed the law of Venice for mercy, and this rule of construction has the approval of all the ages, but the Supreme Court of the United States construed American law against the weak and in the interest of prejudice and brutality. Never before was made so clear the meaning of Paul's saying, "The letter killeth, but the spirit giveth life."[8]

Douglass also sought to establish his intellectual credentials through the use of historical references, examples, and parallels. In an 1862 speech, Douglass recalled several historical examples whereby dominant groups sought to justify the enslavement and submission of others by assigning inferior characteristics to minorities.

The misfortunes of my own race in this respect are not singular. They have happened to all nations, when under the heel of oppression. Whenever and wherever any particular variety of the human family have been enslaved by another, their enslavers and oppressors, in every such instance, have found their best apology for their own base conduct in the bad character of their victims. The cunning, the deceit, the indolence, and the manifold vices and crimes, which naturally grow out of the condition of Slavery, are generally charged as inherent characteristics of the oppressed and enslaved race. The Jews, the Indians, the Saxons, and the ancient Britons, have all had a taste of this bitter experience.[9]

Douglass went on to note how the United States had justified wresting land from Mexico with "charges of Mexican inferiority."

When the United States coveted a part of Mexico, and sought to wrest from that sister Republic her coveted domain, some of you remember how our presses teemed from day to day with charges of Mexican inferiority. How they were assailed as a worn-out race; how they were denounced as a weak, worthless, indolent, and turbulent nation, given up to the sway of animal passions, totally incapable of self-government, and how excellent a thing we were told it would be for civilization if the strong beneficent arm of the Anglo-Saxon could be extended over them; and how, with our usual blending of piety with plunder, we justified our avarice by appeals to the hand-writing of Divine Providence.[10]

Douglass used evidences from history to demonstrate that American blacks had not responded with violence to their enslavers as other oppressed groups had done.

It is to his credit that he has steadily refused to resort to those extreme measures of repression and retaliation to which the cruel wrongs he has suffered might have tempted a less docile and forgiving race. He has not imitated the plan of the oppressed tenant who sneaks in ambush and shoots his landlord, as in Ireland, nor the example of the Indian who meets the invader of his hunting-ground with scalping-knife and tomahawk; he has not learned his lesson from the freed serfs of Russia, and organized assassination against tyrant princes and nobles; nor has he copied the example of his own race in Santo Domingo, who taught their French oppressors by fire and sword the danger of goading too far "the energy that slumbers in the black man's arm."[11]

In the same speech, when Douglass was describing the black exodus from certain southern states, he drew biblical and historical parallels. "If the whole five million are to leave the South, as a doomed country," observed Douglass, it would as "Lot left Sodom, or driven out as the Moors were driven out of Spain."[12]

It was not just his competence that Douglass sought to establish but that of the entire black race. He wanted the black race to be judged by its brightest stars, and Douglass was well aware that he was one of those stars. But there were other stars in the negro sky, and with great frequency Douglass pointed to them. In an 1862 speech, Douglass cited the example of freed slaves in the British West Indies to prove "beyond all controversy that the black man not only has the ability and the disposition to work, but knows well how to take care of his earnings."[13] In an 1865 address, Douglass noted that the Civil War had abolished "a great many delusions" about the negro.

One was, that the negro would not work; but he has proved his ability to work. Another was, that the negro would not fight . . . but the war has proved that there is a great deal of human nature in the negro, and that he will fight, as Mr. Quincy, our President, said, in earlier days than these, "when there is a reasonable probability of his whipping anybody."[14]

At the dedication of the Douglass Institute in Baltimore on September 29, 1865, Douglass pointed to the examples of accomplished free black men to prove what good citizens blacks could be if given the opportunity; yet, they were examples most white people chose to ignore.

Great actions, as shown by Robert Small, the gallant captain of the "Planter," and by William Tilghman, and other brave colored men, which by the war slavery has tossed to the surface, have not been sufficient to change the general estimate formed of the colored race. The eloquence and learning of Doctor Smith, Professors Vashon, Reason, Garnet, Remond, Martin, Rock, Crummel, and many others, have done us service; but they leave us yet under a cloud. The public with the mass of ignorance—notwithstanding that ignorance has been enforced and compelled among our people, hitherto—has sternly denied the representative character of our distinguished men. They are treated as exceptions, individual cases, and the like. They contend that the race, as such, is destitute of the subjective original elemental condition of a high self-originating and self-sustaining civilization.[15]

Those who desired to substantiate their claims of black inferiority often pointed to Haiti, a black republic yet a nation filled with religious superstitions and warring factions. To counter the argument that the black citizens of Haiti were uncivilized because of unsophisticated and superstitious religious practices, Douglass enumerated similar examples that were practiced among the so-called civilized people.

Let it be remembered that superstition and idolatry in one form or another have not been in the past, nor are they in the present, confined to any particular place or locality, and that, even in our enlightened age, we need not travel far from our own country, from England, from Scotland, from Ireland, France, Germany or Spain to find considerable traces of gross superstition. We consult familiar spirits in America. Queen Victoria gets water from the Jordan to christen her children, as if the water of that river were any better than the water of any other river. Many go thousands of miles in this age of light to see an old seamless coat supposed to have some divine virtue. Christians at Rome kiss the great toe of a black image called St. Peter, and go up stairs on their knees, to gain divine favor.[16]

To support his thesis that in time the black nation of Haiti would take its place among the noble nations of the world in spite of present internal problems, Douglass drew supportive analogies from Europe.

Some of the most enlightened and highly civilized states of the world of to-day, were, a few centuries ago, as deeply depraved in morals, manners and customs, as Haiti is alleged to be now. Prussia, which is to-day the arbiter of peace and war in Europe and holds in her borders the profoundest thinkers of the nineteenth century, was, only three centuries ago, like Haiti, the theatre of warring factions, and the scene of flagrant immoralities. France, England, Italy and Spain have all gone through the strife and turmoil of factional war, the like of which now makes Haiti a by-word, and a hissing to a mocking earth. As they have passed through the period of violence, why may not Haiti do the same?[17]

It was important for Douglass not only to his establish his competence, and in so doing the competence of his race, but to affirm his personal character as well. Douglass often made great efforts to assure others of his integrity. In an 1862 speech in Boston, he asserted that his mission was one on behalf of the lowly: "Whether in peace or in war, whether in safety or in peril, whether in evil report or good report, at home or abroad, my mission is to stand up for the down-trodden, to open my mouth for the dumb, to remember those in bonds as bound with them."[18]

Three years later, in Baltimore, Douglass affirmed that he had been faithful to his noble mission.

When I left Maryland, twenty-seven years ago, I did so with the firm resolve never to forget my brothers and sisters in bondage, and to do whatever might be in my power to accomplish their emancipation; and I have to say to-night that in whatever else I may have failed, in this at least I have not failed. No man can truthfully say I ever deserted the post of duty.[19]

Douglass affirmed he had been faithful to his calling, even though there were temptations to follow an easier course. In one speech he noted that he had "a very tempting offer of citizenship in another country [England]," but loyalty to America and his mission compelled him to return to the United States. "I have never regretted that decision," he acknowledged, "although my pathway has been anything than a smooth one; and to-night, I allow no man to exceed me in the desire for the safety and welfare of this country." He further established his moral character by declaring, "Though everywhere spoken against, the most malignant and unscrupulous of all our slanderers have not in this dark and terrible hour of the nation's trial dared to accuse us of a want of patriotism or loyalty."[20]

When speaking to black audiences, Douglass often challenged them to responsibility and hope, basing such challenges solely on his own character and insight. In his 1863 "Call to Arms" speech, Douglass sought to assure potential black recruits that what he was asking them to do was the result of his "best deliberation?": "I have not thought lightly of the words I am now addressing you. The counsel I give comes of close observation of the great struggle now in progress, and of the deep conviction that this is your hour and mine. In good earnest then, and after the best deliberation, I now for the first time during the war feel at liberty to call and counsel your to arms."[21]

In 1886, when the future did not appear promising for blacks, especially in the South, Douglass asked his black audience to trust him when he promised that "progress will still roll on." "I do not despair, and no power that I know of can make me despair of the ultimate triumph of justice and liberty in this country. I have seen too many abuses outgrown, too many evils removed, too many moral and physical improvements made, to doubt that the wheels of progress will still roll on."[22]

An essential element of ethos is the speaker's ability to establish a sense of goodwill with his audience, to demonstrate an interest in and a friendship for his listeners. Once again Douglass was a master of this rhetorical technique. In a speech at Cork, Ireland, on October 14, 1845, Douglass began by expressing his appreciation for and oneness with the people he was addressing. "I never more than at present," he declared, "lacked words to express my feeling. The cordial and manly reception I have met with, and the spirit of freedom that seems to animate the bosoms of the entire audience have filled my heart with feelings I am incapable of expressing."[23]

In a speech at Boston in 1865, some eighteen years after he had moved west to Rochester, New York, Douglass praised his audience for the sense of justice that prevailed in Massachusetts, specifically in Boston, and how much he missed his old associations.

I have felt, since I have lived out west [Rochester], that in going there I parted from a great deal that was valuable; and I feel, every time I come to these meetings, that I have lost a great deal by making my home west of Boston, west of Massachusetts, for, if anywhere in the country there is to be found the highest sense of justice, or the truest demands for my race, I look for it in the East, I look for it here. The ablest discussions of the whole question of our rights occur here, and to be deprived of the privilege of listening to those discussions is a great deprivation.[24]

Four years later, this time speaking in Rochester, Douglass complimented the people there for their progressive attitudes and actions, especially in regard to racial matters.

I have now a word to say of the goodly city [Rochester] in which I have lived for the last twenty years, and where I still reside, a city than which not one in the country is more civilized, refined and cultivated. It abounds in both educational and religious institutions, and its people are generally as liberal and friendly to the colored race as any other in this State, and far more so than most cities outside of the State. Here the common schools have been open to classes alike for a dozen years, and colored and white children have sat on the same benches and played in the same school yards, and at the same sports and games, and they have done so in peace. I can say many good things of Rochester. The fugitive slave bill never took a slave out of its limits, though several attempts were made to do so. When colored people were mobbed and hunted like wild beasts in other cities, and public fury was fanned against them by a malignant pro-slavery press, the colored man was always safe and well-protected in Rochester.[25]

Douglass was greatly concerned with his ethos. It was imperative for this former slave to establish his credibility. For one who had received no formal education, he needed to impress his audiences as to his competence—and not just his competence but the competence of his race as well. Douglass knew that his listeners needed to believe in his integrity and that he could and did identify with them. Ethos has always been an essential element of rhetoric; for Douglass it was especially so, and he did it well.

PATHOS

Every cause that Frederick Douglass addressed was done so with great passion—pathos. Whether he was talking about slavery, its cruelty, and the need for its eradication; on various matters pertaining to the Civil War; on his defense and advocacy of the Republican party; on the injustices inflicted on blacks, especially in the South, in the years following the war; or on any other matters he addressed, Douglass always invested his rhetoric with great emotion. Furthermore, he wanted to transfer his own passion into the lives of those who heard him.

There were many rhetorical tools Douglass used to convey his pathos. Humor—biting, sarcastic, satirical humor—was an important, effective, and powerful tool in Douglass's oratorical arsenal.   Others quickly observed Douglass's skillful use of wit. In 1842, the editor of the *Salem Register,* after hearing this new orator on the New England scene, wrote: "Douglass possesses great powers of humor, which he indulged freely on Monday evening in giving some of the neatest and severest home thrusts at the 'peculiar institution' of which he professed to be a graduate, which it was ever our fortune to hear."[26] Two years later, another observer commented: "[Douglass] gave us part of his experiences while in slavery; a sad tale, truly, but intermingled with humorous bits at the fallacy of the slaveholders' reasoning, if it can be so called."[27] Quite early in his oratorical career Douglass became concerned that perhaps he too often resorted to humor. He recalled that "one of the hardest things I had to learn when I was fairly underway as a public speaker was to stop telling so many funny stories. I could keep my audience in a roar of laughter . . . but I was convinced that I was in danger of becoming something of a clown, and that I must guard against it."[28] As the years went by, Douglass never deserted his use of humor, but learned how to use it more judiciously.

Often that humor was expressed through satire which Douglass used to ridicule something or someone. In an 1862 speech, he satirically characterized the efforts of General George B. McClellan.

He [McClellan] moved upon Manassas when the enemy had been gone from there seven long days. When he gets there he is within sixty miles of Richmond. Does he go on? Oh! no, but he just says hush, to the press and the people. I am going to do something transcendentally brilliant in strategy. Three weeks pass away, and knowing ones wink and smile as much as to say you will see something wonderful soon. And so indeed we do, at the end of three weeks we find that General McClellan has actually marched back from Manassas to the Potomac, gotten together an endless number of vessels at a cost of untold millions, to transport his troops to Yorktown, where he is just as near to Richmond and not a bit nearer than he was just three weeks before, and where he is opposed by an army every way as strongly posted as any he could have met with by marching straight to Richmond from Manassas. Here we have two hundred and thirty thousand men moved to attack empty fortifications, and moved back again.[29]

Douglass often ridiculed the North for its compliance with slavery. In an 1855 speech at Watertown, New York, he accused northern whites of being subservient to the slave powers. A newspaper man reported on Douglass's satirical wit in that Watertown speech.

He said the South and the North might be compared to a master and his dog. The North want offices, and the South have them to sell for a vote in Congress. The master taking a bone (office) from his pocket, calls (imitating with his lips the call of a dog) and the obedient canine comes cheerfully forward. Holding out the bone, the master says speak—and the dog speaks; stand up—and he stands in prayerful attitude; now roll over—and he rolls over, now go and lie down—and he goes and lies down, while the imperious master puts the bone in his pocket.[30]

In an 1863 speech, delivered in Washington, Douglass ridiculed the reasoning of a Reverend Morgan Goodwin, who had published a book in 1680, claiming that the negro's body belonged to his master.

[Dr. Goodwin] conceded the right of the master to own and control the body of the Negro, but insisted that the soul of the Negro belonged to the Lord. His able reasoning on this point, it is true, left the Negro for himself neither soul nor body. When he claimed his body, he found that [it] belonged to his earthly master, and when he looked around for his soul, he found that that belonged to his master in Heaven.[31]

Sometimes Douglass's humor was expressed through irony—the use of words to convey the opposite of their literal meaning. In 1863 he spoke of the slaveholders' definition of "discussion": "They [slaveholders] tell us that discussion has made them wise.—Discussion indeed! Discussion which only permits one side to be heard . . . denouncing by rails, tar and feathers, faggots and fire against any who should dare call in question the accursed system of slavery, and this they call discussion."[32]

There were times when Douglass's humor was expressed through the

analogous joke. One month after the Emancipation Proclamation became
official, Douglass used an analogous joke to illustrate why outlawing slavery in
the rebel states was sufficient to outlaw slavery in all the states: "You have
heard the story of the Irishman who paid the price of two spurs—but refused to
carry away but one; on the ground, as he said, that if he could make one side of
the horse go, he would risk the other. (Laughter and cheering.) So I say, if we
can strike down Slavery in the Rebel States, I will risk the downfall of Slavery
in the Border States."[33]

Douglass's humor was often expressed through mimicry, a technique he
developed as a youth, while still a slave, and a rhetorical tool he employed with
great skill in many of his later orations. Douglass was blessed with a keen and
sensitive ear that quickly detected differences in patterns of speech, and, after
hearing the differences, discovered that he could replicate them. Whether the
slow and cultured speech of his masters; the resounding oratory of the preachers,
black or white; or the unique inflections of New England visitors to a southern
plantation, young Frederick detected the differences and imitated them. For the
enjoyment and amazement of his peers, the youth would imitate the guarded
anger of his masters when they spoke of the abolitionists, or the bombastic
oratory of a preacher defending the institution of slavery. There was another
renowned American orator who, as a boy, was skilled in mimicry. Abraham
Lincoln amused his boyhood friends by imitating the preachers he had heard the
previous Sunday.[34]

Perhaps no one in the long annals of oratory used mimicry with greater skill
and effect than did Frederick Douglass. The noted Unitarian clergyman,
reformer, and orator Thomas Wentworth Higginson declared that Douglass "was
a perfect mimic. He could reproduce anything."[35] His audiences convulsed with
laughter, anger and astonishment as Douglass mimicked a slave auctioneer, a
conversation around his master's dinner table, or an apology for slavery by some
politician. He was, however, most noted for, and thus frequently called upon,
to imitate southern preachers as they defended slavery as a God-ordained and
biblically sanctioned institution. On January 28, 1842, at a public meeting in
Boston's Faneuil Hall, with approximately 5,000 people in attendance, Douglass
rendered one of his first imitations of a southern preacher. This rendering, or
something similar to it, would be repeated many times throughout his oratorical
career.

But what a mockery of this religion is preached at the South! I have been called upon
to describe the style in which it is set forth. And I find our ministers there learn to do
it at the northern colleges! I used to know they went away somewhere, I did not know
where, and came back ministers, and this is the way they would preach. They would take
a text—say this:—"Do unto others as you would have others do unto you." And this is
the way they would apply it. They would explain it to mean, "slaveholders, do unto
slaveholders what you would have them do unto you;—and then, looking impudently up
to the slaves' gallery, (for they have a place set apart for us, though it is said they have
no prejudice), just as is done here in the northern churches; looking high up to the poor

colored drivers and the rest, and spreading his hands gracefully abroad, he says, (mimicking,) "And you too, my friends, have souls of infinite values—souls that will live through endless happiness or misery in eternity. Oh, labor diligently to make your calling and election sure. Oh, receive unto your souls these words of the holy apostle—'Servants, be obedient unto your masters.'"[36]

Douglass's many and varied expressions of humor were often a means of softening, or perhaps making more palatable, his burning indignation. Whether recounting his own days in slavery, the plight of other slaves, the failure to give blacks the right to vote, or the lynchings in post-Reconstruction times, Douglass's speeches were marked by intense anger. Those who heard him could not miss nor mistake the orator's rage. Elizabeth Cady Stanton described Douglass as being "majestic in his wrath."[37] N. P. Rogers, who edited the *Herald of Freedom,* of Concord, New Hampshire, described a speech in his community by Douglass during the year 1844.

He began by a calm, deliberate and very simple narrative of his life. . . . He closed his slave narrative, and gradually let out the outraged humanity that was laboring in him, in indignant and terrible speech. It was not what you could describe as oratory or eloquence. It was sterner-darker-deeper than these. It was the volcanic outbreak of human nature long pent up in slavery and at last bursting its imprisonment.[38]

In his famous 1852 Fourth of July address, Douglass's anger was evident. He had been asked to deliver a speech celebrating the nation's independence, but Douglass used the speech to express his outrage over slavery. "This Fourth [of] July is yours, not mine," he thundered. "You may rejoice, I must mourn. To drag a man in fetters into the grand illuminated temple of liberty, and call upon him to join you in joyous anthems, were inhuman mockery and sacrilegious irony. Do you mean, citizens to mock me, by asking me to speak to-day?" Douglass, in an outpouring of rage, drew the antithesis between what America proclaimed and what it practiced.

This nation never looked blacker to me than on this 4th of July! Whether we turn to the declarations of the past, or to the professions of the present, the conduct of the nation seems equally hideous and revolting. America is false to the past, false to the present, and solemnly binds herself to be false to the future. Standing with God and the crushed and bleeding slaves on this occasion, I will, in the name of humanity which is outraged, in the name of liberty which is fettered, in the name of the constitution and the Bible, which are disregarded and trampled upon, dare to call in question and to denounce, with all the emphasis I can command, everything that serves to perpetuate slavery—the great sin and shame of America! "I will not equivocate; I will not excuse"; I will use the severest language I can command; and yet not one word shall escape me that any man, whose judgment is not blinded by prejudice, or who is not at heart a slaveholder, shall not confess to be right and just.[39]

Douglass's pathos was enhanced by his descriptive powers, especially when he described the terrible brutality of slavery. In that same masterful Fourth of July address, Douglass depicted a group of slaves headed for the slave-market.

These wretched people are to be sold singly, or in lots, to suit purchasers. They are food for the cotton-field, and the deadly sugar-mill. Mark the sad procession, as it moves wearily along, and the inhuman wretch who dives them. Hear his savage yells and his blood-chilling oaths, as he hurries on his affrighted captives! . . . Cast one glance, if you please, upon that young mother, whose shoulders are bare to the scorching sun, her briny tears falling on the brow of the babe in her arms. See, too, that girl of thirteen, weeping, yes! weeping, as she thinks of the mother from whom she has been torn! The drove moves tardily. Heat and sorrow have nearly consumed their strength; suddenly you hear a quick snap, like the discharge of a rifle; the fetters clank, and the chain rattles simultaneously; your ears are saluted with a scream, that seems to have torn its way to the center of your soul! The crack you heard, was the sound of the slave-whip; the scream you heard, was from the woman you saw with the babe. Her speed had faltered under the weight of her child and her chains! that gash on her shoulder tells her to move on. . . . Attend the auction, see men examined like horses; see the forms of women rudely and brutally exposed to the shocking gaze of American slave-buyers. See this drove sold and separated for ever; and never forget the deep, sad sobs that arose from that scattered multitude. . . . This is but a glance at the American slave-trade, as it exists, at this moment, in the ruling part of the United States.[40]

Seven years before Douglass used his descriptive powers in a speech at Cork, Ireland, whereby he sought to alert this foreign audience as to the brutality of American slavery. Excerpts from that speech and various emotional responses from the audience were recorded.

The natural elasticity of the human soul repels the slightest attempt to enslave it. The black slaves of America are not wholly without that elasticity; they are men, and, being so, they do not submit readily to the yoke. (Great cheering.) . . . Oftentimes, when the poor slave, after recovering from the application of the scourge and the branding iron, looks at his master with a face indicating dissatisfaction, he is subjected to fresh punishment. The cross look must at once be repulsed . . . according to his cruel taskmaster's idea, it looks as if he had the devil in him, and it must be whipped out. (Oh,oh.) . . . I stand before you with the marks of the slave-driver's whip, that will go down with me to my grave, but, what is worse, I feel the scourge of slavery itself piercing into my heart, crushing my feeling, and sinking me into the depths of moral and intellectual degradation. (Loud Cheering.) . . . I saw one poor woman who had her ear nailed to a post, for attempting to run away, but the agony she endured was so great, that she tore away, and left her ear behind. (Great sensation.)[41]

At times Douglass stirred pathos, not so much by description but instead through the use of emotionally laden words. In an 1861 speech in Rochester, Douglass associated the slaveholder with such provocative words as "traitor," "rebel," and "robber."

A man cannot be a slaveholder without being a traitor to humanity and a rebel against the law and government of the ever-living God. He is a usurper, a spoiler. His patriotism means plunder, and his principles are those of the highway robber. Out of such miserable stuff you can make nothing but conspirators and rebels. . . . a slaveholder who is a slaveholder at heart is a natural born traitor and rebel. He is a rebel against manhood, womanhood and brotherhood. The essence of his crime is nothing less than the complete destruction of all that dignifies and ennobles human character.[42]

Personification—the investing of abstractions with human qualities—was a method often used by Douglass to enhance the pathos of his oratory. It was a device used by many of the abolitionists in the nineteenth-century when they referred to slavery. Slavery was evil, and evil (in nineteenth century America) was actively malevolent. Slavery needed to be conceived of as actively evil, continually spreading its diabolical shadow over everything and everybody. Personification of slavery was a necessary tool in motivating white people in the North to take a bold stand against this malignant evil. Personification was employed by Douglass again and again in his discussions of slavery.

Slavery has been on its knees, only asking to die in peace. But the Missouri Compromise gave it a new lease on life.[43]

Slavery . . . became in a few years . . . rampant, throttling free speech, fighting friendly Indians, annexing Texas, warring with Mexico, kindling with malicious hand the fires of war and bloodshed on the virgin soil of Kansas, and finally threatening to pull down the pillars of the Republic.[44]

Slavery is humbled in Maryland, threatened in Tennessee, stunned nearly to death in Western Virginia, doomed in Missouri, trembling in Kentucky.[45]

Douglass frequently and skillfully used metaphors—comparisons between things of unlike nature that yet have something in common—to enhance the pathos of his speeches. Aristotle once wrote that "it is the metaphor above all else that gives clearness, charm, and distinction to the style."[46] Harkening back to his earlier days when he worked as a shipyard caulker, Douglass displayed a certain relish for shipboard metaphors. He compared slaveholders to mutineers: "They came on board the national ship subject to these conditions, they signed the articles after having duly read them, and the fact that these rights, plainly written, have been exercised is no apology whatever for the slaveholder's mutiny and their attempt to lay piratical hands on the ship and its officers." Seeking to impart hope, Douglass continued on with his nautical metaphor as he depicted life as a journey on the sea: "Hence, though this life of ours offers a thousand opportunities to drown, to only one of being saved; hence though the sea is broad, and the ship is narrow; hence though the billows are mighty and the bark frail, there is a power on board, a captain at the helm whose presence forbids despair even in the darkest hours."[47]

Douglass often used medical metaphors. He depicted the nation's tolerance of slavery as a disease.

Like the slow convalescence of some patients the fault is less chargeable to the medicine than to the deep-seated character of the disease. We were in a very low condition before the remedy was applied. The whole head was sick and the whole heart faint. Dr. Buchanan and his Democratic friends had given us up, and were preparing to celebrate the nation's funeral.[48]

On several occasions Douglass likened the experience of the Civil War to going to school. In an 1864 speech he made this application.

The most hopeful fact of the hour is that we are now in a salutary school—the school of affliction. If sharp and signal retribution, long protracted, widesweeping and overwhelming, can teach a great nation respect for the long-despised claims of justice, surely we shall be taught now and for all time to come. But if, on the other hand, this potent teacher, whose lessons are written in characters of blood, and thundered to us from a hundred battle-fields, shall fall, we shall go down as we shall deserve to go down, as a warning to all other nations which shall come after us.[49]

Douglass used a prison metaphor in his recruiting speeches during the Civil War. "The iron gate of our prison stands half open," he declared. "One gallant rush from the North will fling it wide open, while four millions of our brothers and sisters shall march out into liberty."[50] After the war, a mountain metaphor was used to describe prejudice, and also to inspire hope. "While we recognize the color line as a hurtful force," Douglass emphasized, "a mountain barrier to our progress, wounding our bleeding feet with its flinty rock at every step, we do not despair."[51]

A primary reason for Douglass's oratorical effectiveness was the unmistakable pathos with which most of his speeches were delivered. Through humor, anger, vivid descriptions, personification and metaphors, this orator left no doubt as to how passionately he felt, and wanted others to feel, about the various issues he addressed.

PARALLELISM

Douglass was a master in the use of oratorical parallelism. One significant way he accomplished this was through the repetition of a certain word or groups of words to begin sentences, clauses, or phrases. Anaphora, as this technique is sometimes called, rendered a rhythmic cadence to Douglass's speeches. In a speech at Cooper Institute in 1863, Douglass mocked the slaveholders who professed to be "wiser than" other great Americans.

The Lords of the Lash have often boasted of late that discussion has convinced them that Slavery is right. That in this respect they are wiser than Washington, who desired to see Slavery abolished, and would gladly give his vote for such abolition; wiser than Jefferson, who said he trembled for his country; when he reflected that God was just, and that his justice would not sleep forever; wiser than Franklin, who was President of the first Abolition Society in America; wiser than Madison, who did not wish to have it seen in the Constitution that there could be any such thing as property in man; wiser than the Congress of 1807, which abolished the Slave Trade, and wiser than the men of 1787, who abolished Slavery in all the Territory then belonging to the United States.[52]

In an 1864 speech, Douglass assailed the Democratic party with a series of sentences beginning, "Ask why."

Ask why it was for the Florida War, and it answers, Slavery. Ask why it was for the annexation of Texas, and it answers, Slavery. Ask why it was opposed to the habeas corpus when a negro was the applicant, and it answers, Slavery. Ask why it is now in favor of the habeas corpus, when Rebels and traitors are the applicants for its benefits, and it answers, Slavery. Ask why it was for mobbing down freedom of speech a few years ago, when that freedom was claimed by the Abolitionists, and it answers, Slavery. Ask why it now asserts freedom of speech, when sympathizers with traitors claim that freedom, and again Slavery is the answer. Ask why it denied the right of a State to protect itself against possible abuses of the Fugitive Slave bill, and you have the same old answer. . . . Ask why it was for war at the beginning of the Rebellion; ask why it has attempted to embarrass and hinder the loyal Government at every step of its progress, and you have but one answer, Slavery.[53]

In an 1876 oration, Douglass pointed out the great problems faced by President Lincoln, noting that "he was assailed" from all sides. The passage is also a superb example of parallel structure: "He was assailed by abolitionists; he was assailed by slaveholders; he was assailed by men who were for peace at any price; he was assailed by those who were for a more vigorous prosecution of the war; he was assailed for not making the war an abolition war; and he was most bitterly assailed for making the war an abolition war."[54]

In his 1893 speech at the World's Columbian Exposition in Chicago, Douglass extolled Haiti with sentences beginning, "Until she spoke."

Until she spoke no Christian nation had abolished slavery. Until she spoke no Christian nation had given to the world an organized effort to abolish slavery. Until she spoke the slave ship, followed by hungry sharks, greedy to devour the dead and dying slaves flung overboard to feed them, ploughed in peace the South Atlantic painting the sea with the Negro's blood. Until she spoke, the slave trade was sanctioned by all the Christian nations of the world, and our land of liberty and light included. . . . Until Haiti spoke, the church was silent, and the pulpit was dumb.[55]

In an 1883 speech, Douglass repeated the word "intention" again and again, as he protested Supreme Court decisions that denied civil rights.

In the dark days of slavery, this Court, on all occasions, gave the greatest importance to *intention* as a guide to interpretation. The object and *intention* of the law, it was said, must prevail. Everything in favor of slavery and against the negro was settled by this object and *intention*. The Constitution was construed according to its *intention*. We were over and over again referred to what the framers meant, and plain language was sacrificed that the so affirmed *intention* of these framers might be positively asserted. When we said in behalf of the negro that the Constitution of the United States was intended to establish justice and to secure the blessings of liberty to ourselves and our posterity, we were told that the words said so, but that was obviously not its *intention;* that it was intended to apply only to white people, and that the *intention* must govern.[56]

An important component of the structure of Douglass's rhetoric was through his posing of questions, the interrogation technique. Sometimes he would pose questions for the purpose of stimulating dialogue, asking questions and then directly answering them. Seeking to demonstrate that persecution has a way of turning on the persecutor, Douglass noted:

In Ireland, persecution has at last reached a point where it reacts terribly upon her persecutors. England to-day is reaping the bitter consequences of her injustice and oppression. Ask any man of intelligence to-day, "What is the chief source of England's weakness?" "What has reduced her to the rank of a second-class power?" and the answer will be Ireland! Poor, ragged, hungry, starving and oppressed as she is, she is strong enough to be a standing menace to the power and glory of England.[57]

At other times Douglass would ask questions to be answered by other questions or by other statements in question form. Here the responses were less direct, but effective.

Now what will be the effect? Suppose colored men are allowed to fight the battles of the Republic. Suppose they do fight and win victories as I am sure they will, what will be the effect upon themselves; Will not the country rejoice in such victories? and will it not extend to the colored man the praise due to his bravery? Will not the colored man himself soon begin to take a more hopeful view of his own destiny?[58]

There were instances when Douglass asked questions in order to enable the audience to infer the answers. In an 1886 speech, Douglass sought to answer those who recommended that persecuted southern blacks move to the West Coast. He posed questions that inferred the answers.

These people are advised to make an exodus to the Pacific slope. With the best intentions they are told of the fertility of the soil and the salubrity of the climate. If they should tell the same as existing in the moon, the simple question, How shall they get there? would knock the life out of it at once. Without money, without friends, without knowledge, and only gaining enough by daily toil to keep them above the starvation point, where they are, how can such a people rise and cross the continent?[59]

Antithesis was another form of rhetoric often and effectively used by Douglass whereby strongly contrasting words and ideas were balanced against each other. Aristotle praised this form of rhetoric, writing that "things are best known by opposition, and are better known when the opposites are put side by side."[60] No orator used antithesis better than Douglass. He used this technique to describe the complexities of Lincoln: "Though high in position, the humblest could approach him and feel at home in his presence. Though deep, he was transparent; though strong, he was gentle; though decided and pronounced in his convictions, he was tolerant towards those who differed from him, and patient under reproaches."[61]

In an 1883 speech, on the occasion of the twenty-first anniversary of emancipation in the District of Columbia, Douglass used antithesis to explain why speakers younger than himself would be better suited to speak: "I represent the past, they the present. I represent the down-fall of slavery, they the glorious triumph of liberty. I speak of deliverance from bondage, they speak of concessions to liberty and equality. Their mission begins where my mission ends."[62]

Irony may well have been Douglass's primary rhetorical tool, enough so, at least, that Gerald Fulkerson refers to Douglass's speeches as "the rhetoric of irony. . . . From the beginning of his career his audiences saw him as an almost unique personification of the ironies that he illuminated with logical precision, wit, and sarcasm."[63] It has been noted in previous pages that Douglass was obsessed with the great irony that existed between what America professed and what it practiced. This was the central them of his 1852 Fourth of July address. To those who advocated that Douglass and other abolitionists should speak with cool and reasoned argument rather than in passionate and denunciatory tones, Douglass replied, "What, then, remains to be argued? . . . The time for such argument is past."

At a time like this, scorching irony, not convincing argument, is needed. O! had I the ability, and could I reach the nation's ear, I would, to-day, pour out a fiery stream of biting ridicule, blasting reproach, withering sarcasm, and stern rebuke. For it is not light than is needed, but fire; it is not the gentle shower, but thunder. We need the storm, the whirlwind, and the earthquake. The feeling of the nation must be quickened; the conscience of the nation must be roused; the propriety of the nation must be startled; the hypocrisy of the nation must be exposed; and its crimes against God and man must be proclaimed and denounced.[64]

The contradiction that Douglass denounced in America was surpassed only by the contradiction he observed in religion. The chasm between profession and practice in religion was, for Douglass, even wider and more hypocritical than that which existed in the nation. N. P. Rogers, editor of the *Herald of Freedom,* reported on Douglass's condemnation of religion in an 1844 speech in Concord, New Hampshire. "It is because of your Religion, he sternly replied, which sanctifies the system under which I suffer, and dooms me to it, and the millions of many of my brethren now in bondage. Your religion justifies our tyrants, and you are yourselves our enslavers."[65] Douglass's inflammatory words directed toward religion in his Concord speech, were similarly and often repeated in other places and on other dates. Too often, in Douglass's experience, religion had been used to condone and support slavery; to justify the worst forms of inhumane brutality. Nevertheless,—and this is another irony—religion had a profound effect in the development of Douglass as an orator. Sophia Auld taught him to read, using the Bible as her textbook. It was from religion in general and "Uncle Lawson" in particular that young Frederick first gained a vision of what he could become. It was as a lay preacher in New Bedford, Massachusetts, that Douglass had his first experiences as a public speaker. These earlier influences of religion show themselves again and again throughout Douglass's oratorical career.[66]

Douglass illustrates Vincent Harding's thesis that religion provided a vital source of inspiration and language for black protest against bondage.[67] Douglass's speeches were replete with biblical quotations, references, and analogies at all stages of his rhetorical career. George A. Hinshaw has culled a partial list of biblical references and analogies from Douglass's speeches.

Fairly direct references as these were used: "We have passed through the furnace and have not been consumed," "Putting new wines into old bottles . . . ," ". . . Righteousness alone can permanently exalt a nation," "Come then, and let us reason together," "There are prodigal sons everywhere, who are ready to demand the portion of goods that would fall to them and betake themselves to a strange country," ". . . like the pestilence that walketh in darkness," "If we find, we shall have to seek."

Some references were analogical, such as the following: "Having taken the sword it [Slavery] is destined to perish by the sword," "What doth it profit a nation if it gain the whole world, but lose its honor," ". . . to help him away from his old home to the modern Canaan of Kansas," "There is no modern Joshua who can command this resplendent orb of popular discussion to stand still," "They have the fate of Pharaoh and his hosts." ". . . endeavoring to put the new wine of liberty in the old bottles of slavery."[68]

An American religious tradition to which Douglass frequently resorted in his oratorical ventures was the use of the jeremiad. Having its American origins in Puritan Massachusetts Bay, the jeremiad was a warning of dire consequences from God if the people failed to follow the precepts of the Almighty. The concept points backward many centuries to the prophet, Jeremiah, who warned his people of conquest by the Babylonians because they had turned their backs on God. It was the kind of rhetoric that Douglass and many blacks evoked in antebellum days. "The Black jeremiad," Wilson Moses has written, consisted of "constant warnings issued by blacks to whites, concerning the judgment that was to come for the sin of slavery. . . . Their use of the jeremiad . . . showed a clever ability to play on the belief that America as a whole was a chosen nation with a covenantal duty to deal justly with the blacks."[69]

Douglass employed the jeremiad with great skill. In an 1848 speech, "The War with Mexico," he warned that if America continued to protect and tolerate slavery within its borders, "we shall not go unpunished," and "a terrible retribution awaits us." Blacks had a duty "to warn our fellow countrymen" and dissuade America from "rushing on in her wicked career."[70]

In 1854, responding to the Kansas-Nebraska Act, Douglass observed that a nation that denies the God-given right of freedom to its citizens does so at its peril. "This mighty government of ours will never be at peace with God until it shall embrace this great truth [universal freedom] as the foundation of all its institutions and the rule of its entire administrations."[71] In 1862, when the war effort was not going well for the Union, Douglass, sounding like the prophets of old, thundered, "the fate of the greatest of all modern Republics trembles in the balance. . . . Nations, not less than individuals, are subjects of the moral government of the universe, and that flagrant, long continued, and persistent transgression of the Laws of Divine government, will certainly bring national sorrow, shame, suffering and death." Later in the speech, Douglass continued his theme: "We have made . . . the deplorable mistake of supposing that we could sow to the wind without reaping the whirlwind. We have attempted to maintain our Union in utter defiance of the Moral Chemistry of the universe." He then prophesied, that "if this nation is destroyed . . . it will be solely owing to the want of moral courage and wise statesmanship in dealing with slavery, the cause and motive of the rebellion."[72]

In 1894, nearly thirty years after the ending of the Civil War, Douglass was still issuing dire warnings to the nation. He noted the crimes against blacks in the South—most especially the crime of lynching--and once more prophesied:

In the order of Divine Providence the man who puts one end of a chain around the ankle of his fellow man will find the other end around his own neck. And it is the same with a nation. Confirmation of this truth is as strong as thunder. "As we sow, we shall reap," is a lesson to be learned here as elsewhere. We tolerated slavery, and it cost us a million graves, and it may be that lawless murder, if permitted to go on, may yet bring vengeance, not only on the revered head of age and upon the heads of helpless women, but upon the innocent babe in the cradle.[73]

For most American prophets the jeremiad was never an end in itself. The ultimate purpose of the jeremiad was never punishment or retribution but rather reformation. It was a cleansing process whereby evil was purged in order that the good might take root and flourish. Therefore, the jeremiad was an apocalyptic process—severe, painful, devastating—which would eventually culminate in the glorious millennium. Thus, the proclaimer of the jeremiad could be stern and awful in predicting the judgment to come, and at the same time be optimistic as to the ultimate future. The words of Frederick Douglass were a part of this judgment-reformation, apocalypse-millennium, doomsayer-optimistic rhetoric.

In an early February of 1863 speech, Douglass noted the Emancipation Proclamation—officially declared the previous month—was part of the millennial hope in the midst of the apocalyptic civil war. "I believe in the millennium," he exclaimed, "the final perfection of the race, and hail this Proclamation, though wrung out under the goading lash of a stern military necessity, as one reason of the hope that is in me. Men may see in it only a military necessity. To me it has a higher significance. It is a grand moral necessity."[74]

On January 9, 1894, Douglass delivered his last major speech. After he had pronounced a destructive judgment coming upon America for allowing the evil of lynching to go on unrestrained and unabated, the speech concluded with a millennial promise, if only America would repent.

But, my friends, I must stop. Time and strength are not equal to the task before me. But could I be heard by this great nation, I would call to mind the sublime and glorious truths with which, at its birth, it saluted a listening world. Its voice then, was as the trump of the archangel, summoning hoary forms of oppression and time honored tyranny to judgment. Crowned heads heard it and shrieked. Toiling millions heard it and clapped their hands for joy. It announced the advent of a nation, based upon human brotherhood and the self-evident truths of liberty and equality. Its mission was the redemption of the world from the bondage of ages. Apply these sublime and glorious truths to the situation now before you. Put away your race prejudice. Banish the idea that one class must rule over another. Recognize the fact that the rights of the humblest citizen are as worthy of protection as are those of the highest, and your problem will be solved, and, whatever may be in store for it in the future, whether prosperity, or adversity; whether it shall have foes without, or foes within; whether there shall be peace, or war; based upon the eternal principles of truth, justice, and humanity, and with no class having any cause of complaint or grievance, your Republic will stand and flourish forever.[75]

Not long after his escape from slavery, Douglass expressed without hesitancy or reservation his bitter disappointment with established religion. Many, including some of his fellow African Americans, were critical of the orator's attacks on what they perceived as the sacred. Douglass's experiences, however, had formulated his negative perceptions of churches and clergy. It was a perception that became more deeply ingrained over the years. Nevertheless, though Douglass tended to abandon formalized religion—or as he might phrase it, formalized religion had abandoned him—he never abandoned the language of Zion which had played such an integral part in his formative years. His words were often the words of the Bible, and with great consistency he appealed to the seeming antithetical theological concepts of judgment (jeremiad, apocalypse) and deliverance (reform, millennium).

Whether in addressing national policies or religious practice, Douglass was superlative in the use of devices that drew contrasts between what was and what was supposed to be. The contrasts were drawn, for the most part, through parallel structures, structures enhanced by the uses of repetition, questions, antithesis and irony.

Now, a few concluding thoughts as to Douglass's rhetorical presence and practices. Douglass physical features were an imposing supplement to his rhetorical skills. Over six feet in height, a strong and muscular physique, broad shouldered, skin more nearly brown than black, and handsome, Douglass's very presence compelled attention. James M'Cune Smith wrote of Douglass's "keen, well set eye, brawny chest, lithe figure, and fair sweep of arm."[76] Ebeneezer D. Bassett, America's first black minister to Haiti, recalled that Douglass's

physical equipment left little to be desired. The tall and manly form of singular grace and vitality; the erect carriage that had something majestic about it; the searching but kindly eye; the whole cut of that strange, strong face, set off with the semblance of a certain scornful expression which told of the gall of early trials to a proud and sensitive nature like his; the never-to-be-forgotten flowing locks; the striking intelligence beaming in the look; the apparently unconscious possession of reserved forces; the perfect self-poise; the rare and happy blending of affability and modesty with dignity of bearing—all this gave him a distinguished appearance, a truly imposing presence, which everywhere stamped him as a man of mark, and were of no mean advantage to him from the beginning to the end of his career.[77]

Douglass's sonorous voice complemented his physical features. A newspaper reported in 1850: "His voice is full and rich, and his enunciation remarkably distinct and musical. He speaks in a low conversational tone most of the time, but occasionally his tones roll out full and deep as those of an organ. The effect is electrical."[78] The Reverend William Henry Crogman recalled hearing Douglass at Boston's Faneuil Hall. "His voice, a heavy baritone, or rendered a little heavier than usual by a slight hoarseness contracted in previous speaking, could be distinctly heard in that historic but most wretched of auditoriums."[79]

Some of Douglass's speeches were entirely extemporaneous in nature, as he was often called on, without prior notice, to address an audience. In his earlier addresses, when he knew in advance that he would be the speaker, he took a few notes to the podium. James Monroe, a Connecticut abolitionist, observed Douglass as he prepared to speak in 1841. "On a table near him was a leaf of paper on which were scrawled perhaps two dozen words. 'What is this?' I said. 'That,' he replied with a laugh, 'is my speech.'"[80] Within a few years, along with his notes, Douglass took books, newspaper articles, magazines and pamphlets to the lectern from which he read appropriate passages.

In the 1850s, as he addressed increasingly diverse audiences, was invited to be a part of lyceum lectures, and spoke before various sophisticated groups, Douglass began to prepare manuscripts from which he read his speeches. This has already been noted in his "What to the Slave Is the Fourth of July?" speech (1852), and his address at Ohio Western Reserve College (1854). Douglass first delivered his "Self-Made Men" speech in 1858, a carefully prepared address. He would deliver revised versions of that speech for the next thirty years.

Douglass seemed to sense those times when his audience was losing interest in speeches read from prepared manuscripts, and he devised two tactics to counteract such situations. The first tactic was to put aside his prepared manuscript and speak extemporaneously. In a speech before a Boston lyceum group in 1861, Douglass knew his listeners were growing restless, so he abandoned his manuscript and spoke from his heart on matters of interest to his audience. The group which had been "particularly listless and inattentive," suddenly "became attentive and enthusiastic."[81] The second tactic Douglass employed to bring a prepared and ponderous speech alive was to combine reading with extemporaneous remarks. His driest lectures took on new energy after he perfected this technique. Someone who heard Douglass deliver his "Self-Made Men" speech in 1865, commented on the mixture of prepared and extemporaneous material.

The address was a noble and eloquent one, pervaded by richness of thought and manly sentiment; abounding in wisdom and wit; seasoned by a pleasing diffusion of choice bits of sarcasm, and presented with that power of utterance and soul stirring vigor for which the orator is distinguished. Many interesting facts were interspersed and the few incidents of personal narrative that were introduced, showing how the speaker acquired rudiments of education, contributed to the entertainment.

It would be impossible for Mr. Douglass to deliver a lecture, no matter what title he might give it, without checkering it with thoughts and views pertaining to the great subject nearest his heart, and which has monopolized the service and devotion of his life. On this occasion the welfare of the black man was not forgotten.[82]

Douglass's speeches were often two hours in length, not unusual for nineteenth-century orators. In a time undistracted by television, the cinema, radio, or quick sound bites, audiences were prepared and willing to listen to what today would be considered overly long speeches. Because nineteenth-century oratory was an important source of education, information, inspiration, and entertainment, orators such as Douglass worked hard to make sure that they had something worthwhile to say and that it would be said in an engaging manner. One reporter wrote of a Douglass speech delivered in 1852. The speaker, he noted,

spoke for two hours to an audience which filled every seat and packed the aisles. Ten o'clock came and he stopped amid the cries, "Go on! go on!" He stopped and said: "I don't often have a chance to talk to such an audience of friends. You who are standing are certainly wearied. We will take a five minute recess and allow any to retire." The time was up and he spoke for another hour and a quarter, and not a man or woman left the audience.[83]

Such an account is of great credit to both speaker and audience.

In the days following Frederick Douglass's death on February 20, 1895, newspapers across the nation eulogized this significant man. As would be expected, many of the eulogies focused on his oratorical skills. On February 21 the *Springfield Republican* (Massachusetts) noted:

[Douglass] was a slave born in disgrace, suffering abuse and degradation, friendless and alone, save for other slaves, as hopeless as himself. He won recognition as a master of the rare faculty of eloquence, the moving power over men which marks the orator from the days of Demosthenes to our own. No one who has heard Douglass speak will ever forget that most impressive presence.

Three days after Douglass's death, the *Times,* of Oakland, California, extolled his rhetorical powers.

Few living orators surpassed Frederick Douglass in declamatory eloquence. He was not argumentative or so logical as many of his contemporaries, but few living men of his day ever produced a more powerful impression upon an audience. His manner was wonderfully eloquent, and his language copious and impressive. He stood before an audience a natural orator like the African Cinque who, without the aid of schools, poured forth with burning zeal the thoughts which crowded his brain. His voice was good, his form manly and graceful, and his electric words leaped forth like the flashes of lightning clothed with beauty and power.

The writer of this listened to him when a boy, and was spellbound with his bold imagery, pictures gorgeously beautiful, voice as musical and deep as the organ and captivating as the songs of the sirens. He held the audience entranced from start to finish.[84]

6

SPEECHES

The speeches included in this chapter are printed in their entirety, or nearly so. One speech is taken from each of the three periods in Frederick Douglass's life following his escape from slavery as outlined in chapter 1; the prewar years, the war years, and the postwar years. The setting of the speech and significant matters relating to it will be briefly noted before each text.

"WHAT TO THE SLAVE IS THE FOURTH OF JULY?" (1852)

Somewhere between 500 and 600 people, mostly abolitionists, packed Corinthian Hall in Rochester, New York, on Monday morning, July 5, 1852, where they paid twelve and a half cents each to hear the principal address delivered by Frederick Douglass. He had been invited by the Rochester Ladies' Anti-Slavery Society, and those who heard Douglass that morning heard the orator at his very best. William L. Andrews agrees with most others when he writes that this address "is the most famous anti-slavery speech Douglass ever gave."[1] William S. McFeely goes a step further when he evaluates that this speech is "perhaps the greatest antislavery oration ever given."[2] Just to read the address is a thrilling experience. It can only be imagined what it would have been like to have been there and heard Douglass deliver it. It was reported that at the conclusion of the speech the audience responded with a great burst of applause (this in addition to the applause interspersed throughout the delivery).

Douglass reported that he spent all of his spare moments during the last three weeks of June preparing the text of this address. Whether he read the speech that day in Rochester, or whether it had a more extemporaneous quality, is not known. Combining accounts from his own experiences, along with emphasis on the current conditions of African Americans in the North as well as the South, Douglass employed a wide range of rhetorical devices: irony, satire, hyperbole, metaphors, personification, anger, antithesis, and various argumentative skills. To support his points he drew illustrative material from experience, literature, the Bible, and American and European history.

He reminded his listeners that the Fourth of July celebration "is yours, not mine." He then began vivid descriptions of what life was like for black people in America. His account of "the internal slave trade" is descriptive language at its very best. He castigated the Fugitive Slave Act, then less than two years old, as "an act of the American Congress" wherein "slavery has been nationalized." He severely chastised the clergy and churches, North and South, for their roles in supporting or condoning slavery. Yet, the speech is filled with religious metaphors and biblical quotations, with Douglass sounding very much like an Old Testament prophet or a Puritan Divine, warning his audience of dire consequences if America did not change its ways. He took time to defend the American Constitution, indicating a major difference with Garrison who looked upon the Constitution as a document supporting slavery.

Douglass first published a text of the speech in the *Frederick Douglass' Paper* on July 9. He then had the speech printed in pamphlet form about July 16.[3] The audience on July 5 demonstrated its appreciation for the speech by subscribing for 700 copies of the proposed pamphlet, and donating money to help with printing expenses.

Mr. President, Friends and Fellow Citizens: He who could address this audience without a quailing sensation, has stronger nerves than I have. I do not remember ever to have appeared as a speaker before any assembly more shrinkingly, nor with greater distrust of my ability, than I do this day. A feeling has crept over me, quite unfavorable to the exercise of my limited powers of speech. The task before me is one which requires much previous thought and study for its proper performance. I know that apologies of this sort are generally considered flat and unmeaning. I trust, however, that mine will not be so considered. Should I seem at ease, my appearance would much misrepresent me. The little experience I have had in addressing public meetings, in country school houses, avails me nothing on the present occasion.

The papers and placards say, that I am to deliver a 4th [of] July oration. This certainly, sounds large, and out of the common way, for me. It is true that I have often had the privilege to speak in this beautiful Hall, and to address many who now honor me with their presence. But neither their familiar faces, nor the perfect gage I think I have of Corinthian Hall, seems to free me from embarrassment.

The fact is, ladies and gentlemen, the distance between this platform and the slave plantation, from which I escaped, is considerable—and the difficulties to be overcome in getting from the latter to the former, are by no means slight. That I am here to-day, is, to me, a matter of astonishment as well as of gratitude. You will not, therefore, be surprised, if in what I have to say, I evince no elaborate preparation, nor grace my speech with any high sounding exordium. With little experience and with less learning, I have been able to throw my thoughts hastily and imperfectly together; and trusting to your patient and generous indulgence, I will proceed to lay them before you.

This, for the purpose of this celebration, is the 4th of July. It is the birthday of your National Independence, and of your political freedom. This, to you, is what the Passover was to the emancipated people of God. It carries your minds back to the day, and to the act of your great deliverance; and to the signs, and to the wonders, associated with that act, and that day. This celebration also marks the beginning of another year of your national life; and reminds you that the Republic of America is now 76 years old. I am glad, fellow-citizens, that your nation is so young. Seventy-six years, though a good old age for a man, is but a mere speck in the life of a nation. Three score years and ten is the allotted time for individual men; but nations number their years by thousands. According to this fact, you are, even now only in the beginning of your national career, still lingering in the period of childhood. I repeat, I am glad this is so. There is hope in the thought, and hope is much needed, under the dark clouds which lower above the horizon. The eye of the reformer is met with angry flashes, portending disastrous times; but his heart may well beat lighter at the thought that America is young, and that she is still in the impressible stage of her existence. May he not hope that high lessons of wisdom, of justice and of truth, will yet give direction to her destiny? Were the nation older, the patriot's heart might be sadder, and the reformer's brow heavier. Its future might be shrouded in gloom, and the hope of its prophets go out in sorrow. There is consolation in the thought, that America is young.—Great streams are not easily turned from channels, worn deep in the course of ages. They may sometimes rise in quiet and stately majesty, and inundate the land, refreshing and fertilizing the earth with their mysterious properties. They may also rise in wrath and fury, and bear away, on their angry waves, the accumulated wealth of years of toil and hardship. They, however, gradually flow back to the same old channel, and flow on as serenely as ever. But, while the river may not be turned aside, it may dry up, and leave nothing behind but the withered branch, and the unsightly rock, to howl in the abyss-sweeping wind, the sad tale of departed glory. As with rivers so with nations.

Fellow-citizens, I shall not presume to dwell at length on the associations that cluster about this day. The simple story of it is, that, 76 years ago, the people of this country were British subjects. The style and title of your "sovereign people" (in which you now glory) was not then born. You were under the British Crown. Your fathers esteemed the English Government as the home government; and England as the fatherland. This home government, you know, although a considerable distance from your home, did, in the exercise of its parental prerogatives, impose upon its colonial children, such restraints, burdens and limitations, as, in its mature judgment, it deemed wise, right and proper.

But, your fathers, who had not adopted the fashionable idea of this day, of the infallibility of government, and the absolute character of its acts, presumed to differ from the home government in respect to the wisdom and the justice of some of those burdens and restraints. They went so far in their excitement as to pronounce the measure of government unjust, unreasonable, and oppressive, and altogether such as ought not to be quietly submitted to. I scarcely need say, fellow-citizens, that my opinion of those measures fully accords with that of your fathers. Such a declaration of agreement on my part, would not be worth much to anybody. It would, certainly, prove nothing, as to what part I might have taken, had I lived during the great controversy of 1776. To say *now* that America was right, and England wrong, is exceedingly easy. Everybody can say it; the dastard, not less than the noble brave, can flippantly descant on the tyranny of England towards the American Colonies. It is fashionable to do so; but there was a time when, to pronounce against England, and in favor of the cause of the colonies, tried men's souls. They who did so were accounted in their day, plotters of mischief, agitators and rebels, dangerous men. To side with the right, against the wrong, with the weak against the strong, and with the oppressed against the oppressor! *here* lies the merit, and the one which, of all others, seems unfashionable in our day. The cause of liberty may be stabbed by the men who glory in the deeds of your fathers. But, to proceed.

Feeling themselves harshly and unjustly treated, by the home government, your fathers, like men of honesty, and men of spirit, earnestly sought redress. They petitioned and remonstrated; they did so in a decorous, respectful, and loyal manner. Their conduct was wholly unexceptionable. This, however, did not answer the purpose. They saw themselves treated with sovereign indifference, coldness and scorn. Yet they persevered. They were not the men to look back.

As the sheet anchor takes a firmer hold, when the ship is tossed by the storm, so did the cause of your fathers grow stronger, as it breasted the chilling blasts of kingly displeasure. The greatest and best of British statesmen admitted its justice, and the loftiest eloquence of the British Senate came to its support. But, with that blindness which seems to be the unvarying characteristic of tyrants, since Pharaoh and his hosts were drowned in the Red sea, the British Government persisted in the exactions complained of.

The madness of this course, we believe, is admitted now, even by England; but we fear the lesson is wholly lost on our present rulers.

Oppression makes a wise man mad. Your fathers were wise men, and if they did not go mad, they became restive under this treatment. They felt themselves the victims of grievous wrongs, wholly incurable in their colonial capacity. With brave men there is always a remedy for oppression. Just here, the idea of a total separation of the colonies from the crown was born! It was a startling idea, much more so, than we, at this distance of time, regard it. The timid and the prudent (as has been intimated) of that day, were, of course, shocked and alarmed by it.

Such people lived then, had lived before, and will, probably, ever have a place on this planet; and their course, in respect to any great change, (no matter how great the good to be attained, or the wrong to be redressed by it), may be calculated with as much precision as can be the course of the stars. They hate all changes, but silver, gold and copper change! Of this sort of change they are always strongly in favor.

These people were called tories in the days of your fathers; and the appellation, probably, conveyed the same idea that is meant by a more modern, though a somewhat less euphonious term, which we often find in our papers, applied to some of our old politicians.

Their opposition to the then dangerous thought was earnest and powerful; but, amid all their terror and affrighted vociferations against it, the alarming and revolutionary idea moved on, and the country with it.

On the 2d of July, 1776, the old Continental Congress, to the dismay of the lovers of ease, and the worshippers of property, clothed that dreadful idea with all the authority of national sanction. They did so in the form of a resolution; and as we seldom hit upon resolutions, drawn up in our day, whose transparency is at all equal to this, it may refresh your minds and help my story if I read it.

Resolved, That these united colonies *are*, and of right, ought to be free and Independent States; that they are absolved from all allegiance to the British Crown; and that all political connection between them and the State of Great Britain *is*, and ought to be, dissolved.

Citizens, your fathers made good that resolution. They succeeded; and to-day you reap the fruits of their success. The freedom gained is yours; and you, therefore, may properly celebrate this anniversary. The 4th of July is the first great fact in your nation's history—the very ring-bolt in the chain of your yet undeveloped destiny.

Pride and patriotism, not less than gratitude, prompt you to celebrate and to hold it in perpetual remembrance. I have said that the Declaration of Independence is the RING-BOLT to the chain of your nation's destiny; so, indeed, I regard it. The principles contained in that instrument are saving principles. Stand by those principles, be true to them on all occasions, in all places, against all foes, and at whatever cost.

From the round top of your ship of state, dark and threatening clouds may be seen. Heavy billows, like mountains in the distance, disclose to the leeward huge forms of flinty rocks! That *bolt* drawn, that *chain* broken, and all is lost. *Cling to this day—cling to it,* and to its principles, with the grasp of a storm-tossed mariner to a spar at midnight.

The coming into being of a nation, in any circumstances, is an interesting event. But, besides general considerations, there were peculiar circumstances which make the advent of this republic an event of special attractiveness.

The whole scene, as I look back to it, was simple, dignified and sublime.

The population of the country, at the time, stood at the insignificant number of three millions. The country was poor in the munitions of war. The population was weak and scattered, and the country a wilderness unsubdued. There were then no means of concert and combination, such as exist now. Neither stream nor lightning had then been reduced to order and discipline. From the Potomac to the Delaware was a journey of many days. Under these, and innumerable other disadvantages, your fathers declared for liberty and independence and triumphed.

Fellow Citizens, I am not wanting in respect for the fathers of this republic. The signers of the Declaration of Independence were brave men. They were great men too—great enough to give fame to a great age. It does not often happen to a nation to raise, at one time, such a number of truly great men. The point from which I am compelled to view them is not, certainly, the most favorable; and yet I cannot contemplate their great deeds with less than admiration. They were statesmen, patriots and heroes, and for the good they did, and the principles they contended for, I will unite with you to honor their memory.

They loved their country better than their own private interests; and, though this is not the highest form of human excellence, all will concede that it is a rare virtue, and that when it is exhibited, it ought to command respect. He who will, intelligently, lay down his life for his country, is a man whom it is not in human nature to despise. Your fathers staked their lives, their fortunes, and their sacred honor, on the cause of their country. In their admiration of liberty, they lost sight of all other interests.

They were peace men; but they preferred revolution to peaceful submission to bondage. They were quiet men; but they did not shrink from agitating against oppression. They showed forbearance; but that they knew its limits. They believed in order; but not in the order of tyranny. With them, nothing was *"settled"* that was not right. With them, justice, liberty and humanity were *"final";* not slavery and oppression. You may well cherish the memory of such men. They were great in their day and generation. Their solid manhood stands out the more as we contrast it with these degenerate times.

How circumspect, exact and proportionate were all their movements! How unlike the politicians of an hour! Their statesmanship looked beyond the passing moment, and stretched away in strength into the distant future. They seized upon eternal principles, and set a glorious example in their defence. Mark them!

Fully appreciating the hardship to be encountered, firmly believing in the right of their cause, honorably inviting the scrutiny of an onlooking world, reverently appealing to heaven to attest their sincerity, soundly comprehending the solemn responsibility they were about to assume, wisely measuring the terrible odds against them, your fathers, the fathers of this republic, did, most deliberately, under the inspiration of a glorious patriotism, and with a sublime faith in the great principles of justice and freedom, lay deep, the corner-stone of the national superstructure, which has risen and still rises in grandeur around you.

Of this fundamental work, this day is the anniversary. Our eyes are met with demonstrations of joyous enthusiasm. Banners and pennants wave exultingly on the breeze. The din of business, too, is hushed. Even mammon seems to have quitted his grasp on this day. The ear-piercing fife and the stirring drum unite their accents with the ascending peal of a thousand church bells. Prayers are made, hymns are sung, and sermons are preached in honor of this day; while the quick martial tramp of a great and multitudinous nation, echoed back by all the hills, valleys and mountains of a vast continent, bespeak the occasion one of thrilling and universal interest—a nation's jubilee.

Friends and citizens, I need not enter further into the causes which led to this anniversary. Many of you understand them better than I do. You could instruct me in regard to them. That is a branch of knowledge in which you feel, perhaps, a much deeper interest than your speaker. The causes which led to the separation of the colonies from the British crown have never lacked for a tongue. They have all been taught in your common schools, narrated at your firesides, unfolded from your pulpits, and thundered from your legislative halls, and are as familiar to you as household words. They form the staple of your national poetry and eloquence.

I remember, also, that, as a people, Americans are remarkably familiar with all facts which make in their own favor. This is esteemed by some as a national trait—perhaps a national weakness. It is a fact, that whatever makes for the wealth or for the reputation of Americans, and can be had *cheap!* will be found by Americans. I shall not be charged with slandering Americans, if I say I think the American side of any question may be safely left in American hands.

I leave, therefore, the great deeds of your fathers to other gentlemen whose claim to have been regularly descended will be less likely to be disputed than mine!

The Present. My business, if I have any here to-day, is with the present. The accepted time with God and his cause is the ever-living now.

> Trust no future, however pleasant,
> Let the dead past bury its dead;
> Act, act in the living present,
> Heart within, and God overhead.

We have to do with the past only as we can make it useful to the present and to the future. To all inspiring motives, to noble deeds which can be gained from the past, we are welcome. But now is the time, the important time. Your fathers have lived, died, and have done their work, and have done much of it well. You live and must die, and you must do your work. You have no right to enjoy a child's share in the labor of your fathers, unless your children are to be blest by your labors. You have no right to wear out and waste the hard-earned fame of your fathers to cover your indolence. Sydney Smith tells us that men seldom eulogize the wisdom and virtues of their fathers, but to excuse some folly or wickedness of their own. This truth is not a doubtful one. There are illustrations of it near and remote, ancient and modern. It was fashionable, hundreds of years ago, for the children of Jacob to boast, we have "Abraham to our father," when they had long lost Abraham's faith and spirit. That people contented themselves under the shadow of Abraham's great name, while they repudiated the deeds which made his name great. Need I remind you that a similar thing is being done all over this country to-day? Need I tell you that the Jews are not the only people who built the tombs of the prophets, and garnished the sepulchers of the righteous? Washington could not die till he had broken the chains of his slaves. Yet his monument is built up by the price of human blood, and the traders in the bodies and souls of men, shout—"We have Washington to *our father.*" Alas! that it should be so; yet so it is.

> The evil that men do, lives after them,
> The good is oft' interred with their bones.

Fellow-citizens, pardon me, allow me to ask, why am I called upon to speak here to-day? What have I, or those I represent, to do with your national independence? Are the great principles of political freedom and of natural justice, embodied in that Declaration of Independence, extended to us? and am I, therefore, called upon to bring our humble offering to the national altar, and to confess the benefits and express devout gratitude for the blessings resulting from your independence to us?

Would to God, both for your sakes and ours, that an affirmative answer could be truthfully returned to these questions! Then would my task be light, and my burden easy and delightful. For *who* is there so cold, that a nation's sympathy could not warm him? Who so obdurate and dead to the claims of gratitude, that would not thankfully acknowledge such priceless benefits? Who so stolid and selfish, that would not give his voice to swell the hallelujahs of a nation's jubilee, when the chains of servitude had been torn from his limbs? I am not that man. In a case like that, the dumb might eloquently speak, and the "lame man leap as an hart."

But, such is not the state of the case. I say it with a sad sense of the disparity between us. I am not included within the pale of this glorious anniversary! Your high independence only reveals the immeasurable distance between us. The blessings in which you, this day rejoice, are not enjoyed in common.—The rich inheritance of justice, liberty, prosperity and independence, bequeathed by your fathers, is shared by you, not by me. The sunlight that brought life and healing to you, has brought stripes and death to me. This Fourth [of] July is *yours,* not *mine.* You may rejoice, *I* must mourn. To drag a man in fetters into the grand illuminated temple of liberty, and call upon him to join you in joyous anthems, were inhuman mockery and sacrilegious irony. Do you mean, citizens, to mock me, by asking me to speak to-day? If so, there is a parallel to your conduct. And let me warn you that it is dangerous to copy the example of a nation whose crimes, towering up to heaven, were thrown down by the breath of the Almighty, burying that nation in irrecoverable ruin! I can to-day take up the plaintive lament of a peeled and woe-smitten people!

"By the rivers of Babylon, there we sat down. Yea! we wept when we remembered Zion. We hanged our harps upon the willows in the midst thereof. For there, they that carried us away captive, required of us a song; and they who wasted us required of us mirth, saying, Sing us one of the songs of Zion. How can we sing the Lord's song in a strange land? If I forget thee, O Jerusalem, let my right hand forget her cunning. If I do not remember thee, let my tongue cleave to the roof of my mouth."

Fellow-citizens; above your national, tumultuous joy, I hear the mournful wail of millions! whose chains, heavy and grievous yesterday, are, to-day, rendered more intolerable by the jubilee shouts that reach them. If I do forget, if I do not faithfully remember those bleeding children of sorrow this day, "may my right hand forget her cunning, and may my tongue cleave to the roof of my mouth!" To forget them, to pass lightly over their wrongs, and to chime in with the popular theme, would be treason most scandalous and shocking, and would make me a reproach before God and the world. My subject, then, fellow-citizens, is AMERICAN SLAVERY. I shall see, this day, and its popular characteristics, from the slave's point of view. Standing, there, identified with the

American bondman, making his wrongs mine, I do not hesitate to declare, with all my soul, that the character and conduct of this nation never looked blacker to me than on this 4th of July! Whether we turn to the declarations of the past, or to the professions of the present, the conduct of the nation seems equally hideous and revolting. America is false to the past, false to the present, and solemnly binds herself to be false to the future. Standing with God and the crushed and bleeding slaves on this occasion, I will, in the name of humanity which is outraged, in the name of liberty which is fettered, in the name of the constitution and the Bible, which are disregarded and trampled upon, dare to call in question and to denounce, with all the emphasis I can command, everything that serves to perpetuate slavery—the great sin and shame of America! "I will not equivocate; I will not excuse;" I will use the severest language I can command; and yet not one word shall escape me that any man, whose judgment is not blinded by prejudice, or who is not at heart a slaveholder, shall not confess to be right and just.

But I fancy I hear some one of my audience say, it is just in this circumstance that you and your brother abolitionists fail to make a favorable impression on the public mind. Would you argue more, and denounce less, would you persuade more, and rebuke less, your cause would be much more likely to succeed. But, I submit, where all is plain there is nothing to be argued. What point in the anti-slavery creed would you have me argue? On what branch of the subject do the people of this country need light? Must I undertake to prove that the slave is a man? That point is conceded already. Nobody doubts it. The slaveholders themselves acknowledge it in the enactment of laws for their government. They acknowledge it when they punish disobedience on the part of the slave. There are seventy-two crimes in the State of Virginia, which, if committed by a black man, (no matter how ignorant he be,) subject him to the punishment of death; while only two of the same crimes will subject a white man to the like punishment.—What is this but the acknowledgement that the slave is a moral, intellectual and responsible being? The manhood of the slave is conceded. It is admitted in the fact that Southern statute books are covered with enactments forbidding, under severe fines and penalties, the teaching of the slave to read or to write.—When you can point to any such laws, in reference to the beasts of the field, then I may consent to argue the manhood of the slave. When the dogs in your streets, when the fowls of the air, when the cattle on your hills, when the fish of the sea, and the reptiles that crawl, shall be unable to distinguish the slave from a brute, *then* will I argue with you that the slave is a man!

For the present, it is enough to affirm the equal manhood of the negro race. Is it not astonishing that, while we are ploughing, planting and reaping, using all kinds of mechanical tools, erecting houses, constructing bridges, building ships, working in metals of brass, iron, copper, silver and gold; that, while we are reading, writing and ciphering, acting as clerks, merchants and secretaries, having among us lawyers, doctors, ministers, poets, authors, editors, orators and teachers; that, while we are engaged in all manner of enterprises common to other men, digging gold in California, capturing the whale in the Pacific, feeding sheep and cattle on the hill-side, living, moving, acting, thinking, planning, living in families as husbands, wives and children, and, above all, confessing and worshipping the Christian's God, and looking hopefully for life and immortality beyond the grave, we are called upon to prove that we are men!

Would you have me argue that man is entitled to liberty? that he is the rightful owner of his own body? You have already declared it. Must I argue the wrongfulness of slavery? Is that a question for Republicans? Is it to be settled by the rules of logic and argumentation, as a matter beset with great difficulty, involving a doubtful application of the principle of justice, hard to be understood? How should I look today, in the presence of Americans, dividing, and subdividing a discourse, to show that men have a natural right to freedom? speaking of it relatively, and positively, negatively, and affirmatively. To do so, would be to make myself ridiculous, and to offer an insult to your understanding.—There is not a man beneath the canopy of heaven, that does not know that slavery is wrong *for him*.

What, am I to argue that it is wrong to make men brutes, to rob them of their liberty, to work them without wages, to keep them ignorant of their relations to their fellow men, to beat them with sticks, to flay their flesh with the lash, to load their limbs with irons, to hunt them with dogs, to sell them at auction, to sunder their families, to knock out their teeth, to burn their flesh, to starve them into obedience and submission to their masters? Must I argue that a system thus marked with blood, and stained with pollution, is *wrong*? No! I will not. I have better employments for my time and strength, than such arguments would imply.

What, then, remains to be argued? Is it that slavery is not divine; that God did not establish it; that our doctors of divinity are mistaken? There is blasphemy in the thought. That which is inhuman, cannot be divine! *Who* can reason on such a proposition? They that can, may; I cannot. The time for such argument is past.

At a time like this, scorching irony, not convincing argument, is needed. O! had I the ability, and could I reach the nation's ear, I would, to-day, pour out a fiery stream of biting ridicule, blasting reproach, withering sarcasm, and stern rebuke. For it is not light that is needed, but fire; it is not the gentle shower, but thunder. We need the storm, the whirlwind, and the earthquake. The feeling of the nation must be quickened; the conscience of the nation must be roused; the propriety of the nation must be startled; the hypocrisy of the nation must be exposed; and its crimes against God and man must be proclaimed and denounced.

What, to the American slave, is your 4th of July? I answer; a day that reveals to him, more than all other days in the year, the gross injustice and cruelty to which he is the constant victim. To him, your celebration is a sham; your boasted liberty, an unholy license; your national greatness, swelling vanity; your sounds of rejoicing are empty and heartless; your denunciations of tyrants, brass fronted impudence; your shouts of liberty and equality, hollow mockery; your prayers and hymns, your sermons and thanksgivings, with all your religious parade, and solemnity, are, to him, mere bombast, fraud, deception, impiety, and hypocrisy—a thin veil to cover up crimes which would disgrace a nation of savages. There is not a nation on the earth guilty of practices, more shocking and bloody, than are the people of these United States, at this very hour.

Go where you may, search where you will, roam through all the monarchies and despotisms of the old world, travel through South America, search out every abuse, and when you have found the last, lay your facts by the side of the every day practices of this nation, and you will say with me, that, for revolting barbarity and shameless hypocrisy, America reigns without a rival.

The Internal Slave Trade. Take the American slave-trade, which, we are told by the papers, is especially prosperous just now. Ex-Senator Benton tells us that the price of men was never higher than now. He mentions that fact to show that slavery is in no danger. This trade is one of the peculiarities of American institutions. It is carried on in all the large towns and cities in one half of this confederacy; and millions are pocketed every year, by dealers in this horrid traffic. In several states, this trade is a chief source of wealth. It is called (in contradistinction to the foreign slave-trade) *"the internal slave-trade."* It is, probably, called so, too, in order to divert from it the horror with which the foreign slave-trade is contemplated. That trade has long since been denounced by this government, as piracy. It has been denounced with burning words, from the high places of the nation, as an execrable traffic. To arrest it, to put an end to it, this nation keeps a squadron, at immense cost, on the coast of Africa. Everywhere, in this country, it is safe to speak of this foreign slave-trade, as a most inhuman traffic, opposed alike to the laws of God and of man. The duty to extirpate and destroy it, is admitted even by our DOCTORS OF DIVINITY. In order to put an end to it, some of these last have consented that their colored brethren (nominally free) should leave this country, and establish themselves on the western coast of Africa! It is, however, a notable fact, that, while so much execration is poured out by Americans, upon those engaged in the foreign slave-trade, the men engaged in the slave-trade between the states pass without condemnation, and their business is deemed honorable.

Behold the practical operation of this internal slave-trade, sustained by American politics and American religion. Here you will see men and women, reared like swine, for the market. You know what is a swine-drover? I will show you a man-drover. They inhabit all our Southern States. They perambulate the country, and crowd the highways of the nation, with droves of human stock. You will see one of these human flesh jobbers, armed with pistol, whip and bowie-knife, driving a company of a hundred men, women, and children, from the Potomac to the slave market at New Orleans. These wretched people are to be sold singly, or in lots, to suit purchasers. They are food for the cotton-field, and the deadly sugar-mill. Mark the sad procession, as it moves wearily along, and the inhuman wretch who drives them. Hear his savage yells and his blood-chilling oaths, as he hurries on his affrighted captives! There, see the old man, with locks thinned and gray. Cast one glance, if you please, upon that young mother, whose shoulders are bare to the scorching sun, her briny tears falling on the brow of the babe in her arms. See, too, that girl of thirteen, weeping, *yes!* weeping, as she thinks of the mother from whom she has been torn! The drove moves tardily. Heat and sorrow have nearly consumed their strength; suddenly you hear a quick snap, like the discharge of a rifle; the fetters clank, and the chain rattles simultaneously; your ears are saluted with a scream, that seems to have torn its way to the centre of your soul! The crack you heard, was the sound of the slave-whip; the scream you heard, was from the woman you saw with the babe. Her speed had faltered under the weight of her child and her chains! that gash on her shoulder tells her to move on. Follow this drove to New Orleans. Attend the auction; see men examined like horses; see the forms of women rudely and brutally exposed to the shocking gaze of American slave-buyers. See this drove sold and separated for ever; and never forget the deep, sad sobs that arose from that scattered multitude. Tell me citizens, WHERE, under the sun, you can witness a spectacle more fiendish and shocking. Yet this is but a glance at the American slave-trade, as it exists, at this moment, in the ruling part of the United States.

I was born amid such sights and scenes. To me the American slave-trade is a terrible reality. When a child, my soul was often pierced with a sense of its horrors. I lived on Philpot Street, Fell's Point, Baltimore, and have watched from the wharves, the slave ships in the Basin, anchored from the shore, with their cargoes of human flesh, waiting for favorable winds to waft them down the Chesapeake. There was, at that time, a grand slave mart kept at the head of Pratt Street, by Austin Woldfolk. His agents were sent into every town and country in Maryland, announcing their arrival, through the papers, and on flaming *"hand-bills,"* headed CASH FOR NEGROES. These men were generally well dressed men, and very captivating in their manners. Ever ready to drink, to treat, and to gamble. The fate of many a slave has depended upon the turn of a single card; and many a child has been snatched from the arms of its mother, by bargains arranged in a state of brutal drunkenness.

The flesh-mongers gather up their victims by dozens, and drive them, chained, to the general depot at Baltimore. When a sufficient number have been collected here, a ship is chartered, for the purpose of conveying the forlorn crew to Mobile, or to New Orleans. From the slave prison to the ship, they are usually driven in the darkness of night; for since the anti-slavery agitation, a certain caution is observed.

In the deep still darkness of midnight, I have been often aroused by the dead heavy footsteps, and the piteous cries of the chained gangs that passed our door. The anguish of my boyish heart was intense; and I was often consoled, when speaking to my mistress in the morning, to hear her say that the custom was very wicked; that she hated to hear the rattle of the chains, and the heart-rending cries. I was glad to find one who sympathized with me in my horror.

Fellow-citizens, this murderous traffic is, to-day, in active operation in this boasted republic. In the solitude of my spirit, I see clouds of dust raised on the highways of the South; I see the bleeding footsteps; I hear the doleful wail of fettered humanity, on the way to the slave-markets, where the victims are to sold like *horses, sheep,* and *swine,* knocked off to the highest bidder. There I see the tenderest ties ruthlessly broken, to gratify the lust, caprice and rapacity of the buyers and sellers of men. My soul sickens at the sight.

Is this the land your Fathers loved,
The freedom which they toiled to win?
Is this the earth whereon they moved?
Are these the graves they slumber in?

But a still more inhuman, disgraceful, and scandalous state of things remains to be presented.

By an act of the American Congress, not yet two years old, slavery has been nationalized in its most horrible and revolting form. By that act, Mason & Dixon's line has been obliterated; New York has become as Virginia; and the power to hold, hunt, and sell men, women, and children, as slaves remains no longer a mere state institution, but is now an institution of the whole United States. The power is co-extensive with the star-spangled banner, and American Christianity. Where these go, may also go the merciless slave-hunter. Where these are, man is not sacred. He is a bird for the sportsman's gun. By that most foul and fiendish of all human decrees, the liberty and person of every man are put in peril. Your broad republican domain is hunting ground for *men. Not* for thieves and robbers, enemies of society, merely, but for men guilty of no crime. Your law-makers have commanded all good citizens to engage in this hellish sport. Your President, your Secretary of State, your *lords, nobles,* and ecclesiastics, enforce, as a duty you owe to your free and glorious country, and to your God, that you do this accursed thing. Not fewer than forty Americans have, within the past two years, been hunted down, and, without a moment's warning, hurried away in chains, and consigned to slavery, and excruciating torture. Some of these have had wives and children, dependent on them for bread; but of this, no account was made. The right of the hunter to his prey stands superior to the right of marriage, and to *all* rights in this republic, the rights of God included! For black men there are neither law, justice, humanity, nor religion. The Fugitive Slave *Law* makes MERCY TO THEM, A CRIME; and bribes the judge who tries them. An American JUDGE GETS TEN DOLLARS FOR EVERY VICTIM HE CONSIGNS to slavery, and five, when he fails to do so. The oath of any two villains is sufficient, under this hell-black enactment, to send the most pious and exemplary black man into the remorseless jaws of slavery! His own testimony is nothing. He can bring no witnesses for himself. The minister of American justice is bound by the law to hear but *one* side; and *that* side, is the side of the oppressor. Let this damning fact be perpetually told. Let it be thundered around the world, that, in tyrant-killing, king-hating, people-loving, democratic, Christian America, the seats of justice are filled with judges, who hold their offices under an open and palpable *bribe,* and are bound, in deciding in the case of a man's liberty, *to hear only his accusers!*

In glaring violation of justice, in shameless disregard of the forms of administering law, in cunning arrangement to entrap the defenseless, and in diabolical intent, this Fugitive Slave Law stands alone in the annals of tyrannical legislation. I doubt if there be another nation on the globe, having the brass and the baseness to put such a law on the statute-book. If any man in this assembly thinks differently from me in this matter, and feels able to disprove my statements, I will gladly confront him at any suitable time and place he may select.

Religious Liberty. I take this law to be one of the grossest infringements of Christian Liberty, and, if the churches and ministers of our country were not stupidly blind, or most wickedly indifferent, they, too, would so regard it.

At the very moment that they are thanking God for the enjoyment of civil and religious liberty, and for the right to worship God according to the dictates of their own consciences, they are utterly silent in respect to a law which robs religion of its chief significance, and makes it utterly worthless to a world lying in wickedness. Did this law concern the *"mint, anise* and *cummin"*—abridge the right to sing psalms, to partake of the sacrament, or to engage in any of the ceremonies of religion, it would be smitten by the thunder of a thousand pulpits. A general shout would go up from the church, demanding *repeal, repeal, instant repeal!*—And it would go hard with that politician who presumed to solicit the votes of the people without inscribing this motto on his banner.   Further, if this demand were not complied with, another Scotland would be added to the history of religious liberty, and the stern old covenanters would be thrown into the shade.   A John Knox would be seen at every church door, and heard from every pulpit, and Fillmore would have no more quarter than was shown by Knox, to the beautiful, but treacherous Queen Mary of Scotland.—The fact that the church of our country, (with fractional exceptions,) does not esteem "the Fugitive Slave Law" as a declaration of war against religious liberty, implies that that church regards religion simply as a form of worship, an empty ceremony, and *not* a vital principle, requiring active benevolence, justice, love and good will towards man.   It esteems sacrifice above mercy; psalm-singing above right doing; solemn meetings above practical righteousness.   A worship that can be conducted by persons who refuse to give shelter to the houseless, to give bread to the hungry, clothing to the naked, and who enjoin obedience to a law forbidding these acts of mercy, is a curse, not a blessing to mankind.   The Bible addresses all such persons as "scribes, pharisees, hypocrites, who pay tithe of *mint, anise,* and *cummin,* and have omitted the weightier matters of the law, judgment, mercy and faith."

The Church Responsible.   But the church of this country is not only indifferent to the wrongs of the slave, it actually takes sides with the oppressors.   It has made itself the bulwark of American slavery, and the shield of American slave-hunters.   Many of its most eloquent Divines, who stand as the very lights of the church, have shamelessly given the sanction of religion, and the Bible, to the whole slave system.—They have taught that man may, properly, be a slave; that the relation of master and slave is ordained of God; that to send back an escaped bondman to his master is clearly the duty of all the followers of the Lord Jesus Christ; and this horrible blasphemy is palmed off upon the world for Christianity.

For my part, I would say, welcome infidelity! welcome atheism! welcome anything! in preference to the gospel, *as preached by those Divines!*   They convert the very name of religion into an engine of tyranny, and barbarous cruelty, and serve to confirm more infidels, in this age, than all the infidel writings of Thomas Paine, Voltaire, and Bolingbroke, put together, have done!   These ministers make religion a cold and flinty-hearted thing, having neither principles of right action, nor bowels of compassion.   They strip the love of God of its beauty, and leave the throne of religion a huge, horrible, repulsive form.   It is a religion for oppressors, tyrants, man-stealers, and *thugs.*   It is not that *"pure and undefiled religion"* which is from above, and which is *"first pure, then peaceable, easy to be entreated,* full of mercy and good fruits, *without partiality, and without hypocrisy."*   But a religion which favors the rich against the poor; which exalts the proud above the humble; which divides mankind into two classes, tyrants and slaves; which says to the man in chains, *stay there;* and to the oppressor, *oppress on;* it is a religion which may be professed and enjoyed by all the robbers and enslavers of mankind; it makes God a respecter of persons, denies his fatherhood of the race, and tramples in the dust the great truth of the brotherhood of man. All this we affirm to be true of the popular church, and the popular worship of our land and nation—a religion, a church, and a worship which, on the authority of inspired wisdom, we pronounce to be an abomination in the sight of God. In the language of Isaiah, the American church might be well addressed, "Bring no more vain oblations; incense is an abomination unto me: the new moons and Sabbaths, the calling of assemblies, I cannot away with; it is iniquity, even the solemn meeting. Your new moons, and your appointed feasts my soul hateth. They are a trouble to me; I am weary to bear them; and when ye spread forth your hands I will hide mine eyes from you. Yea! when ye make many prayers, I will not hear. YOUR HANDS ARE FULL OF BLOOD; cease to do evil, learn to do well; seek judgment; relieve the oppressed; judge for the fatherless; plead for the widow."

The American church is guilty, when viewed in connection with what it is doing to uphold slavery; but it is superlatively guilty when viewed in connection with its ability to abolish slavery.

The sin of which it is guilty is one of omission as well as of commission. Albert Barnes but uttered what the common sense of every man at all observant of the actual state of the case will receive as truth, when he declared that "There is no power out of the church that could sustain slavery an hour, if it were not sustained in it."

Let the religious press, the pulpit, the sunday school, the conference meeting, the great ecclesiastical, missionary, Bible and tract associations of the land array their immense powers against slavery, and slave-holding; and the whole system of crime and blood would be scattered to the winds, and that they do not do this involves them in the most awful responsibility of which the mind can conceive.

In prosecuting the anti-slavery enterprise, we have been asked to spare the church, to spare the ministry; but *how,* we ask, could such a thing be done? We are met on the threshold of our efforts for the redemption of the slave, by the church and ministry of the country, in battle arrayed against us; and we are compelled to fight or flee. From *what* quarter, I beg to know, has proceeded a fire so deadly upon our ranks, during the last two years, as from the Northern pulpit? As the champions of oppressors, the chosen men of American theology have appeared—men, honored for their so-called piety, and their real learning. The LORDS of Buffalo, the SPRINGS of New York, the LATHROPS of Auburn, the COXES and SPENCERS of Brooklyn, the GANNETS and SHARPS of Boston, the DEWEYS of Washington, and other great religious lights of the land, have, in utter denial of the authority of *Him,* by whom they professed to be called to the ministry, deliberately taught us, against the example of the Hebrews, and against the remonstrance of the Apostles, they teach *"that we ought to obey man's law before the law of God."*

My spirit wearies of such blasphemy; and how such men can be supported, as the "standing types and representatives of Jesus Christ," is a mystery which I leave others to penetrate. In speaking of the American church, however, let it be distinctly understood that I mean the *great mass* of the religious organizations of our land. There are exceptions, and I thank God that there are. Noble men may be found, scattered all over these Northern States, of whom Henry Ward Beecher of Brooklyn, Samuel J. May of Syracuse, and my esteemed friend [R. R. Raymond] on the platform, are shining examples; and let me say further, that, upon these men lies the duty to inspire our ranks with high religious faith and zeal, and to cheer us on in the great mission of the slave's redemption from his chains.

Religion in England and Religion in America. One is struck with the difference between the attitude of the American church towards the anti-slavery movement, and that occupied by the churches in England towards a similar movement in that country. There, the church, true to its mission of ameliorating, elevating, and improving the condition of mankind, came forward promptly, bound up the wounds of the West Indian slave, and restored him to his liberty. There, the question of emancipation was a high religious question. It was demanded, in the name of humanity, and according to the law of the living God. The Sharps, the Clarksons, the Wilberforces, the Buxtons, and Burchells and the Knibbs, were alike famous for their piety, and for their philanthropy. The anti-slavery movement *there,* was not an anti-church movement, for the reason that the church took its full share in prosecuting that movement: and the anti-slavery movement in this country will cease to be an anti-church movement, when the church of this country shall assume a favorable, instead of a hostile position towards that movement.

Americans! your republican politics, not less than your republican religion, are flagrantly inconsistent. You boast of your love of liberty, your superior civilization, and your pure Christianity, while the whole political power of the nation, as embodied in the two great political parties, is solemnly pledged to support and perpetuate the enslavement of three millions of your countrymen. You hurl your anathemas at the crowned headed tyrants of Russia and Austria, and pride yourselves on your Democratic institutions, while you yourselves consent to be the mere *tools* and *body-guards* of the tyrants of Virginia and Carolina. You invite to your shores fugitives of oppression from abroad, honor them with banquets, greet them with ovations, cheer them, toast them, salute them, protect them, and pour out your money to them like water; but the fugitives from your own land, you advertise, hunt, arreśt, shoot and kill. You glory in your refinement and your universal education; yet you maintain a system as barbarous and dreadful, as ever stained the character of a nation—a system begun in avarice, supported in pride, and perpetuated in cruelty. You shed tears over fallen Hungary, and make the sad story of her wrongs the theme of your poets, statesmen and orators, till your gallant sons are ready to fly to arms to vindicate her cause against her oppressors; but, in regard to the ten thousand wrongs of the American slave, you would enforce the strictest silence, and would hail him as an enemy of the nation who dares to make those wrongs the subject of public discourse! You are all on fire at the mention of liberty for France or for Ireland; but are as cold as an iceberg at the thought of liberty for the enslaved of America.—You discourse eloquently on the dignity of labor; yet, you sustain a system which, in its very essence, casts a stigma upon labor. You can bare your bosom to the storm of British artillery, to throw off a threepenny tax on tea; and yet wring the last hard-earned farthing from the grasp of the black laborers of your country. You profess to believe "that, of one blood, God made all nations of men to dwell on the face of all the earth." and hath commanded all men, everywhere to love one another; yet you notoriously hate, (and glory in your hatred,) all men whose skins are not colored like your own. You declare, before the world, and are understood by the world to declare, that you *"hold these truths to be self evident, that all men are created equal; and are endowed by their Creator with certain inalienable rights; and that, among these are, life, liberty, and the pursuit of happiness;"* and yet, you hold securely, in a bondage, which according to your own Thomas Jefferson, *"is worse than ages of that which your fathers rose in rebellion to oppose,"* a *seventh part* of the inhabitants of your country.

Fellow-citizens! I will not enlarge further on your national inconsistencies. The existence of slavery in this country brands your republicanism as a sham, your humanity as a base pretence, and your Christianity as a lie. It destroys your moral power abroad; it corrupts your politicians at home. It saps the foundation of religion; it makes your name a hissing, and a by-word to a mocking earth. It is the antagonistic force in your government, the only thing that seriously disturbs and endangers your *Union.* It fetters your progress; it is the enemy of improvement, the deadly foe of education; it fosters pride; it breeds insolence; it promotes vice; it shelters crime; it is a curse to the earth that supports it; and yet, you cling to it, as if it were the sheet anchor of all your hopes. Oh! be warned! be warned! a horrible reptile is coiled up in your nation's bosom; the venomous creature is nursing at the tender breast of your youthful republic; *for the love of God, tear away,* and fling from you the hideous monster, and *let the weight of twenty millions, crush and destroy it forever!*

The Constitution. But it is answered in reply to all this, that precisely what I have now denounced is, in fact, guaranteed and sanctioned by the Constitution of the United States; that the right to hold, and to hunt slaves is a part of that Constitution framed by the illustrious Fathers of this Republic.

Then, I dare to affirm, notwithstanding all I have said before, your fathers stooped, basely stooped

To palter with us in a double sense:
And keep the word of promise to the ear,
But break it to the heart.

And instead of being the honest men I have before declared them to be, they were the veriest imposters that ever practiced on mankind. *This is the inevitable conclusion,* and from it there is no escape; but I differ from those who charge this baseness on the framers of the Constitution of the United States. *It is a slander upon their memory,* at least, so I believe. There is not time now to argue the constitutional question at length; nor have I the ability to discuss it as it ought to be discussed. The subject has been handled with masterly power by Lysander Spooner, Esq., by William Goodell, by Samuel E. Sewall, Esq., and last, though not least, by Gerritt Smith, Esq. These gentlemen have, as I think, fully and clearly vindicated the Constitution from any design to support slavery for an hour.

Fellow-citizens! there is no matter in respect to which, the people of the North have allowed themselves to be so ruinously imposed upon, as that of the pro-slavery character of the Constitution. In *that* instrument I hold there is neither warrant, license, nor sanction of the hateful thing; but, interpreted, as it *ought* to be interpreted, the Constitution is a GLORIOUS LIBERTY DOCUMENT. Read its preamble, consider its purposes. Is slavery among them? Is it at the gateway? or is it in the temple? it is neither. While I do not intend to argue this question on the present occasion, let me ask, if it be not somewhat singular that, if the Constitution were intended to be, by its framers and adopters, a slave-holding instrument, why neither *slavery, slaveholding,* nor *slave* can anywhere be found in it. What would be thought of an instrument, drawn up, *legally* drawn up, for the purpose of entitling the city of Rochester to a track of land, in which no mention of land was made? Now, there are certain rules of interpretation, for the proper understanding of all legal instruments. These rules are well established. They are plain, common-sense rules, such as you and I, and all of us, can understand and apply, without having passed years in the study of law. I scout the idea that the question of the constitutionality, or unconstitutionality of slavery is not a question for the people. I hold that every American citizen has a right to form an opinion of the Constitution, and to propagate that opinion, and to use all honorable means to make his opinion the prevailing one. Without this right, the liberty of an American citizen would be as insecure as that of a Frenchman. Ex-Vice-President Dallas tells us that the Constitution is an object to which no American mind can be too attentive, and no American heart too devoted. He further says, the Constitution, in its words, is plain and intelligible, and is meant for the home-bred, unsophisticated understandings of our fellow-citizens. Senator Berrien tells us that the Constitution is the fundamental law, that which controls all others. The charter of our liberties, which every citizen has a personal interest in understanding thoroughly. The testimony of Senator Breese, Lewis Cass, and many others that might be named, who are everywhere esteemed as sound lawyers, so regard the Constitution. I take it, therefore, that it is not presumption in a private citizen to form an opinion of that instrument.

Now, take the Constitution according to its plain reading, and I defy the presentation of a single pro-slavery clause in it. On the other hand it will be found to contain principles and purposes, entirely hostile to the existence of slavery.

I have detained my audience entirely too long already. At some future period I will gladly avail myself of an opportunity to give this subject a full and fair discussion.

Allow me to say, in conclusion, notwithstanding the dark picture I have this day presented, of the state of the nation, I do not despair of this country. There are forces in operation, which must inevitably, work the downfall of slavery. *"The arm of the Lord is not shortened,"* and the doom of slavery is certain. I, therefore, leave off where I began, with *hope.* While drawing encouragement from the Declaration of Independence, the great principles it contains, and the genius of American Institutions, my spirit is also cheered by the obvious tendencies of the age. Nations do not now stand in the same relation to each other that they did ages ago. No nation can now shut itself up, from the surrounding world, and trot round in the same old path of its fathers without interference. The time *was* when such could be done. Long established customs of hurtful character could formerly fence themselves in, and do their evil work with social impunity. Knowledge was then confined and enjoyed by the privileged few, and the multitude walked on in mental darkness. But a change has now come over the affairs of mankind. Walled cities and empires have become unfashionable. The arm of commerce has borne away the gates of the strong city. Intelligence is penetrating the darkest corners of the globe. It makes its pathway over and under the sea, as well as on the earth. Wind, steam, and lightning are its chartered agents. Oceans no longer divide, but link nations together. From Boston to London is now a holiday excursion. Space is comparatively annihilated.—Thoughts expressed on one side of the Atlantic are distinctly heard on the other.

The far off and almost fabulous Pacific rolls in grandeur at our feet. The Celestial Empire, the mystery of ages, is being solved. The fiat of the Almighty, *"Let there be Light,"* has not yet spent its force. No abuse, no outrage whether in taste, sport or avarice, can now hide itself from the all-pervading light. The iron shoe, and crippled foot of China must be seen, in contrast with nature. *Africa must rise and put on her yet unwoven garment. "Ethiopia shall stretch out her hand unto God."* In the fervent aspirations of William Lloyd Garrison, I say, and let every heart join in saying it:

God speed the year of jubilee
The wide world o'er!
When from their galling chains set free,
Th' oppress'd shall vilely bend the knee,
And wear the yoke of tyranny
Like brutes no more.
That year will come, and freedom's reign,
To man his plundered rights again
Restore.

God speed the day when human blood
Shall cease to flow!
In every clime be understood,
The claims of human brotherhood,
And each return for evil, good,
Not blow for blow;
That day will come all feuds to end,
And change into a faithful friend
Each foe.

God speed the hour, the glorious hour,
When none on earth
Shall exercise a lordly power,
Nor in a tyrant's presence cower;
But all to manhood's stature tower,
By equal birth!
THAT HOUR WILL COME, to each, to all,
And from his prison-house, the thrall
Go forth.

Until that year, day, hour, arrive,
With head, and heart, and hand I'll strive,
To break the rod, and rend the gyve,
The spoiler of his prey deprive—
So witness Heaven!

And never from my chosen post,
Whate'er the peril or the cost,

Be driven.

"NEGROES AND THE NATIONAL WAR EFFORT" (1863)

On June 23, 1863, permission was granted by the War Department for three black regiments to be recruited from the Pennsylvania area. Because black men in the area had heard of discriminatory practices in the army against black troops, they were slow in responding to the call to arms. Frederick Douglass was invited to Philadelphia to stimulate black recruitment. In a speech at National Hall on July 6, 1863, Douglass directly engaged the issue of discrimination in the military. Acknowledging its reality, Douglass urged black men to enlist anyway. For him it was an easy choice. A Union victory offered far more promise and hope for the black man than a Confederate triumph. The government of Jefferson Davis was committed to the preservation and extension of slavery. Admitting great wrongs against black people in the North, Douglass urged the potential recruits to forget the past and fight for what could be a promising future.

Mr. President and Fellow Citizens—I shall not attempt to follow Judge Kelley and Miss Dickinson in their eloquent and thrilling appeals to colored men to enlist in the service of the United States. They have left nothing to be desired on that point. I propose to look at the subject in a plain and practical common-sense light. There are obviously two views to be taken of such enlistments—a broad view and a narrow view. I am willing to take both and consider both. The narrow view of this subject is that which respects the matter of dollars and cents. There are those among us who say they are in favor of taking a hand in this tremendous war, but they add they wish to do so on terms of equality with white men. They say if they enter the service, endure all the hardships, perils and suffering—if they make bare their breasts, and with strong arms and courageous hearts confront rebel cannons, and wring victory from the jaws of death, they should have the same pay, the same rations, the same bounty, and the same favorable conditions every way afforded to other men.

I shall not oppose this view. There is something deep down in the soul of every man present which assents to the justice of the claim thus made, and honors the manhood and self-respect which insist upon it. I say at once, in peace and war, I am content with nothing for the black man short of equal and exact justice. The only question I have, and the point at which I differ from those who refuse to enlist, is whether the colored man is more likely to obtain justice and equality while refusing to assist in putting down this tremendous rebellion than he would be if he should promptly, generously and earnestly give his hand and heart to the salvation of the country in this day of calamity and peril. Nothing can be more plain, nothing more certain than that the speediest and best possible way open to us to manhood, equal rights and elevation, is that we enter this service. For my own part, I hold that if the Government of the United States offered nothing more, as an inducement to colored men to enlist, than bare subsistence and arms, considering the moral effect of compliance upon ourselves, it would be the wisest and best thing for us to enlist. There is something ennobling in the possession of arms, and we of all other people in the world stand in need of their ennobling influence.

\   The case presented in the present war, and the light in which every colored man is bound to view it, may be stated thus. There are two governments struggling now for the possession of and endeavoring to bear rule over the United States—one has its capital in Richmond and is represented by Mr. Jefferson Davis, and the other has its capital at Washington, and is represented by "Honest Old Abe." These two governments are to-day face to face, confronting each other with vast armies, and grappling each other upon many a bloody field, north and south, on the banks of the Mississippi, and under the shadows of the Alleghenies. Now, the question for every colored man is, or ought to be, what attitude is assumed by these respective governments and armies towards the rights and liberties of the colored race in this country? Which is for us, and which against us?

Now, I think there can be no doubt as to the attitude of the Richmond or Confederate government. Wherever else there has been concealment, here all is frank, open, and diabolically straightforward. Jefferson Davis and his government make no secret as to the cause of this war, and they do not conceal the purpose of the war. That purpose is nothing more nor less than to make the slavery of the African race universal and perpetual on this continent. It is not only evident from the history and logic of events, but the declared purpose of the atrocious war now being waged against the country. Some, indeed, have denied that slavery has anything to do with the war, but the very same men who do this affirm it in the same breath in which they deny it, for they tell you that the abolitionists are the cause of the war. Now, if the abolitionists are the cause of the war, they are the cause of it only because they have sought the abolition of slavery. View it in any way you please, therefore, the rebels are fighting for the existence of slavery—they are fighting for the privilege, the horrid privilege, of sundering the dearest ties of human nature—of trafficking in slaves and the souls of men—for the ghastly privilege of scourging women and selling innocent children.

I say this is not the concealed object of the war, but the openly confessed and shamelessly proclaimed object of the war. Vice-President Stephens has stated, with the utmost clearness and precision, the difference between the fundamental ideas of the Confederate Government and those of the Federal Government. One is based upon the idea that colored men are an inferior race, who may be enslaved and plundered forever, and to the heart's content of any men of a different complexion, while the Federal Government recognizes the natural and fundamental equality of all men.

I say, again, we all know that this Jefferson Davis government holds out to us nothing but fetters, chains, auction-blocks, bludgeons, branding-irons, and eternal slavery and degradation. If it triumphs in this contest, woe, woe, ten thousand woes, to the black man! Such of us as are free, in all the likelihoods of the case, would be given over to the most excruciating tortures, while the last hope of the long-crushed bondman would be extinguished forever.

Now, what is the attitude of the Washington government towards the colored race? What reasons have we to desire its triumph in the present contest? Mind, I do not ask what was its attitude towards us before this bloody rebellion broke out. I do not ask what was its disposition when it was controlled by the very men who are now fighting to destroy it, when they could no longer control it. I do not even ask what it was two years ago, when McClellan shamelessly gave out that in a war between loyal slaves and disloyal masters, he would take the side of the masters against the slaves—when he openly proclaimed his purpose to put down slave insurrection with an iron hand—when glorious Ben Butler now stunned into a conversion to anti-slavery principles (which I have every reason to believe sincere), proffered his services to the Governor of Maryland to suppress a slave insurrection, while treason ran riot in that State, and the warm, red blood of Massachusetts soldiers still stained the pavements of Baltimore.

I do not ask what was the attitude of this government when many of the officers and men who had undertaken to defend it, openly threatened to throw down their arms and leave the service, if men of color should step forward to defend it, and be invested with the dignity of soldiers. Moreover, I do not ask what was the position of this government when our loyal camps were made slave-hunting grounds, and United States officers performed the disgusting duty of slave dogs to hunt down slaves for rebel masters. These were all dark and terrible days for the republic. I do not ask you about the dead past. I bring you to the living present. Events more mighty than men, eternal Providence, all-wise, and all-controlling, have placed us in new relations to the government, and the government to us. What that government is to us to-day, and what it will be to-morrow, is made evident by a very few facts. Look at them, colored men! Slavery in the District of Columbia is abolished forever; slavery in all the territories of the United States is abolished forever; the foreign slave trade, with its ten thousand revolting abominations, is rendered impossible; slavery in ten States of the Union is abolished forever; slavery in the five remaining States is as certain to follow the same fate as the night is to follow the day. The independence of Hayti is recognized; her minister sits beside our Prime Minister, Mr. Seward, and dines at his table in Washington, while colored men are excluded from the cars in Philadelphia; showing that a black man's complexion in Washington, in the presence of the Federal government, is less offensive than in the city of brotherly love.   Citizenship is no longer denied us under this government.

Under the interpretation of our rights by Attorney General Bates, we are American citizens. We can import goods, own and sail ships, and travel in foreign countries with American passports in our pockets; and now, so far from there being any opposition, so far from excluding us from the army as soldiers, the President at Washington, the Cabinet and the Congress, the generals commanding, and the whole army of the nation unite in giving us one thunderous welcome to share with them in the honor and glory of suppressing treason and upholding the star-spangled banner. The revolution is tremendous, and it becomes us as wise men to recognize the change, and to shape our action accordingly.

I hold that the Federal Government was never, in its essence, anything but an anti-slavery Government. Abolish slavery to-morrow, and not a sentence or syllable of the Constitution need be altered. It was purposely so framed as to give no claim, no sanction to the claim of property in man.   If in its origin slavery had any relation to the Government, it was only as the scaffolding to the magnificent structure, to be removed as soon as the building was completed. There is in the Constitution no East, no West, no North, no South, no black, no white, no slave, no slaveholder, but all are citizens who are of American birth.

Such is the Government, fellow-citizens, you are now called upon to uphold with your arms. Such is the Government that you are called upon to co-operate with in burying rebellion and slavery in a common grave. Never since the world began was a better chance offered to a long enslaved and oppressed people. The opportunity is given us to be men. With one courageous resolution we may blot out the hand-writing of ages against us. Once let the black man get upon his person the brass letters U.S.; let him get an eagle on his button, and a musket on his shoulder, and bullets in his pocket, and there is no power on the earth or under the earth which can deny that he has earned the right of citizenship in the United States. I say again, this is our chance, and woe betide us if we fail to embrace it! The immortal bard hath told us:

There is a tide in the affairs of men,

Which, taken at the flood, leads on to fortune.
Omitted, all the voyage of their life
Is bound in shallows and in miseries.
We must take the current when it serves,
Or lose our ventures.

Do not flatter yourselves, my friends, that you are more important to the Government than the Government is to you. You stand but as the plank to the ship. This rebellion can be put down without your help. Slavery can be abolished by white men: but liberty so won for the black man, while it may leave him an object of pity, can never make him an object of respect.

Depend upon it, this is no time for hesitation. Do you say you want the same pay that white men get? I believe that the justice and magnanimity of your country will speedily grant it. But will you be over-nice about this matter? Do you get as good wages now as white men get by staying out of the service? Don't you work for less every day than white men get? You know you do. Do I hear you say you want black officers? Very well, and I have not the slightest doubt that, in the progress of this war, we shall see black officers, black colonels, and generals even. But is it not ridiculous in us in all at once refusing to be commanded by white men in time of war, when we are everywhere commanded by white men in time of peace? Do I hear you say still that you are a son, and want your mother provided for in your absence?—a husband, and want your wife cared for?—a brother, and want your sister secured against want? I honor you for your solicitude. Your mothers, your wives and your sisters ought to be cared for, and an association of gentlemen, composed of responsible white and colored men, is now being organized in this city for this very purpose.

Do I hear you say you offered your services to Pennsylvania, and were refused? I know it. But what of that? The State is not more than the nation. The greater includes the lesser. Because the State refuses, you should all the more readily turn to the United States. When the children fall out, they should refer their quarrel to the parent. "You came unto your own, and your own received you not." But the broad gates of the United States stand open night and day. Citizenship in the United States will, in the end, secure your citizenship in the State.

Young men of Philadelphia, you are without excuse. The hour has arrived, and your place is in the Union army. Remember that the musket—the United States musket with its bayonet of steel—is better than all mere parchment guarantees of liberty. In your hands that musket means liberty; and should your constitutional right at the close of this war be denied, which, in the nature of things, it cannot be, your brethren are safe while you have a Constitution which proclaims your right to keep and bear arms.

"THE LESSONS OF THE HOUR" (1894)

Between 1889 and 1899, a lynching took place at the rate of one every other day in America. The greatest proportion of them happened in the South, and two-thirds of the victims were African Americans. In 1892 156 African Americans were lynched, often under the most sadistic and tortuous means imaginable. Those in the South who defended such brutal lawlessness claimed that it was a necessary means to keep unrestrained black men from raping white women. Such defenders referred to the "negro problem." Later studies on lynching demonstrated that in most instances, charges of rape were not even made against the supposed perpetrators. Lynching was a means of warning blacks in the South not to challenge policies of segregation and discrimination.

In 1892 Frederick Douglass began to use his writing and oratorical skills to attack lynching and those, North and South, who made excuses for such barbaric behavior. An article, "Lynch Law in the South," was published in the July 1892 issue of the *North American Review.* Douglass developed a speech, "The Lessons of the Hour," in which he denounced lynching and dismantled the arguments used to defend its practice. The speech was delivered in Detroit, Chicago, Washington, Boston, Providence, and many other northern cities. The text below is from the version delivered at the Metropolitan A.M.E. Church in Washington on January 9, 1894. The speech, Douglass's last major oration, was printed in pamphlet form and was widely distributed. Because of the length of the speech, portions have been edited out of the discourse as it is printed here. Hopefully, this has not altered the fervor or the meaning of the address.

Friends and Fellow Citizens. . . . Now the special charge against the negro by which this ferocity is justified, and by which mob law is defended by good men North and South, is alleged to be assaults by negroes upon white women. This charge once fairly stated, no matter by whom or in what manner, whether well or ill-founded, whether true or false, is certain to subject the accused to immediate death. It is nothing, that in the case there may be a mistake as to identity. It is nothing that the victim pleads "not guilty." It is nothing that he only asks for time to establish his innocence. It is nothing that the accused is of fair reputation and his accuser is of an abandoned character. It is nothing that the majesty of the law is defied and insulted; no time is allowed for defense or explanation; he is bound with cords, hurried off amid the frantic yells and cursing of the mob to the scaffold and under its shadow he is tortured till by pain or promises, he is made to think he can possibly gain time or save his life by confession, and then whether innocent or guilty, he is shot, hanged, stabbed or burned to death amid the wild shouts of the mob. When the will of the mob has been accomplished, when its thirst for blood has been quenched, when its victim is speechless, silent and dead, his mobocratic accusers and murderers of course have the ear of the world all to themselves, and the world generally approves their verdict. . . .

Now it is important to know how this state of affairs is viewed by the better classes of the Southern States. I will tell you, and I venture to say if our hearts were not already hardened by familiarity with such crimes against the negro, we should be shocked and astonished by the attitude of these so-called better classes of the Southern people and their lawmakers. With a few noble exceptions the upper classes of the South are in full sympathy with the mob and its deeds. Press, platform and pulpit are either generally silent or they openly apologize for the mob. The mobocratic murderers are not only permitted to go free, untired and unpunished, but are lauded and applauded as honorable men and good citizens, the guardians of Southern women. If lynch law is in any case condemned, it is only condemned in one breath, and excused in another.

The great trouble with the negro in the South is, that all presumptions are against him. A white man has but to blacken his face and commit a crime, to have some negro lynched in his stead. An abandoned woman has only to start the cry that she has been insulted by a black man, to have him arrested and summarily murdered by the mob. Frightened and tortured by his captors, confused into telling crooked stories about his whereabouts at the time when the alleged crime was committed and the death penalty is at once inflicted, though his story may be but the incoherency of ignorance or distraction caused by terror.

Now in confirmation of what I have said of the better classes of the South, I have before me the utterances of some of the best people of that section, and also the testimony of one from the North, a lady, from whom, considering her antecedents, we should have expected a more considerate, just and humane utterance.

In a late number of the "Forum" Bishop Haygood, author of the "Brother in Black," says that "The most alarming fact is, that execution by lynching has ceased to surprise us. The burning of a human being for any crime, it is thought, is a horror that does not occur outside of the Southern States of the American Union, yet unless assaults by negroes come to an end, there will most probably be still further display of vengeance that will shock the world, and men who are just will consider the provocation."

In an open letter addressed to me by ex-Governor Chamberlain, of South Carolina, and published in the "Charleston News and Courier," a letter which I have but lately seen, in reply to an article of mine on the subject published in the "North American Review," the ex-Governor says: "Your denunciation of the South on this point is directed exclusively, or nearly so, against the application of lynch law for the punishment of one crime, or one sort of crime, the existence, I suppose, I might say the prevalence of this crime at the South is undeniable. But I read your (my) article in vain for any special denunciation of the crime itself. As you say your people are lynched, tortured and burned for assault on white women. As you value your own good fame and safety as a race, stamp out the infamous crime." He further says, the way to stop lynching is to stamp out the crime.

And now comes the sweet voice of a Northern woman, of Southern principles, in the same tone and the same accusation, the good Miss Frances Willard, of the W.C.T.U. [Women's Christian Temperance Union] She says in a letter now before me, "I pity the Southerner. The problem on their hands is immeasurable. The colored race," she says, "multiplies like the locusts of Egypt. The safety of woman, of childhood, of the home, is menaced in a thousand localities at this moment, so that men dare not go beyond the sight of their own roof tree." Such then is the crushing indictment drawn up against the Southern negroes, drawn up, too, by persons who are perhaps the fairest and most humane of the negro's accusers. But even they paint him as a moral monster ferociously invading the sacred rights of women and endangering the homes of the whites.

The crime they allege against the negro, is the most revolting which men can commit. It is a crime that awakens the intensest abhorrence and invites mankind to kill the criminal on sight. This charge thus brought against the negro, and as constantly reiterated by his enemies, is not merely against the individual culprit, as would be in the case with an individual culprit of any other race, but it is in a large measure a charge against the colored race as such. It throws over every colored man a mantle of odium and sets upon him a mark for popular hate, more distressing than the mark set upon the first murderer. It points him out as an object of suspicion and avoidance. Now it is in this form that you and I, and all of us, are required to meet it and refute it, if that can be done. In the opinion of some of us, it is thought that it were well to say nothing about it, that the least said about it the better. In this opinion I do not concur. Taking this charge in its broad and comprehensive sense in which it is presented, and as now stated, I feel that it ought to be met, and as a colored man, I am grateful for the opportunity now afforded me to meet it. For I believe it can be met and successfully met. I am of opinion that a people too spiritless to defend themselves are not worth defending. . . .

But I want to be understood at the outset. I do not pretend that negroes are saints or angels. I do not deny that they are capable of committing the crime imputed to them, but I utterly deny that they are any more addicted to the commission of that crime than is true of any other variety of the human family. In entering upon my argument, I may be allowed to say, that I appear here this evening not as the defender of any man guilty of this atrocious crime, but as the defender of the colored people as a class. . . .

It is the misfortune of the colored people in this country that the sins of the few are visited upon the many, and I am here to speak for the many whose reputation is put in peril by the sweeping charge in question. With General Grant and every other honest man, my motto is, "Let no guilty man escape." But while I am here to say this, I am here also to say, let no innocent man be condemned and killed by the mob, or crushed under the weight of a charge of which he is not guilty. . . .

At the outset I deny that a fierce and frenzied mob is or ought to be deemed a competent witness against any man accused of any crime whatever. The ease with which a mob can be collected and the slight causes by which it may be set in motion, and the elements of which it is composed, deprives its testimony of the qualities that should inspire confidence and command belief. It is moved by impulses utterly unfavorable to an impartial statement of the truth. At the outset, therefore, I challenge the credibility of the mob, and as the mob is the main witness in the case against the negro, I appeal to the common sense of mankind in support of my challenge. It is the mob that brings this charge, and it is the mob that arraigns, condemns and executes, and it is the mob that the country has accepted as its witness.

Again, I impeach and discredit the veracity of southern men generally, whether mobocrats or otherwise, who now openly and deliberately nullify and violate the provisions of the constitution of their country, a constitution, which they have solemnly sworn to support and execute. I apply to them the legal maxim, "False in one, false in all."

Again I arraign the negro's accuser on another ground, I have no confidence in the truthfulness of men who justify themselves in cheating the negro out of his constitutional right to vote. The men, who either by false returns, or by taking advantage of his illiteracy or surrounding the ballot-box with obstacles and sinuosities intended to bewilder him and defeat his rightful exercise of the elective franchise, are men who are not to be believed on oath. That this is done in the Southern States is not only admitted, but openly defended and justified by so-called honorable men inside and outside of Congress. . . .

But I come to a stronger position. I rest my conclusion not merely upon general principles, but upon well known facts. I reject the charge brought against the negro as a class, but all through the late war, while the slave masters of the South were absent from their homes in the field of rebellion, with bullets in their pockets, treason in their hearts, broad blades in their blood stained hands, seeking the life of the nation, with the vile purpose of perpetuating the enslavement of the negro, their wives, their daughters, their sisters and their mothers were left in the absolute custody of these same negroes, and during all those long four years of terrible conflict, when the negro had every opportunity to commit the abominable crime now alleged against him, there was never a single instance of such crime reported or charged against him. He was never accused of assault, insult, or an attempt to commit an assault upon any white woman in the whole South. A fact like this, although negative, speaks volumes and ought to have some weight with the American people.

Then, again on general principles, I do not believe the charge because it implies an improbable, if not impossible, change in the mental and moral character and composition of the negro. It implies a change wholly inconsistent with well known facts of human nature. It is a contradiction to well known human experience. History does not present an example of such a transformation in the character of any class of men so extreme, so unnatural and so complete as is implied in this charge. The change is too great and the period too brief. Instances may be cited where men fall like stars from heaven, but such is not the usual experience. Decline in the moral character of a people is not sudden, but gradual. The downward steps are marked at first by degrees and by increasing momentum from bad to worse. Time is an element in such changes, and I contend that the negroes of the South have not had time to experience this great change and reach this lower depth of infamy. On the contrary, in point of fact, they have been and still are, improving and ascending to higher levels of moral and social worth.

Again, I do not believe it and utterly deny it, because those who bring the charge do not and dare not, give the negro a chance to be heard in his own defence. He is not allowed to explain any part of his alleged offense. He is not allowed to vindicate his own character or to criminate the character and motives of his accusers. Even the mobocrats themselves admit that it would be fatal to their purpose to have the character of his accusers brought into court. They pretend to a delicate regard for the feelings of the parties assaulted, and therefore object to giving a fair trial to the accused. The excuse in this case is contemptible. It is not only mock modesty but mob modesty. Men who can collect hundreds and thousands, if we may believe them, and can spread before them in the tempest and whirlwind of vulgar passion, the most disgusting details of crime with the names of women, with the alleged offense, should not be allowed to shelter themselves under the pretense of modesty. Such a pretense is absurd and shameless. Who does not know that the modesty of womanhood is always an object for protection in a court of law? Who does not know that a lawless mob composed in part of the basest of men can have no such respect for the modesty of women as a court of law. No woman need be ashamed to confront one who has insulted or assaulted her in a court of law. Besides innocence does not hesitate to come to the rescue of justice.

Again, I do not believe it, and deny it because if the evidence were deemed sufficient to bring the accused to the scaffold, through the action of an impartial jury, there could be, and would be, no objection to having the alleged offender tried in conformity to due process of law.

Any pretence that a guilty negro, especially one guilty of the crime now charged, would in any case be permitted to escape condign punishment, is an insult to common sense. Nobody believes or can believe such a thing as escape possible, in a country like the South, where public opinion, the laws, the courts, the juries, and the advocates are all known to be against him, he could hardly escape if innocent. I repeat, therefore, I do not believe it, because I know, and you know, that a passionate and violent mob bent upon taking life, from the nature of the case, is not a more competent and trustworthy body to determine the guilt or innocence of a negro accused in such a case, than is a court of law. I would not, and you would not, convict a dog on such testimony.

But I come to another fact, and an all-important fact, bearing upon this case. You will remember that during all the first years of reconstruction and long after the war when the Southern press and people found it necessary to invent, adopt, and propagate almost every species of falsehood to create sympathy for themselves and to formulate an excuse for gratifying their brutal instincts, there was never a charge then made against a negro involving an assault upon any white woman or upon any little white child. During all this time the white women and children were absolutely safe. During all this time there was no call for Miss Willard's pity, or Bishop Haygood's defense of burning negroes to death.

You will remember also that during this time the justification for the murder of negroes was said to be negro conspiracies, insurrections, schemes to murder all the white people, to burn the town, and commit violence generally. These were the excuses then depended upon, but never a word was then said or whispered about negro outrages upon white women and children. So far as the history of that time is concerned, white women and children were absolutely safe, and husbands and fathers could leave home without the slightest anxiety on account of their families.

But when events proved that no such conspiracies; no such insurrections as were then pretended to exist and were paraded before the world in glaring head-lines, had ever existed or were even meditated; when these excuses had run their course and served their wicked purpose; when the huts of negroes had been searched, and searched in vain, for guns and ammunition to prove these charges, and no evidence was found, when there was no way open thereafter to prove these charges against the negro and no way to make the North believe in these excuses for murder, they did not even then bring forward the present allegation against the negro. They, however, went on harassing and killing just the same. But this time they based the right thus to kill on the ground that it was necessary to check the domination and supremacy of the negro and to secure the absolute rule of the Anglo-Saxon race.

It is important to notice that there has been three distinct periods of persecution of negroes in the South, and three distinct sets of excuses for persecution. They have come along precisely in the order in which they were most needed. First you remember it was insurrection. When that was worn out, negro supremacy became the excuse. When that is worn out, now it is assault upon defenseless women. I undertake to say, that this order and periodicity is significant and means something and should not be overlooked. And now that negro supremacy and negro domination are no longer defensible as an excuse for negro persecutions, there has come in due course, this heart-rending cry about the white women and little white children of the South. . . .

This new charge has come at the call of new conditions, and nothing could have been hit upon better calculated to accomplish its purpose. It clouds the character of the negro with a crime the most revolting, and is fitted to drive from him all sympathy and all fair play and all mercy. It is a crime that places him outside of the pale of the law, and settles upon his shoulders a mantle of wrath and fire that blisters and burns into his very soul.

It is for this purpose, as I believe, that this new charge unthought of in the times to which I have referred, has been largely invited, if not entirely trumped up. It is for this purpose that it has been constantly reiterated and adopted. It was to blast and ruin the negro's character as a man and a citizen.

I need not tell you how thoroughly it has already done its wonted work. You may feel its malign influence in the very air. You may read it in the faces of men. It has cooled our friends. It has heated our enemies, and arrested in some measure the efforts that good men were wont to make for the colored man's improvement and elevation. It has deceived our friends at the North and many good friends at the South, for nearly all have in some measure accepted the charge as true. Its perpetual reiteration in our newspapers and magazines has led men and women to regard us with averted eyes, increasing hate and dark suspicion. . . .

To sum up my argument on this lynching business. It remains to be said that I have shown that the negro's accusers in this case have violated their oaths and have cheated the negro out of his vote; that they have robbed and defrauded the negro systematically and persistently, and have boasted of it. I have shown that when the negro had every opportunity to commit the crime now charged against him he was never accused of it by his bitterest enemies. I have shown that during all the years of reconstruction, when he was being murdered at Hamburg, Yazoo, New Orleans, Copiah and elsewhere, he was never accused of the crime now charged against him. I have shown that in the nature of things no such change in the character and composition of a people as this charge implies could have taken place in the limited period allowed for it. I have shown that those who accuse him dare not confront him in a court of law and have their witnesses subjected to proper legal inquiry. And in showing all this, and more, I have shown that they who charge him with this foul crime may be justly doubted and deemed unworthy of belief.

But I shall be told by many of my Northern friends that my argument, though plausible, is not conclusive. It will be said that the charges against the negro are specific and positive, and that there must be some foundation for them, because as they allege men in their normal condition do not shoot and hang their fellowmen who are guiltless of crime. Well! This assumption is very just, very charitable. I only ask something like the same justice and charity could be shown to the negro as well as to the mob. It is creditable to the justice and humanity of the good people of the North by whom it is entertained. They rightly assume that men do not shoot and hang their fellowmen without just cause. But the vice of their argument is in their assumption that the lynchers are like other men. The answer to that argument is what may be truly predicated of human nature under one condition is not what may be true of human nature under another. Uncorrupted human nature may shudder at the commission of such crimes as those of which the Southern mob is guilty.

But human nature uncorrupted is one thing and human nature corrupted and perverted by long abuse of irresponsible power, is quite another and different thing. No man can reason correctly on this question who reasons on the assumption that the lynchers are like ordinary men.

We are not, in this case, dealing with men in their natural condition, but with men brought up in the exercise of arbitrary power. We are dealing with men whose ideas, habits and customs are entirely different from those of ordinary men. It is, therefore, quite gratuitous to assume that the principles that apply to other men apply to the Southern murderers of the negro, and just here is the mistake of the Northern people. They do not see that the rules resting upon the justice and benevolence of human nature do not apply to the mobocrats, or to those who were educated in the habits and customs of a slave-holding community. What these habits are I have a right to know, both in theory and in practice.

I repeat: The mistake made by those who on this ground object to my theory of the charge against the negro, is that they overlook the natural effect and influence of the life, education and habits of the lynchers. We must remember that these people have not now and have never had any such respect for human life as is common to other men. They have had among them for centuries a peculiar institution, and that peculiar institution has stamped them as a peculiar people. They were not before the war, they were not during the war and have not been since the war in their spirit or in their civilization, a people in common with the people of the North. I will not here harrow up your feelings by detailing their treatment of Northern prisoners during the war. Their institutions have taught them no respect for human life and especially the life of the negro. It has in fact taught them absolute contempt for his life. The sacredness of life which ordinary men feel does not touch them anywhere. A dead negro is with them a common jest. . . .

Again, I cannot dwell too much upon the fact that colored people are much damaged by this charge. As an injured class we have a right to appeal from the judgment of the mob to the judgment of the law and the American people. Our enemies have known well where to strike and how to stab us most fatally. Owing to popular prejudice it has become the misfortune of the colored people of the South and of the North as well, to have as I have said, the sins of the few visited upon the many. When a white man steals, robs or murders, his crime is visited upon his own head alone. But not so with the black man. When he commits a crime the whole race is made to suffer. The cause before us is an example. This unfairness confronts us not only here, but it confronts us everywhere else. . . .

But call this problem what you may, or will, the all important question is: How can it be solved? How can the peace and tranquility of the South, and of the country, be secured and established?

There is nothing occult or mysterious about the answer to this question. Some things are to be kept in mind when dealing with this subject and never be forgotten. It should be remembered that in the order of Divine Providence the man who puts one end of a chain around the ankle of his fellow man will find the other end around his own neck. And it is the same with a nation. Confirmation of this truth is as strong as thunder. "As we sow, we shall reap," is a lesson to be learned here as elsewhere. We tolerated slavery, and it cost us a million graves, and it may be that lawless murder, if permitted to go on, may yet bring vengeance, not only on the reverend head of age and upon the heads of helpless women, but upon the innocent babe in the cradle.

But how can this problem be solved? I will tell you how it can *not* be solved. It cannot be solved by keeping the negro poor, degraded, ignorant and half-starved, as I have shown is now being done in the Southern States.

It cannot be solved by keeping the wages of the laborer back by fraud, as is now being done by the landlords of the South.

It cannot be done by ballot-box stuffing, by falsifying election returns, or by confusing the negro voter by cunning devices.

It cannot be done by repealing all federal laws enacted to secure honest elections.

It can, however, be done, and very easily done, for where there's a will, there's a way!

Let the white people of the North and South conquer their prejudices.

Let the great Northern press and pulpit proclaim the gospel of truth and justice against war now being made upon the negro.

Let the American people cultivate kindness and humanity.

Let the South abandon the system of "mortgage" labor, and cease to make the negro a pauper, by paying him scrip for his labor.

Let them give up the idea that they can be free, while making the negro a slave. Let them give up the idea that to degrade the colored man, is to elevate the white man.

Let them cease putting new wine into old bottles, and mending old garments with new cloth.

They are not required to do much. They are only required to undo the evil that they have done, in order to solve this problem.

In old times when it was asked, "How can we abolish slavery?" the answer was "Quit stealing."

The same is the solution of the Race problem to-day. The whole thing can be done by simply no longer violating the amendments of the Constitution of the United States, and no longer evading the claims of justice. If this were done, there would be no negro problem to vex the South, or to vex the nation.

Let the organic law of the land be honestly sustained and obeyed.

Let the political parties cease to palter in a double sense and live up to the noble declarations we find in their platforms.

Let the statesmen of the country live up to their convictions.

In the language of Senator Ingalls: "Let the nation try justice and the problem will be solved." . . .

Put away your race prejudice. Banish the idea that one class must rule over another. Recognize the fact that the rights of the humblest citizen are as worthy of protection as are those of the highest, and your problem will be solved; and, whatever may be in store for it in the future, whether prosperity, or adversity; whether it shall have foes without, or foes within, whether there shall be peace, or war; based upon the eternal principles of truth, justice and humanity, and with no class having any cause of complaint or grievance, your Republic will stand and flourish forever.

NOTES

INTRODUCTION

1. Robert T. Oliver, *History of Public Speaking in America* (Boston: Allyn and Bacon, Inc., 1965), p. 246.

2. As quoted in John W. Blassingame, ed., "Introduction," *The Frederick Douglass Papers* (New Haven, CT: Yale University Press, 1979), pp. 1:xli–xlii.

3. Helen Pitts Douglass, *In Memoriam: Frederick Douglass* (Freeport, NY: Books for Libraries Press, 1971; repr. of 1897 ed.), pp. 287, 288.

4. Waldo E. Martin Jr., "Frederick Douglass (1818–1895)," in *American Orators before 1900: Critical Studies and Sources,* Bernard K. Duffy and Halford R. Ryan, eds. (Westport, CT: Greenwood Press, 1987), p. 129.

CHAPTER 1: THE YEARS OF SLAVERY

1. Frederick Douglass, *Narrative of the Life of Frederick Douglass, An American Slave* (New York: Penguin Books, 1986; first published in 1845), p. 49.

2. Ibid., p. 47.

3. Ibid., p. 48.

4. Ibid., p. 49.

5. Frederick Douglass, *The Life and Times of Frederick Douglass* (New York: Macmillan, 1962; first published in 1881, expanded in 1892), p. 36.

6. James M'Cune Smith, "Introduction," in Frederick Douglass, *My Bondage and My Freedom* (New York: Dover Publications, 1969; first published in 1855), p. xix.

7. John W. Blassingame, ed., *The Frederick Douglass Papers* (New Haven, CT: Yale University Press, 1979), pp. 1:31–32.

8. William S. McFeely, *Frederick Douglass* (New York: W. W. Norton, 1991), p. 10.

9. Douglass, *My Bondage and My Freedom,* p. 132.

10. Douglass, *Narrative of the Life of Frederick Douglass,* pp. 78–79. Frederick's evaluation of Sophia Auld underwent a sad change. The woman whom he at first found so caring and helpful became corrupted, he claimed, by slavery. "When I went there, she was a pious, warm, and tender-hearted woman. . . . Slavery soon proved its ability to divest her of these heavenly qualities. Under its influence, the tender heart became stone,

and the lamb-like disposition gave way to tiger-like fierceness." Ibid., pp. 81–82.

11. Douglass, *My Bondage and My Freedom*, p. 155.

12. Ibid., 158.

13. Caleb Bingham, *The Columbian Orator: Containing a Variety of Original and Selected Pieces; Together with Rules, Calculated to Improve Youth and Others in the Ornamental and Useful Art of Eloquence* (Boston: Manning and Loring, 1797), pp. 240-42.

14. Douglass, *My Bondage and My Freedom*, p. 158.

15. Waldo E. Martin Jr., "Frederick Douglass (1818–1895)," *American Orators before 1900: Critical Studies and Sources*, Bernard K. Duffy and Halford R. Ryan, eds. (Westport, CT: Greenwood Press, 1987), p. 139.

16. Douglass, *My Bondage and My Freedom*, pp. 167–69.

17. Douglass, *Narrative of the Life of Frederick Douglass*, pp. 95–96, 97.

18. Ibid., pp. 98–99.

19. Ibid., pp. 105–6.

20. Douglass, *My Bondage and My Freedom*, p. 248.

21. Douglass, *Narrative of the Life of Frederick Douglass*, p. 113.

22. Ibid., p. 121.

23. Ibid., p. 117.

24. Ibid., pp. 117–19.

25. Douglass, *My Bondage and My Freedom*, p. 263.

26. Such an arrangement between masters and city slaves was common. See Richard C. Wade, *Slavery in the Cities: The South 1820–1860* (New York: Oxford University Press, 1964), pp. 38–54.

27. R. Gerald Fulkerson, "Frederick Douglass and the Anti-Slavery Crusade: His Career and Speeches, 1817–1861" (Ph.D. dissertation, University of Illinois, 1971), p. 28.

28. Douglass, *My Bondage and My Freedom*, p. 319.

29. Ibid., p. 330.

CHAPTER 2: THE PREWAR YEARS OF FREEDOM

1. Douglass, *Narrative of the Life of Frederick Douglass, An American Slave* (New York: Penguin Books, 1986; first published in 1845), p. 148.

2. Ibid., p. 150.

3. As quoted in William S. McFeely, *Frederick Douglass* (New York: W. W. Norton, 1991), p. 82.

4. Douglass, *Narrative of the Life of Frederick Douglass*, p. 151.

5. *Liberator*, March 29, 1839, p. 50.

6. Frederick Douglass, *My Bondage and My Freedom* (New York: Dover Publications, 1969; first published in 1855), p. 358.

7. "Introduction" to Douglass, *My Bondage and My Freedom*, p. xxi.

8. "Preface" to Douglass, *Narrative of the Life of Frederick Douglass*, pp. 34–35.

9. Ibid.

10. *Anti-Slavery Standard*, August 26, 1841.

11. *Herald of Freedom* (Concord, NH), December 10, 1841.

12. R. Gerald Fulkerson, "Frederick Douglass and the Anti-Slavery Crusade: His Career and Speeches" (Ph.D. dissertation, University of Illinois, 1971), p. 442.

13. John W. Blassingame, ed., *The Frederick Douglass Papers* (New Haven, CT:

Yale University Press), p. 1:6.

14. Ibid., p. 8.

15. Ibid., pp. 10–12.

16. Ibid., p. 12.

17. *Liberator,* December 10, 1841, p. 197.

18. Ibid., December 3, 1841, p. 193.

19. See Fulkerson, "Frederick Douglass and the Anti-Slavery Crusade," p. 440.

20. *Liberator,* January 21, 1842, p. 11.

21. James G. Birney had been a slaveholder in Alabama and Kentucky but had been converted to the antislavery cause by Theodore Weld. Birney attempted, without success, to publish an antislavery paper in Danville, Kentucky. He moved to Ohio and in 1837 became the executive secretary of the American Anti-Slavery Society.

22. Blassingame, *The Frederick Douglass Papers,* pp. 1:14–15. Birney and the Liberty party were much more successful in the 1844 election. They polled over 62,000 votes, as compared with 7,000 votes in 1840. This represented, however, only 2.3 percent of the popular vote. It is important to recall that this small percentage does not reflect the true strength of antislavery sentiment, for the Garrisonians—ardent antislavery proponents—did not vote for Birney and the Liberty party. The significance of the Liberty party in the 1844 election was that it drew enough votes away from Clay and the Whigs to give the election to Polk and the Democrats. In the western counties of New York alone, the Liberty party siphoned enough votes away from the Whigs to give the state to Polk. With New York State, Clay would have carried the election by seven electoral votes.

23. Charles Lenox Remond was born a free black man in Salem, Massachusetts. He had the advantage of an excellent education and at an early age was recognized as possessing a gift for eloquence. As a young man he frequently addressed public meetings on antislavery subjects, and he was the first black to speak before public gatherings on behalf of abolition. In 1838 he became an agent of the Massachusetts Anti-Slavery Society. In 1840 he was a delegate to the World's Anti-Slavery Convention in London. He delivered antislavery speeches before large audiences in England and Ireland and was highly commended for both his content and style. When he returned to the United States in December 1841, he soon learned that another black man, Frederick Douglass, had risen to first place in the pantheon of antislavery speakers. Though Douglass and Remond did not always agree on the means to achieve a common end, the two worked together—as in the Latimer case—to bring about an end to slavery. Both black men, coming from very different backgrounds, used their oratorical skills effectively in the antislavery cause.

24. *Liberator,* November 18, 1842, p. 182.

25. As reprinted in *Liberator,* December 9, 1842, p. 3.

26. Blassingame, *The Frederick Douglass Papers,* pp. 1:21–22.

27. David Walker, *Walker's Appeal in Four Articles* (New York: Arno Press, 1969; repr. of 1848 ed.), p. 56.

28. Frederick Douglass, *The Life and Times of Frederick Douglass* (New York: Macmillan, 1962; first published in 1881, expanded in 1892), p. 230.

29. *Liberator,* October 13, 1843, p. 163.

30. As recorded in *Liberator,* November 24, 1843, p. 186.

31. *Herald of Freedom* (Concord, NH), February 16, 1844, p. 208.

32. Douglass, *My Bondage and My Freedom,* p. 362.

33. Blassingame, *The Frederick Douglass Papers,* p. 1:30.

34. Ibid., p. 1:56.

35. Ibid., p. 1:42. Cf. Theodore Dwight Weld, *American Slavery as It Is: Testimony of a Thousand Witnesses* (New York: American Anti-Slavery Society, 1839), p. 144.

36. Ibid., p. 35.

37. Ibid.

38. R. Gerald Fulkerson, "Frederick Douglass and the Anti-Slavery Crusade," pp. 469–73.

39. R. Gerald Fulkerson, "Exile as Emergence: Frederick Douglass in Great Britain, 1845–1847," *Quarterly Journal of Speech* 60 (February 1974), p. 73.

40. As reported in the *Liberator,* February 27, 1846, p. 34.

41. Blassingame, *The Frederick Douglass Papers,* p. 1:149.

42. Ibid., pp. 1:167, 159, 161–62, 164.

43. *Liberator,* May 15, 1846, pp. 78–79.

44. William M. Merrill, ed., *The Letters of William Lloyd Garrison: No Union with Slaveholders* (Cambridge, MA: Belknap Press of Harvard University, 1971), p. 3:151.

45. Ibid., p. 160.

46. Blassingame, *The Frederick Douglass Papers,* p. 1:408.

47. Ibid., p. 409.

48. Ibid., pp. 409–10.

49. Ibid., p. 413.

50. Ibid., pp. 2:19–52.

51. For an evaluation of Douglass by these men, see Douglass, *Life and Times,* chapter 6, pp. 232–58.

52. *Liberator,* June 25, 1847, p. 203.

53. *North Star,* December 3, 1847, p. 2. In this same issue, Douglass explained his choice of the paper's name by quoting lines from a noted fugitive slave song: "I kept my eye on the bright north star, And thought of liberty."

54. As quoted in Fulkerson, "Frederick Douglass and the Anti-Slavery Crusade," p. 162.

55. *North Star,* November 23, 1849, p. 2.

56. *Woman's Journal,* April 14, 1888, p. 62.

57. Blassingame, *The Frederick Douglass Papers,* p. 2:249.

58. Ibid., pp. 2:210, 211, 212.

59. Fulkerson, "Frederick Douglass and the Anti-Slavery Crusade," p. 189.

60. Blassingame, *The Frederick Douglass Papers,* pp. 2:235–43.

61. Ibid., p. 2:245.

62. *Liberator,* October 18, 1850, p. 166.

63. E. O. Preston Jr., "The Genesis of the Underground Railroad," *Journal of Negro History* 18 (April 1933), pp. 144–70.

64. Sarah H. Bradford, *Scenes in the Life of Harriet Tubman* (Auburn, NY: W. J. Moses, 1869), p. 233.

65. *North Star,* February 9, 1849, p. 3.

66. Blassingame, *The Frederick Douglass Papers,* p. 2:179. John R. McKivigan has written that "in the decade and a half before the beginning of the Civil War . . . there was a significant growth of antislavery sentiment in many northern denominations. . . . By the war's end . . . only Catholics and Episcopalians had failed to condemn slavery and to demand its speedy destruction." *The War against Proslavery Religion: Abolitionism; and the Northern Churches, 1830–1865* (Ithaca, NY: Cornell University Press, 1984), p. 160.

67. Blassingame, *The Frederick Douglass Papers*, pp. 2:180–81.

68. Ibid., p. 2:194.

69. Julia Griffiths's position with the *North Star* was a combination of associate editor and business manager. She saw to it that the paper was published with impeccable style and is generally credited with keeping the publication on a sound financial basis.

70. *North Star*, October 5, 1849, p. 2.

71. The essence of this debate can be found in Blassingame, *The Frederick Douglass Papers*, pp. 2:217–35.

72. *North Star*, January 25, 1850, pp. 2–3.

73. As recorded in Fulkerson, "Frederick Douglass and the Anti-Slavery Crusade," p. 199.

74. Ibid., p. 202.

75. Blassingame, *The Frederick Douglass Papers*, pp. 2:389, 390–91.

76. As recorded in Fulkerson, "Frederick Douglass and the Anti-Slavery Crusade," p. 242.

77. Blassingame, *The Frederick Douglass Papers*, pp. 3:141–42.

78. *Frederick Douglass' Paper*, August 15, 1856, p. 2.

79. *Liberator*, September 5, 1856, p. 146.

80. James Buchanan received slightly over 45 percent of the popular vote with 174 electoral votes; and Millard Filmore, candidate of the American party received 22.5 percent of the popular vote with 8 electoral votes (Maryland).

81. *Douglass' Monthly*, June 1860, p. 276.

82. Ibid., pp. 327–30.

83. As quoted in George A. Hinshaw, "A Rhetorical Analysis of the Speeches of Frederick Douglass during and after the Civil War" (Ph.D. dissertation, University of Nebraska, 1972), pp. 65–66.

84. Letter dated June 26, 1852. The original copy of this letter is located in the archives of the Rush Rhees Library at the University of Rochester.

85. Neil Leroux, "Frederick Douglass and the Attention Shift," *Rhetoric Society Quarterly* 21 (spring 1991), pp. 34, 90.

86. Blassingame, *The Frederick Douglass Papers*, p. 2:371.

87. Ibid., pp. 2:497–525.

88. Ibid., pp. 2:538–59.

89. McFeely, *Frederick Douglass*, p. 181.

90. Blassingame, *The Frederick Douglass Papers*, p. 3:167.

91. Ibid.

92. Ibid., pp. 3:242–46.

93. Benjamin Quarles, *Black Abolitionists* (New York: Oxford University Press, 1969), p. 173.

94. *Douglass' Monthly*, December 1860, p. 369.

95. Truman Nelson, ed., *Documents of Upheaval: Selections from William Lloyd Garrison's The Liberator, 1831–1865* (New York: Hill and Wang, 1966), pp. 121–22.

96. Douglass, *Narrative of the Life of Frederick Douglas*, p. 113.

97. *North Star*, January 14, 1848, p. 1.

98. Blassingame, *The Frederick Douglass Papers*, p. 2:390. An excellent article that traces Douglass's various stances on violence is Leslie Friedman Goldstein, "Violence as an Instrument for Social Change: The Views of Frederick Douglass (1817–1895)," *Journal of Negro History* 61 (January 1976), pp. 61–72.

99. As quoted in Hinshaw, "Rhetorical Analysis of the Speeches of Frederick Douglass," pp. 59–60.

100. Ibid., p. 60.

101. *Liberator,* July 27, 1860, p. 67.

102. Blassingame, *The Frederick Douglass Papers,* pp. 3:386–87.

CHAPTER 3: THE WAR YEARS

1. *Douglass' Monthly,* May 1861, p. 3.

2. John W. Blassingame, ed., *The Frederick Douglass Papers* (New Haven, CT: Yale University Press), pp. 3:424–28.

3. Ibid., p. 3:433.

4. Ibid., p. 3:451.

5. Ibid., p. 3:473.

6. Ibid., pp. 3:473–88.

7. *Douglass' Monthly,* October 1862, p. 2.

8. Frederick Douglass, *The Life and Times of Frederick Douglass* (New York: Macmillan, 1962; first published in 1881, expanded in 1892), p. 354.

9. Blassingame, *The Frederick Douglass Papers,* pp. 3:549–69.

10. Philip S. Foner, *The Life and Writings of Frederick Douglass* (New York: International Publishers, 1950), pp. 3:317–19.

11. Herbert Aptheker, *Essays in the History of the American Negro* (New York: International Publishers, 1945), p. 195.

12. *Douglass' Monthly,* February 1863, p. 3.

13. Blassingame, *The Frederick Douglass Papers,* p. 3:596.

14. *Douglass' Monthly,* August 1863, p. 2.

15. Douglass, *Life and Times,* pp. 347–49.

16. Ibid., pp. 350, 357.

17. Blassingame, *The Frederick Douglass Papers,* pp. 4:8, 12, 24.

18. Ibid., pp. 4:25, 28.

19. Douglass, *Life and Times,* pp. 358–59.

20. Blassingame, *The Frederick Douglass Papers,* pp. 4:74–79.

CHAPTER 4: THE POSTWAR YEARS

1. Frederick Douglass, *The Life and Times of Frederick Douglass* (New York: Macmillan, 1962; first published in 1881, expanded in 1892), p. 364.

2. John W. Blassingame and John R. McKivigan, eds., *The Frederick Douglass Papers* (New Haven, CT: Yale University Press), pp. 4:96–106.

3. Douglass, *Life and Times,* p. 382.

4. Frederick May Holland, *Frederick Douglass: The Colored Orator* (New York: Haskell House Publishers, Ltd., 1969; first published in 1891), pp. 250–55.

5. Blassingame, *The Frederick Douglass Papers,* pp. 4:176–77.

6. As quoted in George A. Hinshaw, "A Rhetorical Analysis of the Speeches of Frederick Douglass during and after the Civil War" (Ph.D. dissertation, University of Nebraska, 1972), p. 112.

7. *New Era,* December 15, 1870.

8. Blassingame, *The Frederick Douglass Papers,* pp. 4:280–81.

9. Ibid., pp. 4:311–12.

10. Ibid., pp. 4:317, 321–22.

11. Douglass, *Life and Times,* p. 403.

12. Hinshaw, "Rhetorical Analysis of the Speeches of Frederick Douglass," p. 128.

13. Blassingame, *The Frederick Douglass Papers,* p. 4:401.

14. Ibid., pp. 4:412–13.

15. Ibid., pp. 4:427–40.

16. Ibid., pp. 4:485–86.

17. Douglass, *Life and Times,* pp. 442–43.

18. Blassingame, *The Frederick Douglass Papers,* pp. 4:527, 530–31.

19. William S. McFeely, *Frederick Douglass* (New York: W. W. Norton, 1991), pp. 299, 300.

20. Blassingame, *The Frederick Douglass Papers,* pp. 5:357–73.

21. As quoted in Hinshaw, "Rhetorical Analysis of the Speeches of Frederick Douglass," p. 140.

22. Benjamin Quarles, *Frederick Douglass* (Washington, DC: Associated Publishers, 1948), p. 387.

23. Francis J. Grimke, "The Second Marriage of Frederick Douglass," *Journal of Negro History* 19 (July 1934), p. 325.

24. Philip S. Foner, ed., *The Life and Writings of Frederick Douglass* (New York: International Publishers, 1950), pp. 4:116, 117.

25. Frederick May Holland, *Frederick Douglass: The Colored Orator* (New York: Haskell House Publishers, Ltd., 1969; first published in 1891), pp. 356–57.

26. Foner, *The Life and Writings of Frederick Douglass,* pp. 4:126–27.

27. Blassingame, *The Frederick Douglass Papers,* pp. 5:338–44. Mary Lincoln gave away four of her husband's canes. The other three went to Charles Sumner, Henry Highland Garnet, and William Slade. Ishbel Ross, *The President's Wife: Mary Todd Lincoln, A Biography* (New York: Putnam, 1973), p. 247.

28. Blassingame, *The Frederick Douglass Papers,* pp. 5:348–57.

29. Ibid., pp. 5:390–98.

30. As quoted in Quarles, *Frederick Douglass,* pp. 322, 320.

31. As quoted in Hinshaw, "Rhetorical Analysis of Frederick Douglass," p. 147.

32. Ibid., p. 148.

33. Blassingame, *The Frederick Douglass Papers,* pp. 5:509–34.

34. McFeely, *Frederick Douglass,* p. 371.

35. Theodore Stanton and Harriet Stanton Blanche, eds., *Elizabeth Cady Stanton, As Revealed in Her Letters, Diary, and Reminiscences* (New York: Harper and Brothers, 1922), pp. 2:311–12.

CHAPTER 5: RHETORICAL TECHNIQUES

1. Lane Cooper, *The Rhetoric of Aristotle: An Expanded Translation with Supplementary Examples for Students of Composition and Public Speaking* (New York: Appleton-Century-Crofts, Inc., 1932), p. 9.

2. John W. Blassingame, ed., *The Frederick Douglass Papers* (New Haven, CT: Yale University Press, 1979), p. 1:3.

3. William L. Andrews, ed., *The Oxford Frederick Douglass Reader* (New York: Oxford University Press, 1996), p. 109.

4. Blassingame, *The Frederick Douglass Papers,* p. 3:492.

5. George L. Ruffin, "Introduction," in Frederick Douglass, *The Life and Times of Frederick Douglass* (New York: Macmillan, 1962; first published in 1881, expanded in 1892), p. 20.

6. Blassingame, *The Frederick Douglass Papers,* p. 3:596.

7. Ibid., p. 5:177.

8. Ibid., p. 5:188.

9. Ibid., p. 3:502.

10. Ibid., p. 3:503.

11. Ibid., pp. 4:511–12.

12. Ibid., p. 4:520.

13. Ibid., p. 3:505.

14. Ibid., p. 4:69.

15. Ibid., pp. 4:91–93. Robert Small and William Tilghman were two black heroes in the Civil War. Dr. Smith was James M'Cune Smith. George Boyer Vashon was a lawyer, educator, and poet from Pittsburgh. Charles Lewis Reason, Henry Highland Garnet, Charles Lenox Remond, and John Seller Martin were eloquent abolitionists. John Sweat Rock was an educator, dentist, medical doctor, lawyer, and lecturer. Crummell was Alexander Crummell, the noted orator.

16. Ibid., pp. 5:524–25.

17. Ibid., pp. 533–34.

18. Ibid., pp. 3:493–94.

19. Ibid., p. 4:87.

20. Ibid., p. 3:493.

21. Philip S. Foner, ed., *The Life and Writings of Frederick Douglass* (New York: International Publishers, 1950), p. 3:318.

22. Blassingame, *The Frederick Douglass Papers,* p. 5:257.

23. Ibid., p. 1:29.

24. Ibid., p. 4:61.

25. Ibid., p. 235.

26. *Liberator,* December 9, 1842, p. 3.

27. Ibid., May 10, 1844, p. 75.

28. Jane Marsh Parker, "Reminiscences of Frederick Douglass," *Outlook* 51 (April 1895), p. 533.

29. Blassingame, *The Frederick Douglass Papers,* p. 3:537.

30. Ibid., pp. 1:xxxiii–xxxiv.

31. Ibid., pp. 5:70–71.

32. Ibid., p. 3:569.

33. Ibid., p. 3:563.

34. Ward Hill Lamon, in one of the earlier Lincoln biographies, has written that "on Monday mornings [Lincoln] would mount a stump and deliver, with a wonderful approach, to exactness the sermon he had heard the day before." *The Life of Abraham Lincoln, From His Birth to His Inauguration* (Boston: James R. Osgood and Company, 1872), p. 39.

35. Thomas Wentworth Higginson, *American Orators and Oratory* (Cleveland, OH: Imperial Press, 1901), pp. 87–89. Only 500 copies of this work were published.

36. *Liberator,* February 4, 1842, p. 19.

37. Theodore Stanton and Harriet Stanton Blanche, eds., *Elizabeth Cady Stanton As*

Revealed in Her Letters, Diary, and Reminiscences (New York: Harper and Brothers, 1922), p. 2:312.

38. *Herald of Freedom,* February 16, 1844, p. 208.

39. Blassingame, The Frederick Douglass Papers, pp. 2:368–69.

40. Ibid., p. 2:273.

41. Ibid., p. 1:41–42.

42. Ibid., pp. 3:440–41.

43. Ibid., p. 3:528.

44. Ibid., p. 3:529.

45. Ibid., p. 4:23.

46. Cooper, *The Rhetoric of Aristotle,* p. 187.

47. As quoted in George A. Hinshaw, "A Rhetorical Analysis of the Speeches of Frederick Douglass during and after the Civil War" (Ph.D. dissertation, University of Nebraska, 1972), p. 335.

48. Blassingame, *The Frederick Douglass Papers,* p. 4:8.

49. Ibid., p. 4:4.

50. Foner, *The Life and Writings of Frederick Douglass,* p. 3:319.

51. Blassingame, *The Frederick Douglass Papers,* p. 5:94.

52. Ibid., pp. 4:9–10.

53. Ibid., p. 4:437.

54. Ibid., p. 3:558.

55. Ibid., p. 5:529.

56. Ibid., p. 5:119.

57. Ibid., p. 5:117.

58. Ibid., p. 3:584.

59. Ibid., p. 5:232.

60. Cooper, *The Rhetoric of Aristotle,* p. 204.

61. Blassingame, *The Frederick Douglass Papers,* p. 4:436.

62. Ibid., 5:60.

63. Raymond Gerald Fulkerson, "Frederick Douglass (1818–1895), Abolitionist, Reformer," in *African-American Orators: A Bio-Critical Sourcebook,* Richard W. Leeman, ed. (Westport, CT: Greenwood Press, 1996), pp. 85–96.

64. Blassingame, *The Frederick Douglass Papers,* p. 2:371.

65. *Herald of Freedom,* February 16, 1844, p. 208.

66. For a good account of Douglass's spiritual journey, see William Van Deburg, "Frederick Douglass: Maryland Slave to Religious Liberal," *Maryland Historical Magazine* 69 (Spring 1974), pp. 27–43.

67. Vincent Harding, "Religion and Resistance among Antebellum Negroes, 1800–1860," in *The Making of Black America,* August Meier and Elliot Rudwick, eds. (New York: Atheneum, 1969), p. 1:179.

68. Hinshaw, "Rhetorical Analysis of the Speeches of Frederick Douglass," pp. 348–49.

69. Wilson Jeremiah Moses, *Black Messiahs and Uncle Toms: Social and Literary Manipulations of a Religious Myth* (University Park: Pennsylvania State University Press, 1982), pp. 30–31. Even slave owner Thomas Jefferson employed jeremiad rhetoric when he wrote of slavery: "Liberties are the gift of God. They are not to be violated but with his wrath. Indeed, I tremble for my country when I reflect that God is just, that his justice cannot sleep forever." Ibid. An excellent article on Douglass's use of the jeremiad

is David Howard-Pitney, "The Enduring Black Jeremiad: The American Jeremiad and Black Protest Rhetoric, From Frederick Douglass to W.E.B. Du Bois, 1841–1919," *American Quarterly* 38 (fall 1986), pp. 481–92. For a lengthy treatment of the jeremiad, see Sacvan Bercovitch, *The American Jeremiad* (Madison: University of Wisconsin Press, 1978).

70. As quoted in Howard-Pitney, "The Enduring Black Jeremiad," p. 484.

71. Blassingame, *The Frederick Douglass Papers*, p. 2:559.

72. Ibid., pp. 3:474, 479, 483.

73. Ibid., pp. 5:603–4.

74. Ibid., p. 3:552.

75. Ibid., p. 5:607.

76. James M'Cune Smith, "Introduction," in Frederick Douglass, *My Bondage and My Freedom* (New York: Dover Publications, 1969; first published in 1855), p. xxix.

77. Helen Pitts Douglass, *In Memoriam: Frederick Douglass* (Freeport, NY: Books for Libraries Press, 1971; repr. of 1897 ed.), p. 198.

78. *Anti-Slavery Bugle,* August 17, 1850, p. 2.

79. William Henry Crogman, *Talks for the Times* (Atlanta: Franklin Printing and Publishing Co., 1896), p. 13.

80. Parker, "Reminiscences of Frederick Douglass," p. 553.

81. As quoted in Blassingame, "Introduction," *The Frederick Douglass Papers*, p. 1:lxvii.

82. Ibid., pp. 1:lxvii–lxviii.

83. Ibid., p. 1:xxviii.

84. These newspaper tributes, along with many others, can be found in Helen Pitts Douglass, *In Memoriam: Frederick Douglass*, pp. 285–326. These two specific quotations are located on pp. 290 and 300.

CHAPTER 6: SPEECHES

1. William L. Andrews, ed., *The Oxford Frederick Douglass Reader* (New York: Oxford University Press, 1996), p. 108.

2. William S. McFeely, *Frederick Douglass* (New York: W. W. Norton), p. 173.

3. The pamphlet is titled, *Oration Delivered in Corinthian Hall, Rochester, by Frederick Douglass, July 5th, 1852* (Rochester, 1852).

Chronology of
Selected Speeches

Frederick Douglass's oratorical career spanned nearly sixty years. Over that time
he delivered many hundreds of speeches. Some of the more significant ones are
listed below. Most of the speeches are referred to in the text, and most can be
located in the five-volume work, *The Frederick Douglass Papers,* edited by John
W. Blassingame and John R. McKivigan.

1841

August 12   A speech before the Massachusetts Anti-Slavery Society in Nantucket.
                 This was the speech that caught the attention of the abolitionists and
                 launched Douglass's oratorical career.

November 4   Douglass delivered two speeches on this date before the Old Colony
                 Anti-Slavery Society, meeting in Hingham, Massachusetts: "The
                 Union, Slavery, and Abolitionist Petitions" and "American Prejudice
                 and Southern Religion."

1842

January 26   "Abolitionists and Third Parties." Douglass affirmed the Garrisonian
                 position of noninvolvement in politics before the Massachusetts Anti-
                 Slavery Society, Boston.

January 28   "The Southern Style of Preaching to Slaves." Delivered at Faneuil
                 Hall, Boston.

May 28   "The Church is the Bulwark of Slavery." New England Anti-Slavery
                 Society, Chardon Street Chapel, Boston.

1843

May 9   "The Anti-Slavery Movement, the Slave's Only Earthly Hope."

American Anti-Slavery Society, New York City.

September 17   After a speech near Pendleton, Indiana, Douglass and William A. White were attacked by a mob.

1844

February 11   "Southern Slavery and Northern Religion."   Concord, New Hampshire.

1845

May 6   "My Slave Experience in Maryland."   Delivered just before the publication of *Narrative of the Life of Frederick Douglass,* this speech marked the first time in public address wherein Douglass related the names of former masters and overseers.

October 1   "Irish Christians and Non-Fellowship with Man-Stealers." Dublin, Ireland.

October 14   "My Experience and My Mission to Great Britain." Cork, Ireland.

October 20   "Intemperance and Slavery." Cork, Ireland.

October 23   "American Prejudice Against Color." Cork, Ireland.

1846

January 20   "The Free Church of Scotland and American Slavery."   Dundee, Scotland.

February 12   "The Free Church Connection with the Slave Church."   Arbroath, Scotland.

September 14   "Slavery in the Pulpit of the Evangelical Alliance." London, England.

December 23   "England Shall Lead the Cause of Emancipation." Leeds, England.

1847

March 30   "Farewell to the British People." London, England.

1848

May 9   "The Triumphs and Challenges of the Abolitionist Crusade." American Anti-Slavery Society, New York City.

May 30	"The Slaves Right to Revolt." New England Anti-Slavery Society, Boston.

1849

May 9	"Too Much Religion. Too Little Humanity." American Anti-Slavery Society, New York City.
May 31	"The Colonization Revival." A bitter attack on the concept of colonization, at Faneuil Hall, Boston.

1850

January 17	"Is the Constitution Pro-Slavery?" Douglass's remarks were part of a debate at Syracuse, New York.
October 14	"Do Not Send Back the Slave." Faneuil Hall, Boston.
October 24	"Let Woman Taker Her Rights." National Women's Convention, Worcester, Massachusetts.

1851

February 2	"Henry Clay and Colonization Cant, Sophistry, and Falsehood." Rochester, New York.
April 3	"An Appeal to Canada." Toronto, Canada.

1852

July 5	"What to the Slave Is the Fourth of July?" Delivered in Rochester, New York, this may well be Douglass's best and most famous speech.
August 11	"Let All Soil Be Free Soil." Free Soil Convention, Pittsburgh, Ohio.
August 23	"Agitate, Agitate." Salem, Ohio.

1853

May 11	"No Peace for the Slaveholder." American Anti-Slavery Society, New York City.

1854

July 12	"The Claims of the Negro Ethnologically Considered." Delivered at Ohio's Western Reserve College, this was Douglass's first speech on

a college campus. The speech may stand as the most sophisticated of all Douglass's orations.

October 30   "Slavery, Freedom, and the Kansas-Nebraska Act." Douglass attacked this piece of legislation and Stephen Douglas's part in it, Chicago, Illinois.

1855

September 4   "We Ask Only for Our Rights." State convention of black New Yorkers, Troy, New York.

1856

May 28   "The Political Response to Slavery's Aggressions." A speech before New York State Republicans in which Douglass challenged their right to be called "Black Republicans."

May (?)   "The Dred Scott Decision." New York City.

1858

In this year, Douglass delivered the first rendition of "Self-Made Men." It would be revised and repeated many times during future years.

October 7   "Capital Punishment Is a Mockery of Justice." Rochester, New York.

1860

January 30   "John Brown and the Slaveholder's Insurrection." This speech was delivered in Edinburgh, Scotland. Douglass had fled to the British Isles because of accusations he was involved in Brown's raid on Harpers Ferry.

August 1   "Slavery and the Irrepressible Conflict." Douglass praised the memory and deeds of John Brown in a speech in Geneva, New York.

December 3   "The Legacy of John Brown." Delivered in Boston on the first anniversary of Brown's death.
               "John Brown's Contributions to the Abolition Movement." Boston.

December 9   "A Plea for Freedom of Speech in Boston," Boston.

1861

April 28   "Hope and Despair in These Cowardly Times." Two weeks after the shelling of Fort Sumter, Douglass affirmed his loyalty to the Union and urged the use of black troops, in a speech in Rochester, New York.

May 5   "Revolutions Never Go Backward." In a speech in Rochester, New York, Douglass urged the government not to compromise on principles in order to bring about a hasty end to the war.

June 1   "The American Apocalypse." Rochester, New York.

June 30   "America before the Global Tribunal." Douglass reminded listeners in Rochester, New York, that the abolition of slavery must be the primary focus of the war.

1862

January 14   "Fighting the Rebels with One Hand." In one of his best-known speeches, Douglass told a Philadelphia audience that the North must fight with greater vigor and commitment.

February 5   "The Black Man's Future in the Southern States." Before the Emancipation League, Boston.

July 4   "The Slaveholders' Rebellion." In a speech in Himrods, New York, Douglass strongly criticized Lincoln's and McClellan's conduct of the war.

December 28   "The Day of Jubilee Comes." A speech in Rochester, New York, anticipating the Emancipation Proclamation.

1863

February 6   "The Proclamation and a Negro Army." In a speech in New York City, Douglass praised the Emancipation Proclamation and declared his belief that slavery would be abolished in all the states.

March (?)   "Men of Color, To Arms!" A recruitment speech that Douglass delivered on several occasions and was reprinted in several publications.

July 6   "Negroes and the National War Effort." Recruitment speech delivered in Philadelphia to potential black recruits.

1864

January 13   "The Mission of the War." A plea to make the war one for the abolition of slavery, at Cooper Institute in New York. One of

Douglass's most memorable addresses.

April 12   "Representatives of the Future South." A Boston speech honoring Jean-Baptiste Roudanez and Arnold Bertonneau, free blacks from New Orleans.

1865

January 26   "What the Black Man Wants." Massachusetts Anti-Slavery Society, Boston.

April 4   "The Fall of Richmond." Faneuil Hall, Boston.

April 15   "Our Martyred President." Impromptu remarks at Rochester's City Hall on the day of Lincoln's death.

May 10   "In What New Skin Will the Old Snake Come Forth?" American Anti-Slavery Society, Church of the Puritans, New York City.

September 29   "The Douglass Institute." Dedication service of the Douglass Institute in Baltimore.

1866

February 13   "The Assassination and Its Lessons." First Presbyterian Church, Washington, DC.

September 4   "We Are Here and Want the Ballot-Box." Philadelphia.

1868

May 14   "Equal Rights for All." American Equal Rights Association, New York City.

December 11   "Women and Negroes Must Work Together." Rhode Island Woman's Suffrage Convention, Providence.

1869

August 3   "We Are Not Quite Free." A speech highly critical of American progress in race relations, Medina, New York.

1870

November 5   "I Am a Republican." Election eve, Rochester, New York.

1872

July 24   "Which Greeley Are We Voting For?" Republican rally in Richmond, Virginia.

July 25   "Vote the Regular Republican Ticket." Raleigh, North Carolina.

September 25   "This Democratic Conversion Should Not Be Trusted." Republican rally at the Cooper Institute, New York City.

1874

March 16   "Eulogy for Charles Sumner." Washington, DC.

1875

April 14   "Celebrating the Past, Anticipating the Future." In Philadelphia, Douglass sought to answer those who claimed that enough had been done for the negro.

1876

April 14   "The Freedman's Monument to Abraham Lincoln." Washington, DC.

1878

May 30   "The President's Southern Policy." A defense of Hayes's "southern policy," delivered in Washington, DC.

1879

September 12   "The Negro Exodus from the South." A speech by Douglass, read by another before the American Social Science Association, Saratoga, New York.

1881

September 26   "Garfield, the Friend of a People Oppressed and Proscribed." Eulogy for President Garfield at the Fifteenth Street Presbyterian Church, Washington, DC.

1883

April 16   "Our Destiny Is Largely in Our Own Hands." Washington, DC.

October 22   "This Decision Has Humbled the Nation." A speech responding to a

Supreme Court decision that had declared the 1875 Civil Rights Act
to be null and void. Washington, DC.

1885

April 16   "We Are Confronted by a New Administration." Washington, DC.

August 6   "Great Britain's Example Is High, Noble, and Grand." Before a black
                    audience in Rochester, New York.

1886

April 16   "Strong to Suffer, and yet Strong to Strive." Washington, DC.

1888

February 12   "The Black Man's Debt to Abraham Lincoln." A tribute to Lincoln
                    before the Republican National League in Washington, DC.

March 31   "Give Women Fair Play." Delivered before the International Council
                    of Women in Washington, DC.

April 16   "In Law, Free; in Fact, a Slave." Douglass spoke of the deplorable
                    conditions for blacks in the southern states in a speech at Washington,
                    DC.

October 25   "Parties Are to Be Judged by Their Fruits." Campaign speech for
                    Benjamin Harrison in New Haven, Connecticut.

1890

October 21   "The Negro Problem." An address delivered in Washington's African
                    Methodist Episcopal Church on contemporary racial problems.

1893

January 2   "Haiti and the Haitian People." In a speech at Quinn Chapel in
                    Chicago, in connection with the Columbian Exposition, Douglass
                    extolled the progress and promise of Haiti.

February 13   "Abraham Lincoln, the Great Man of Our Century." A tribute to
                    Lincoln before 300 prominent Republicans in Brooklyn, New York.

1894

January 9   "The Lessons of the Hour." Douglass's last major address, delivered in Washington, DC, focused on the injustices against blacks in the South, especially the terror of lynching.

February 16   "Lucy Stone, Her Memory Is Safe." A tribute to Lucy Stone before the National-American Woman Suffrage Association meeting in Washington, DC.

BIBLIOGRAPHY

SPEECHES, LETTERS, AND AUTOBIOGRAPHIES OF FREDERICK DOUGLASS

Blassingame, John W. and John R. McKivigan for vols. 4 and 5, eds. *The Frederick Douglass Papers.* 5 vols. New Haven: Yale University Press, 1979–1992.

Douglass, Frederick. *The Life and Times of Frederick Douglass.* Intro. by Rayford W. Logan. New York: Macmillan, 1962; first published 1881, expanded version in 1892.

———. *My Bondage and My Freedom.* Original Intro. by James McCune Smith and later Intro. by Philip S. Foner. New York: Dover Publications, Inc., 1969; first published in 1855.

———. *Narrative of the Life of Frederick Douglass, An American Slave.* New York: Penguin Books, 1986; first published in 1845.

Foner, Philip S., ed. *The Life and Writings of Frederick Douglass.* 5 vols. New York: International Publishers, 1950.

EIGHTEENTH-CENTURY SOURCES

Bingham, Caleb. *The Columbian Orator: Containing a Variety of Original and Selected Pieces, Together with Rules; Calculated to Improve Youth and Others in the Ornamented and Useful Art of Eloquence.* Boston: Manning and Loring, 1797.

Campell, George. *Philosophy of Rhetoric.* Lloyd F. Bitzer, ed. Carbondale: Southern Illinois University Press, 1963; first published in 1776.

NINETEENTH-CENTURY SOURCES

Books

Bartlett, David. *Modern Agitators: Pen Portraits of Living American Reformers.* New York: Miller, Orton, and Milligan, 1855.

Bradford, Sarah H. *Scenes in the Life of Harriet Tubman.* Auburn, NY: W. J. Moses, 1869.

Chestnutt, Charles W. *Frederick Douglass.* Boston: Small, Maynard, 1899.

Crogman, William Henry. *Talks for the Times.* Atlanta, GA: Franklin Printing and Publishing Co., 1896.

Douglass, Helen Pitts. *In Memoriam: Frederick Douglass.* Freeport, NY: Books for Libraries Press, 1971; repr. of 1897 ed.

Goodell, William. *Views of American Constitutional Law in Its Bearing upon American Slavery.* Utica, NY: Lawson & Chaplin, 1845.

Gregory, James M. *Frederick Douglass: The Orator.* Springfield, MA: Willey and Co., 1893.

Grimke, Archibald H. *William Lloyd Garrison: The Abolitionist.* New York: Funk and Wagnalls, 1891.

Holland, Frederick May. *Frederick Douglass: The Colored Orator.* New York: Funk and Wagnalls, 1891.

McPherson, Edward. *The Political History of the United States during the Period of Reconstruction.* New York: Negro Universities Press, 1969; repr. of 1887 ed.

Martyn, Carlos. *Wendell Phillips: The Agitator.* 2nd ed. New York: Funk and Wagnalls, 1890.

May, Samuel J. *Some Recollections of Our Antislavery Conflict.* New York: Arno Press, 1968; first published in 1869.

Rice, Allen Thorndike, ed. *Reminiscences of Abraham Lincoln by Distinguished Men of His Time.* 8th ed. New York: North American Review, 1889.

Tilton, Theodore. *Sonnets to the Memory of Frederick Douglass.* 2nd ed. Paris: Brentano's, 1895.

Walker, David. *Walker's Appeal in Four Articles.* New York: Arno Press, 1969; repr. of 1848 ed.

Weld, Theodore Dwight. *American Slavery as It Is: Testimony of a Thousand Witnesses.* New York: American Anti-Slavery Society, 1839.

Wilson, Henry. *History of the Rise and Fall of the Slave Power.* 3 vols. Boston: James R. Osgood and Co., 1872–1877.

Newspapers, Periodicals, Pamphlets, and Articles

Anti-Slavery Bugle (Salem, Ohio)

Anti-Slavery Standard (New York)

Douglass, Frederick. *Oration, Delivered in Corinthian Hall, Rochester, by Frederick Douglass, July 5th, 1852.* Rochester, New York, 1852.

Douglass Letters and Papers: Rush Rhees Library, University of Rochester, New York.

Douglass' Monthly (Rochester, New York)

Frederick Douglass' Paper (Rochester, New York)

Herald of Freedom (Concord, New Hampshire)

Liberator (Boston)

New Era (Washington, DC)

New National Era (Washington, DC)

North Star (Rochester, New York)

Parker, Jane Marsh. "Reminiscences of Frederick Douglass." *Outlook* 51 (April 1895).

Woman's Journal

TWENTIETH-CENTURY SOURCES

Books

Andrews, William L., ed. *Critical Essays on Frederick Douglass*. Boston: G. K. Hall & Co., 1991.

————, ed. *The Oxford Frederick Douglass Reader*. New York: Oxford University Press, 1996.

Aptheker, Herbert. *Essays in the History of the American Negro*. New York: International Publishers, 1945.

Bercovitch, Sacvan. *The American Jeremiad*. Madison: University of Wisconsin Press, 1978.

Blackott, R. J. M. *Building An Antislavery Wall: Black Americans in the Atlantic Abolitionist Movement*. Baton Rouge: Louisiana State University Press, 1983.

Blassingame, John W., ed. *Slave Testimony*. Baton Rouge: Louisiana State University Press, 1977.

Blassingame, John W. et al., eds. *Antislavery Newspapers and Periodicals*. 5 vols. Boston: G. K. Hall, 1980–1984.

Blight, David W. *Frederick Douglass' Civil War: Keeping Faith in Jubilee*. Baton Rouge: Louisiana State University Press, 1989.

Bontempts, Arna. *Free At Last: The Life of Frederick Douglass*. New York: Dodd, Mead & Company, 1971.

Brown, Norma. *A Black Diplomat in Haiti: The Diplomatic Correspondence of U. S. Minister Frederick Douglass From Haiti, 1889-1891*. 2 vols. Salisbury, NC: Documentary Publications, 1977.

Campbell, Stanley W. *The Slave Catchers: Enforcement of the Fugitive Slave Law, 1850–1860*. Chapel Hill: University of North Carolina Press, 1970.

Chapman, John Jay. *William Lloyd Garrison*. 2nd ed. Boston: Atlantic Monthly Press, 1921.

Chesebrough, David B. *"God Ordained This War": Sermons on the Sectional Crisis, 1830–1865*. Columbia: University of South Carolina Press, 1991.

Coles, Howard W. *The Cradle of Freedom: A History of the Negro in Rochester, Western New York and Canada*. Rochester, NY: Oxford Press, 1941.

Cooper, Lane. *The Rhetoric of Aristotle: An Expanded Translation with Supplementary Examples for Students of Composition and Public Speaking*. New York: Appleton-Century-Crofts, Inc., 1932.

Cox, Lawanda. *Lincoln and Black Freedom: A Study in Presidential Leadership*. Columbia: University of South Carolina Press, 1981.

Duberman, Martin, ed. *The Anti-Slavery Vanguard: Essays on the New Abolitionists*. Princeton: Princeton University Press, 1965.

Duffy, Bernard K., and Halford R. Ryan, eds. *American Orators before 1900: Critical Studies and Sources*. Westport, CT: Greenwood Press, 1987.

Fisher, Dexter, and Robert B. Stepto, eds. *Afro-American Literature: The Reconstruction of Instruction*. New York: Modern Languages Association, 1979.

Fladeland, Betty. *Men and Brothers: Anglo-American Antislavery Cooperation*. Urbana: University of Illinois Press, 1972.

Fleming, Walter L. *The Freemen's Savings Bank*. Chapel Hill: University of North Carolina Press, 1927.

Foner, Philip S. *Frederick Douglass: A Biography*. New York: Citadel Press, 1964.

————, ed. *Frederick Douglass on Women's Rights*. Contributions in Afro-American and African Studies, No. 25. Westport, CT: Greenwood Press, 1976.

Frederickson, George M. *The Inner Civil War: Northern Intellectuals and the Crisis of the*

Union. New York: Harper and Row, 1965.

Graham, Shirley. *There Was Once a Slave: The Heroic Story of Frederick Douglass.* New York: Julian Messner, Inc., 1947.

Higginson, Thomas Wentworth. *American Orators and Their Oratory.* Cleveland: Imperial Press, 1901. Only 500 copies of this work were published.

Huggins, Nathan Irvin. *Slave and Citizen: The Life of Frederick Douglass.* Oscar Hanlin, ed. Boston: Little, Brown, 1980.

Hyman Harold W., and Leonard W. Levy, eds. *Freedom and Reform: Essays in Honor of Henry Steele Commager.* New York: Harper and Row, 1967.

Korngold, Ralph. *Two Friends of Man: The Story of William Lloyd Garrison and Wendell Phillips and Their Relationship with Abraham Lincoln.* Boston: Little, Brown and Company, 1950.

Kraditor, Aileea S. Means and Ends in American Abolitionism: Garrison and His Critics on Strategy and Tactics, 1834–1850. New York: Pantheon Books, 1969.

Leeman, Richard W., ed. *African-American Orators: A Bio-Critical Sourcebook.* Westport, CT: Greenwood Press, 1996.

Litwack, Leon, and August Meier, eds. *Black Leaders of the Nineteenth Century.* Urbana: University of Illinois Press, 1988.

Mabee, Carleton. *Black Freedom: The Non-violent Abolitionists from 1830 through the Civil War.* London: Collier-Macmillan, Ltd., 1970.

McFeely, William S. *Frederick Douglass.* New York: W. W. Norton & Company, 1991.

McKivigan, John R. *The War against Proslavery Religion: Abolitionism and the Northern Churches, 1830–1865.* Ithaca, NY: Cornell University Press, 1984.

McPherson, James M. *The Negro's Civil War: How American Negroes Felt and Acted during the War for the Union.* New York: Pantheon Books, 1965.

———. *The Struggle for Equality: Abolitionists and the Negro in the Civil War and Reconstruction.* Princeton: Princeton University Press, 1964.

Martin, Waldo E., Jr. *The Mind of Frederick Douglass.* Chapel Hill: University of North Carolina Press, 1982.

Mays, Benjamin. *The Negro's God as Reflected in His Literature.* New York: Russell & Russell, 1968.

Meier, August. *Negro Thought in America, 1880–1915.* Ann Arbor: University of Michigan Press, 1966.

Meier, August, and Elliot Rudwick, eds. *The Making of Black America.* New York: Atheneum, 1969.

Merrill, Walter M. *Against Wind and Tide: A Biography of William Lloyd Garrison.* Cambridge, MA: Harvard University Press, 1963.

———, ed. *The Letters of William Lloyd Garrison.* 6 vols. Cambridge, MA: Belknap Press of Harvard University, 1971.

Moses, William Jeremiah. *Black Messiahs and Uncle Toms: Social and Literary Manipulations of a Religious Myth.* University Park: Pennsylvania State University Press, 1982.

Nelson, Truman, ed. *Documents of Upheaval: Selections from William Lloyd Garrison's The Liberator, 1831–1965.* New York: Hill and Wang, 1966.

Nye, Russel B. *William Lloyd Garrison and the Humanitarian Reformers.* Boston: Little, Brown and Co., 1955.

Oliver, Robert T. *History of Public Speaking in America.* Boston: Allyn and Bacon, Inc.,

1965.

Pease, Jane H., and William H. *Bound With Them in Chains: A Biographical History of the Antislavery Movement.* Westport, CT: Greenwood Press, 1972.

——. *They Who Would Be Free: Blacks Search for Freedom, 1830–1861.* New York: Atheneum, 1974.

Preston, Dickson J. *Young Frederick Douglass: The Maryland Years.* Baltimore: John Hopkins University Press, 1980.

Quarles, Benjamin. *Black Abolitionists.* New York: Oxford University Press, 1969.

——. *Frederick Douglass.* Washington, DC: Associated Publishers, 1948.

——, ed. *Frederick Douglass.* Englewood Cliffs, NJ: Prentice-Hall, 1968.

Ross, Ishbel. *The President's Wife: Mary Todd Lincoln, A Biography.* New York: Putnam, 1973.

Rossbach, Jeffrey. *The Ambivalent Conspirators: John Brown, the Secret Six, and a Theory of Black Political Violence.* Philadelphia: University of Pennsylvania Press, 1982.

Scott, Otto J. *The Secret Six: John Brown and the Abolitionist Movement.* New York: Times Books, 1978.

Sherwin, Oscar. *Prophet of Liberty: The Life and Times of Wendell Phillips.* New York: Bookman Associates, 1958.

Smith, Arthur L. *Rhetoric of Black Revolution.* Boston: Allyn and Bacon, 1969.

Stanton, Theodore, and Harriet Stanton Blanche, eds. *Elizabeth Cady Stanton, As Revealed in Her Letters, Diary, and Reminiscences.* 2 vols. New York: Harper and Brothers, 1922.

Sunquist, Eric J., ed. *Frederick Douglass: New Literary and Historical Essays.* Cambridge: Cambridge University Press, 1990.

Taylor, Clare. *British and American Abolitionists: An Episode in Transatlantic Understanding.* Edinburgh, Scotland: Edinburgh University Press, 1974.

Temperly, Howard. *British Antislavery, 1833–1870.* Columbia: University of South Carolina Press, 1972.

Thomas, John L. *The Liberator: William Lloyd Garrison.* Boston: Little, Brown, 1963.

——, ed. *Slavery Attacked: The Abolitionist Crusade.* Englewood Cliffs, NJ: Prentice-Hall, 1965.

Thonssen, Lester, and A. Craig Baird. *Speech Criticism: The Development of Standards for Rhetorical Appraisal.* New York: The Ronald Press, 1948.

Tise, Larry E. *Proslavery: A History of the Defense of Slavery in America, 1702–1840.* Athens: University of Georgia Press, 1987.

Voss, Frederick S. *Majestic in His Wrath: A Pictorial Life of Frederick Douglass.* Washington, DC: Smithsonian Institute Press, 1995.

Wade, Richard C. *Slavery in the Cities: The South 1820–1860.* New York: Oxford University Press, 1964.

Washington, Booker T. *Frederick Douglass.* Philadelphia: G. W. Jacobs & Company, 1906.

Watt, Hush. *Thomas Chalmers and the Disruption.* Edinburgh, Scotland: Nelson, 1943.

Weatherford, W. D. *American Churches and the Negro: An Historical Study from Early Slave Days to the Present.* Boston: Christopher Publishing House, 1957.

Woodson, Carter G. *Negro Orators and Their Orations.* Washington, DC: Associated Publishers, Inc., 1925.

Zarefsky, David. *Public Speaking: Strategies for Sucess.* Boston: Allyn and Bacon, 1996.

Articles

Andrews, William L. "Frederick Douglass, Preacher." *American Literature* 54 (December 1982): pp. 592–97.

Aptheker, Herbert. "An Unpublished Frederick Douglass Letter." *Journal of Negro History* 44 (July 1959): pp. 277–81.

Bellah, Robert. "Civil Religion in America." *Daedulus* 96 (winter 1967): pp. 1–21.

Blight, David W. "Frederick Douglass and the American Apocalypse." *Civil War History* 31 (December 1985): pp. 309–28.

Dyer, Brainerd. "The Treatment of Colored Troops by the Confederates." *Journal of Negro History* 20 (July 1935): pp. 273–86.

Fulkerson, R. Gerald. "Exile As Emergence: Frederick Douglass in Great Britain, 1845–1849." *The Quarterly Speech Journal* 60 (February 1974): pp. 69–82.

———. "Frederick Douglass and the Kansas-Nebraska Act: A Case Study in Agitational Versatility." *Central States Speech Journal* 23 (winter 1972): pp. 261–69.

———. "Frederick Douglass (1818-1895), Abolitionist, Reformer." *African-American Orators: A Bio-Critical Sourcebook.* Richard W. Leeman, ed. Westport, CT: Greenwood Press, 1996, pp. 82–97.

Goldstein, Leslie Friedman. "Violence as an Instrument for Social Change: The Views of Frederick Douglass (1817–1895)." *Journal of Negro History* 61 (January 1976): pp. 61–72.

Grimke, Francis J. "The Second Marriage of Frederick Douglass." *Journal of Negro History* 19 (July 1934): pp. 324–29.

Harding, Vincent. "Religion and Resistance among Antebellum Negroes, 1800–1865." *The Making of Black America.* August Meier and Elliot Rudwick, eds. New York: Atheneum, 1969, pp. 1:179–97.

Howard-Pitney, David. "The Enduring Black Jeremiad: The American Jeremiad and Black Protest Rhetoric, From Frederick Douglass to W.E.B. Du Bois, 1841–1919." *American Quarterly* 38 (fall 1986): pp. 481–92.

Johannesen, Richard L. "Caleb Bingham's American Preceptor and Columbian Orator." *The Speech Teacher* 18 (March 1969): pp. 139–43.

Leroux, Neil. "Frederick Douglass and the Attention Shift." *Rhetoric Society Quarterly* 21 (spring 1991): pp. 36–46.

Litwack, Leon F. "Trouble in Mind: The Bicentennial and the Afro-American Experience." *Journal of American History* 74 (1987): pp. 315–37.

Martin, Waldo E., Jr. "Frederick Douglass (1818–1895)." *American Orators before 1900: Critical Studies and Sources.* Bernard K. Duffy and Halford R. Ryan, eds. Westport, CT: Greenwood Press, 1987, pp. 139–45.

Meier, August. "Frederick Douglass' Vision for America: A Case Study in Nineteenth Century Protest." *Freedom and Reform: Essays in Honor of Henry Steele Commager.* Harold W. Hyman and Leonard W. Levy, eds. New York: Harper and Row, 1967, pp. 127–48.

O'Meally, Robert G. "Frederick Douglass' 1845 Narrative: The Text That Was Meant to Be Preached." *Afro-American Literature: The Reconstruction of Instruction.* Dexter Fisher and Robrt B. Stepto, eds. New York: Modern Languages Association, 1979, pp. 192–211.

Pease, William H., and Jane H. "Boston Garrisonians and the Problem of Frederick Douglass." *Canadian Journal of History* 2 (September 1967): pp. 29–48.

Preston, E. O., Jr. "The Genesis of the Underground Railroad." *Journal of Negro History* 18 (April 1933): pp. 144–70.

Quarles, Benjamin. "The Breach between Douglass and Garrison." *The Journal of Negro History* 23 (April 1938): pp. 144–54.

———. "Frederick Douglass and John Brown." *Rochester Historical Society Publications* 17 (1939): pp. 291–99.

———. "Frederick Douglass and the Women's Rights Movement." *The Journal of Negro History* 25 (January 1940): pp. 35–44.

Shepperson, George. "Frederick Douglass and Scotland." *The Journal of Negro History* 38 (July 1953): pp. 307–21.

———. "The Free Church and American Slavery." *Scottish Historical Review* 30 (October 1951): pp. 126–43.

Stepto, Robert B. "Narration, Authentication, and Authorial Control in Frederick Douglass' Narrative of 1845." *Afro-American Literature: The Reconstruction of Instruction.* Dexter Fisher and Robert B. Stepto, eds. New York: Modern Languages Association, 1979, pp. 178–91.

Van Deburg, William L. "Frederick Douglass: Maryland Slave to Religious Liberal." *Maryland Historical Magazine* 69 (spring 1974): pp. 27–43.

Unpublished Theses and Dissertations

Bowers, Detine. "A Strange Speech of an Estranged People: Theory and Practice of Antebellum African-American Freedom Day Orators." Ph.D. dissertation. Purdue University, 1992.

Fulkerson, R. Gerald. "Frederick Douglass and the Anti-Slavery Crusade: His Career and Speeches, 1817–1861." Ph.D. dissertation. University of Illinois, 1971.

Harwood, Thomas F. "Great Britain and American Anti-Slavery." Ph.D. dissertation. University of Texas, 1959.

Hinshaw, George A. "A Rhetorical Analysis of the Speeches of Frederick Douglass during and after the Civil War." Ph.D. dissertation. University of Nebraska, 1972.

Ladner, Cornelius A. "A Critical Analysis of Four Anti-Slavery Speeches of Frederick Douglass." M.A. thesis. University of Iowa, 1947.

Quarles, Benjamin. "The Public Life of Frederick Douglass." Ph.D. dissertation. University of Wisconsin, 1938.

INDEX

About the Author

DAVID B. CHESEBROUGH is Assistant Chair, Graduate Faculty, Department of History at Illinois State University. He is the author of three previous books: *"God Ordained This War": Sermons on the Sectional Crises, 1830–1865* (1991); *"No Sorrow Like Our Sorrow": Northern Protestant Sermons and the Assassination of Lincoln* (1994); and *Clergy Dissent in the Old South, 1830–1865* (1996).

Great American Orators

Ronald Reagan: The Great Communicator
Kurt Ritter and David Henry

Clarence Darrow: The Creation of an American Myth
Richard J. Jensen

"Do Everything" Reform: The Oratory of Frances E. Willard
Richard W. Leeman

Abraham Lincoln the Orator: Penetrating the Lincoln Legend
Lois J. Einhorn

Mark Twain: Protagonist for the Popular Culture
Marlene Boyd Vallin

Delightful Conviction: Jonathan Edwards and the Rhetoric of Conversion
Stephen R. Yarbrough and John C. Adams

Harry S. Truman: Presidential Rhetoric
Halford R. Ryan

Dwight D. Eisenhower: Strategic Communicator
Martin J. Medhurst

Ralph Waldo Emerson: Preacher and Lecturer
Lloyd Rohler

"In a Perilous Hour": The Public Address of John F. Kennedy
Steven R. Goldzwig and George N. Dionisopoulos

Douglas MacArthur: Warrior as Wordsmith
Bernard K. Duffy and Ronald H. Carpenter

Sojourner Truth as Orator: Wit, Story, and Song
Suzanne Pullon Fitch and Roseann M. Mandziuk

ISBN 0-313-30287-1

90000>

EAN

9 780313 302879

HARDCOVER BAR CODE